SECRETS OF
SUCCESS
FROM CANADA'S
FASTEST-GROWING
COMPANIES

Also available in the series from

PROFIT: The Magazine for Canadian Entrepreneurs

Beyond The Banks, Creative Financing for Canadian Entrepreneurs, by Allan Riding and Barbara Orser (ISBN: 0-471-64208-8)

SECRETS OF
SUCCESS
FROM CANADA'S
FASTEST-GROWING
COMPANIES

RICK SPENCE

JOHN WILEY & SONS CANADA, LTD

Toronto • New York • Chichester • Weinheim • Brisbane • Singapore

John Wiley & Sons Canada, Ltd
22 Worcester Road
Etobicoke, Ontario
M9W 1L1

Canadian Cataloguing in Publication Data

Spence, Rick, 1955-
        Secrets of success from Canada's fastest-growing companies

On cover: Profit: the magazine for Canadian entrepreneurs.
ISBN 0-471-64233-9

1. Small business - Canada.   2. Entrepreneurship - Canada.
3. Success in business - Canada.   I. Profit (Toronto, Ont.).
II. Title.

HD62.7.S636 1997   658.02'2'0971   C97-931810-6

Production Credits:
Cover & text design: Christine Rae, RGD
Cover photography: Mir Lada
Profit 100 Trophy design: Donna Braggins
Printer: Tri-graphic Printing Ltd.

Printed in Canada
10 9 8 7 6 5 4 3 2 1

To my Mother
who believes that anything is possible

and

to my Dad
who believes that only what's right is worth doing

CONTENTS

ACKNOWLEDGEMENTS

This book builds upon the work of many editors, writers, and friends of the PROFIT 100. Much of the research that underlies this book was conducted by freelance writer and ace interviewer Kara Kuryllowicz on behalf of PROFIT magazine. In addition, I gladly acknowledge my debt to Randy Litchfield, who got it all going; to John Southerst, Cathy Callaghan, Jerry Zeidenberg, Joe Dangor, Cathy Hilborn, and Jennifer Low, who supported and expanded this project as staff members of PROFIT magazine; to Ted Hart and Paul Jones of CB Media, the publisher of PROFIT, for their support for the survey and the magazine; to Peter Macdonald, our indefatigable PROFIT 100 statistician; to faithful freelancers Terry Brodie, Michael G. Crawford, Diane Luckow, and Richard Wright; to the PROFIT design team of Donna Braggins, Laura MacNeil, and Ian Philips; and to my ever-patient and valued colleagues at PROFIT, Jennifer Myers and Ian Portsmouth. I confess a lasting debt to my father Clarence, the lifelong banker, and my mother Jean, the family's BSc in economics, with whom I engaged in so many dinner-table arguments over the role of business in society, all of which helped shape my attitudes towards business and my admiration for the creativity of Canada's entrepreneurs. And I owe the biggest debt to my family, Sandy, Jennifer, and Carly, who sacrificed much in the making of this book.

INTRODUCTION

"You mean you found 100 Canadian companies that are growing?!"

The early 1990s were not the best of years for the Canadian economy. Even so, the public feeling of gloom was chilling. Each June when PROFIT magazine tried to spread the news about its latest survey of Canada's Fastest-Growing Companies, some approximation of the above quote was the most common reaction — abject surprise that any business at all was doing well in an economy that just seemed to be imploding.

In fact, that is the main reason why PROFIT magazine produces its PROFIT 100 survey each year: to remind people of the success stories that are all around us. Unknown to the general public, almost alien to the economists and politicians who dominate the headlines, a determined band of Canadian entrepreneurs had actually learned how to do business in the fast-changing economy; and they were succeeding beyond even their own wildest dreams. By bringing their names and their stories to light, PROFIT hoped to focus Canadians' attention on two things:

- the opportunity for individual success even in an economy of despair; and

- the common factors that seem to have some impact on business and personal success in today's global markets.

With the economy now on more solid ground, fewer Canadians are expressing astonishment at the very idea of entrepreneurial success. But the second part of that mandate remains as vital as ever: to explore and communicate the trends, common factors, lessons, secrets, and passions that contribute to the success of Canada's top growth companies.

COMMON CHARACTERISTICS FOR SUCCESS

What are the common characteristics that bind these companies?

- recognition that true success doesn't stem from imitating others, but from providing value and consistent innovation that place your business in a class of its own;

- alliance with change, based on the theory that ever-shifting markets, competition, and technology actually benefit the strongest, the fastest, and the smartest;

- renewed focus on your customers as people with real needs, not just consumers with ready cash;

- recognition of employees as creators of value, not generators of overhead;

- propensity for cooperation, not competition; and

- relentless commitment to improvement.

Taken separately, none of these factors is likely to transform a company. Businesspeople of all ranks across the country are aware of the need to get closer to their customers, to treat their employees as assets instead of liabilities, and to adapt to change. Taken together, however, these precepts amount to a revolution, not just in the way business is conducted, but in how it is actually perceived. An economy based on innovation runs on imagination and education, not natural resources or assembly lines. Business based on cooperation requires an ability to plan — and to trust — that few companies can demonstrate. Few organizations have the vision, commitment or the ability to adapt to all these new challenges. This is all the more reason why Canadians should get to know better the growth companies that are in the vanguard of the new economy, the lessons they can teach, and the stories they can tell.

A NATION OF ENTREPRENEURS

Who needs to study these cases? All of us: big business, small business, doers, and dreamers alike. Technology, splintering markets, and growing international competition are changing the rules of business so quickly that everyone needs help keeping up:

- the established public company with established businesses and brands whose time may now be running out;
- family businesses struggling with questions of succession, focus, teamwork, and the role of professional management;
- small companies trying to expand beyond their first initial success; and
- individual would-be entrepreneurs, looking for a concept of their own and the courage and inspiration to begin.

In recent years, Canada has witnessed record rates of business bankruptcies, unprecedented competition from our new free-trade partners and other offshore rivals, and new challenges from advancing technology that are turning established practices and conventions inside out. It is a time of great peril for Canadian entrepreneurs, but it is equally a time of great potential. All these changes also create new opportunities for smart businesspeople. Entrepreneurs have traditionally thrived on change, upheaval, and uncertainty, and the current climate offers more of all of this than ever before. The question is: how do you turn these problems into successful businesses, products, and profits? The **PROFIT 100** companies don't have all the answers. But based on their success in this same competitive context, their lessons have much to offer the rest of us.

Making this study even more timely is the fact that Canada is undergoing a cultural transformation. The latest trends demonstrate that the country is fast becoming a nation of entrepreneurs — all of whom can benefit from an additional dose of confidence, not to mention exposure to proven strategies and tactics. More than two million of us now declare income from self-employment. And that's just the beginning. A recent Angus Reid survey found that more than 10% of Canadian adults said they intended to start a business within the next year.

Few of these entrepreneurs have ever had formal business training. Many will succeed, some by sheer wit and intuition, others because they have been smart enough to tap the wisdom of experienced partners and advisors. But thousands will stumble and suffer as they fight their way through the diverse range of problems that stymie any young company. Yes, there are myriad sources of information on how to start a business or write a business plan, but lamentably few current references on the tactics, tips, and strategies employed by today's most successful entrepreneurs.

THE PROFIT 100 SURVEY

The PROFIT 100 survey of Canada's Fastest-Growing Companies was created to give Canadians access to some of the latest management ideas and attitudes from the rising stars of business. The purpose of this book is the same: to provide Canadians with the inspiration and the hands-on insights that can inject an extra dose of confidence and entrepreneurial savvy into any business or projected start-up.

No work such as this could be complete or authoritative. But then, business does not usually lend itself to definitive solutions. Each one is different, each market a microcosm. What worked for your business will not work the same way at mine. Still, there are principles that do apply across most sectors, and ideas and inspiration to be gained from the most anecdotal of business case studies. When it comes to ideas, strategies, and success stories, the PROFIT 100 companies offer a storehouse of accumulated experience and wisdom that is unequaled in this country.

The "Fastest 50": How It All Began

Like most business endeavours, the PROFIT 100 wasn't quite an overnight success. When PROFIT magazine, then known as *Small Business*, launched its first survey of Canada's Fastest-Growing Companies in 1988, the result was a little, well, underwhelming. Under then-editor Randall Litchfield, the magazine boldly set out to complete the first-ever study of Canada's 100 top growth firms — and failed. By soliciting nominations solely from the readers of the magazine, the editorial team couldn't muster enough responses to compile a list of 100 genuinely fast-growth companies. The result was that the magazine produced a list that came to be called the "Fastest 50." And it proved a very credible — not to mention the first ever — survey of Canada's fifty fastest-growing public and private companies. The companies' five-year growth rates ranged from a breathless 26,753% at the top end to a "mere" 427% for the company in fiftieth place.

In the ensuing years, the list became more sophisticated, more professional, and more complete. The key to the survey's growth was simple — casting the net a little wider every year. By constantly introducing new means of distributing survey ballots — through postcard-sized entry forms personally distributed by account managers for ten Canadian banks, direct mail, computerized database searches, news releases, a network of regional economic development officers, partnerships with other magazines, and even the Internet — PROFIT's survey touched more and more companies across Canada. By 1992, the "Fastest 50" had become the PROFIT 100 and by 1995, in a fit of let's-bury-the-recession-once-and-for-all bravado, PROFIT published an additional list of fifty more growth firms. It was the first-ever list of Canada's 150 fastest-growing companies — all of whom boasted five-year growth rates that would have earned them a spot on that original 1988 Top-50 roster.

How Do You Measure Growth?

Throughout this evolution, the essential methodology of the PROFIT 100 remained the same. The survey ranks Canadian-owned independent companies in terms of five-year sales (gross revenue) growth. Of course, in order to accumulate a five-year track record, a company has to have been in existence for at least six years. This rule alone has been the bane of many fast-start companies that think that a splashy start-up over just two or three years should be enough to earn them a spot on the list. In many cases, PROFIT recognized such precocious businesses through special stories or profiles in other issues of the magazine. Overall, however, the PROFIT 100 survey has maintained its focus of recognizing companies that have developed a track record and demonstrated true staying power by chalking up six years of achievement.

Some of the details of the magazine's methodology have changed over the years. For instance, in the very first year, companies' base-year revenues (i.e., revenues for the period five years ago) did not have to meet any minimum level. As a result, the standings were skewed in favour of companies that posted minuscule revenues in the base year (fiscal 1982). Indeed, the top three firms had 1982 revenues of just $8,029, $3,537, and $5,425 respectively. With bases such as this to build on, it's no wonder that all three posted percentage growth in the five digits (14,151% to 26,753%).

In all, ten of those first Top 50 companies had 1982 base-year revenues of less than $100,000. Obviously, all of those companies were relatively new start-ups. In fact, in some cases, it wasn't clear they had even been in business a full twelve months. In any case, it was evident that there was something wrong: the lack of a revenue minimum gave undue ranking preference to small start-ups. As a result, for all subsequent surveys, qualifying companies have had to report base-year revenues of at least $100,000. Today, many companies with revenues in the millions now complain that the $100,000 minimum is too low (much less than a decent bank executive's salary, say some). In the meantime, however, it has levelled the playing field, allowing well-established companies to compete with brash new start-ups on more equal footing.

The result is that the PROFIT 100 has yet to record another start-up that has grown more than 20,000% in five years. But by 1997 even the 100th ranked company had grown better than 600% — half again better than the 50th-ranked company in 1988 — proving that Canada's top growth companies have more depth and breadth than most observers ever imagined.

Another new rule created for this survey had a blessedly short life. PROFIT magazine didn't always feel comfortable with some of the big superstar companies that managed to qualify for the list. Just as the magazine staff had imposed a minimum revenue level, they then wrestled with the idea of whether there should be a revenue maximum as well. In fact, one year an otherwise deserving, highly successful software company was disqualified from the list simply because it had been too successful. It had grown too fast, from too big a base. Shortly after making the decision (but unfortunately, after the magazine had gone on the presses), the editors realized their mistake. Surely a big company that grows fast is at least as deserving — and probably more so — of recognition as a smaller company. Ever since then, the PROFIT 100 has been home to small, nascent or regional family companies as well as giant publicly traded firms that are usually more at home on the *Canadian Business* magazine list of Canada's biggest companies. By 1997, giants such as **Hummingbird Communications** ($102 million), **FirstService Corporation** ($171 million), **MDC Communications** ($233 million), **Corel Corp.** ($334 million), and **Call-Net Enterprises**, the long-distance carrier operating as **Sprint Canada** ($712 million), were sharing spots on the list with companies such as **Spider Manufacturing** of Kelowna, BC ($1,017,766).

Yet, in a way, this contrast underscored the objective of the original survey begun nine years earlier. A decade ago, Call-Net, Corel, and Hummingbird were all tiny players searching for their market niche, struggling to develop product, processes, and practices that would sustain them for the long term. In their success they embody the hopes and ideals of a generation of entrepreneurs. And while the magnitude of their accomplishments is staggering, the strategies they followed and decisions they made are little different from those of the smaller companies on the PROFIT 100. Big or small, the survey covers companies with the best growth stories and most stunning accomplishments in contemporary Canadian business. The chapters that follow will identify some of these companies, the paths they trod, and the lessons that others can derive from their successes.

CHAPTER ONE

THE SOUL OF
A NEW ECONOMY

"Companies and management that have been around for twenty-five years tend to manage people and money the old way."

Vital Dumais of Triton Electronique Inc.,
revealing why he hires only young people.

LOOKING FOR SOMETHING BETTER

Dave Jinkerson and Don Matiation were just plain frustrated. Working for a Vancouver manufacturer of sophisticated industrial machinery, they were involved in developing complex control panels to guide operations at the large sawmills that line the British Columbia coast. But the year was 1982 and the computer revolution was under way. The two friends had a vision of building computer-controlled systems that would be more precise, more powerful, and ultimately much cheaper than anything on the market. Unfortunately, the forest-products industry had entered a tailspin that showed no sign of ending.

There was simply no money to develop innovations of the sort that Jinkerson and Matiation envisioned. Their company's current product line-up, they were told, was good enough. It had to be.

No doubt about it. Paul Davis was brilliant. As a law student in his native Britain, he had paid for his education by dealing in antique clocks. At the age of twenty-four, he was an assistant law professor at the University of Ottawa. He was younger than many of his students. Davis adored the law, and even found time to co-author a textbook on sentencing practices. There was just one problem: he found the politics of academia abominable. In 1982, at the age of twenty-six, he took a year off to travel and "to get a real life," he says. To support himself, he returned to a hobby that had first captivated him in his youth. He established his own business buying and selling rare coins.

Maybe Brian Luborsky was never meant to be a chartered accountant. He enjoyed the work and he had a flair for numbers and business strategy. But at Coopers & Lybrand, as at most accounting firms, the greatest rewards are reserved for those smart enough, patient enough, and lucky enough to be named partners. "At Coopers," he says, "eighty people starved while two were made partners." He took more interest — and found more profit — in side ventures, investing in Magicuts discount hair salons as a franchisee in 1984 at the ripe old age of twenty-six, and buying and selling real estate as the Toronto property market heated up. When he finally decided that his job was interfering with the work he enjoyed, Luborsky quit to go out on his own. He had learned a lot about business management at Coopers. Could he use that experience to really make something out of his haircutting business?

THE BUMPY ROAD TO SUCCESS

Frustrated. Ambitious. Alienated. Restless. Despite their varied locations, backgrounds and professions, all these people experienced a remarkably similar sense of dissatisfaction. They were frustrated with the status quo, whether it had to do with conditions at their job or the state of their own career. They all felt that they wanted, or needed, something better. They chafed at having to toe the line, fit in, play the game by other people's rules. In other words, these four people felt exactly the way most Canadians do.

Somewhere, somehow, they knew something better was waiting for them — a way of making a living that was not just less frustrating, but more in tune with themselves, their personalities, what they enjoyed doing and who they wanted to be. They shared an unstoppable conviction that if somehow they could do things their own way, they could make not just a living, but also a difference. Forget the notion that a business is a group of people putting together a product or service to meet the needs of its customers. In the beginning, many businesses are hopelessly intertwined with the hopes, the dreams, the self-image and the innate creativity of their founders — and the impact these entrepreneurs wish to have on the world.

"Two roads diverged in a yellow wood" wrote Robert Frost. ". . . And I took the road less travelled by/And that has made all the difference." These four men took the path less traveled — the risks that most people shun, weighed down as they are with inertia, mortgages, family responsibilities, fear of the unknown and fear of failure. And their journeys became the stuff of which business legends are made.

PROFIT 10 With scant savings, Jinkerson and Matiation quit their jobs and started their own business developing computer-controlled equipment for sawmills. Paul Davis found he enjoyed travelling around the world, "buying coins in one place and selling them in another." He managed to make a healthy profit and never went back to the university. Instead, he opened a store in Ottawa from which to buy and sell coins and stamps and started dabbling in foreign currency exchange for local travellers. And Brian Luborsky discovered he had a good head for the hair-salon business. He turned his first four franchises into eight and then ten. By 1988 he owned all twenty-six Magicuts franchises and had become a minority shareholder in the company. When the company's three original founders began to disagree among themselves, they asked Luborsky to take over as president. In 1990 he bought the rest of the company and started looking for new ways to grow.

Their roads were not always smooth, and certainly not very straight. Jinkerson and Matiation, for instance, found they had to practically give their first ten systems away to get them into clients' hands. It was more than two years before their new business was able to pay either of them a salary. And Paul Davis found that while Ottawa offered a tolerable niche for a coin-and-stamp dealer, what it really needed was someone to do a better job than the local banks in foreign exchange.

SUCCESS AT LAST

One by one, these companies began to see daylight. The combination of hard-won experience, canny instincts, and their growing ability to understand what their markets were telling them helped each of these entrepreneurs grasp success. Within a few years, they began to perceive something else — that they had somehow managed to create businesses that could prove more successful than they had dared to dream. Eventually, each achieved one of the rarest and highest distinctions in Canadian business. They saw the organizations they founded, nurtured, and lovingly built brick by brick, ranked by PROFIT magazine as Canada's Fastest-Growing Company of the year.

These entrepreneurs (along with many others who rated close to them on PROFIT magazine's annual survey of Canada's Fastest-Growing Companies) had rediscovered an eternal truth of business — that positive results can emerge from restlessness, frustration, and alienation. Transforming their dissatisfaction into positive action, they came up with concrete, tangible solutions to the problems they faced. And in doing so, they achieved both material success and a sense of personal accomplishment of the sort that money can't buy.

It is for both these reasons that PROFIT magazine chronicles the stories and lessons of the PROFIT 100. For what they have accomplished, personally as well as in business, the men and women behind Canada's Fastest-Growing Companies have much to teach the rest of us. They have met all the challenges of business in the late 1990s: increasing competition; continuous innovation and quality service; the ongoing urgency of hiring, motivating, and training the right people; harnessing technology; and looking beyond national borders for growth. And they have succeeded through vision, persistence, hard work, personal sacrifice, and the personal conviction that a negative situation can be transformed into an enduring positive.

PROFIT 100 Brian Luborsky, who is now president, chairman, and CEO of **Premier Salons International Inc**. in Markham, Ontario, has come closest to defining what it is that makes an entrepreneur capable of such vision and success. "Most entrepreneurs have a belief, within themselves, that one person can make a difference," says Luborsky, whose $250-million company was named Canada's Number One Fastest-Growing Company in 1996, with five-year revenue growth of 10,190%. Luborsky believes that confidence is key to many entrepreneurs' success. "If you talk to people who have built far bigger companies than I have, you always get the same sense of, 'I know one person can make a difference, and I decided I was going to be that person.' And they do it. I don't know if that's cockiness or confidence, but they have the belief that one person can go a long way, one person can really make a difference, and they decided to be that person and to go ahead with it. Maybe everybody who thinks that isn't successful, but I tell you: Everybody who is successful thinks that."

Indeed, the lesson of the PROFIT 100 is that you don't bet against anyone based on size and you never count anyone out. As the stories of these four entrepreneurs indicate, it is still possible for a small, unknown business to come out of nowhere and dominate its markets. In fact, the evidence of the PROFIT 100 is that it can happen anywhere, anytime.

Canada's Number One Growth Companies, 1989-1997:

Year	Number One Company	City	Industry	Five-Year Growth Rate
1989	Kita Industrial Controls Ltd.	Delta, BC	computerized controls for sawmills	26,743%
1990	1141 Packaging Inc.	St. Leonard, QC	plastic packaging	7,900%
1991	JPL International Inc.	St. Laurent, QC	haircare products manufacturer	4,534%
1992	Softkey Software Products, Inc.	Mississauga, ON	consumer software	9,738%
1993	Star Data Systems	Markham, ON	financial industry information systems	11,353%

Year	Number One Company	City	Industry	Five-Year Growth Rate
1994	Accu-Rate Foreign Exchange	Ottawa, ON	currency exchange service	19,090%
1995	Alex Informatics Inc.	Lachine, QC	parallel computer manufacturer	12,765%
1996	Premier Salons International Inc.	Markham, ON	Hair salon operator/ franchisor	10,190%
1997	Oasis Technology Ltd.	North York, ON	electronic funds transfer software	10,114%

Source: PROFIT 100 surveys, 1989-1997.

The stories of Jinkerson and Matiation, Davis, Luborsky, and the other PROFIT 100 champions reveal much about the problems and hazards in today's economy and the focused strategies and creative tactics required to surmount them. While they are not unalloyed success stories, they attest to the enduring power of a great business idea — and the faith of the entrepreneurial founders.

To carry out their dreams of producing computer controllers for the forest-product industry, in 1982 Dave Jinkerson and Don Matiation revived a dormant company they had created a few years earlier for a one-off project. **Kita Industrial Controls Ltd.** wasn't exactly a dream start-up; the partners lived off savings for the six months it took to devise a salable product. While sales took off only slowly, there was no doubt that the result was a winner: their computerized systems allowed sawmills to control production more precisely and save thousands with more efficient cutting and less waste. Gradually, word got out that their product paid for itself in as little as two months. From just $8,200 in 1982 sales reached $2.2 million in 1987, good for five-year growth of 26,700%, and first place on the first PROFIT 100, published in February 1989. In 1988, meanwhile, revenues had jumped another 30%, to $2.8 million.

When the customers of Paul Davis's coin dealership started asking him to exchange their foreign currency, he couldn't guess he was about to join the ranks of Canada's growth leaders. But with travellers and business people in Ottawa waiting days for the chartered banks to change their money, Davis's commitment to instant service and lower margins attracted a steady stream of customers. In its first year, Davis's currency exchange handled about $200,000. By 1993 **Accu-Rate Foreign Exchange Corp.**, with four Ottawa-area trading booths, was ringing up volume of $37 million in 140 currencies. That 19,000% growth placed Accu-Rate number one on the 1994 PROFIT 100.

Davis says customers were just upset with the banks' handling of foreign exchange: "The service charges were high and the service was zero." PROFIT checked out his claims by calling an Ottawa bank to ask about exchanging $1,000 in Italian lire. The bank said delivery would take 24 hours — but suggested Accu-Rate would probably have the money immediately. (In fact, Accu-Rate also offered a superior exchange rate worth an additional $8.) Davis took pride in his accomplishments, but found the hard work of running four branches exhausting — his practice was to get to the office by 5:00 a.m., go back home at 8:00 to take his daughter to school, and then return to the office till 5:00 p.m. In recent years he has closed his suburban outlets to concentrate on higher-value corporate exchange services. Today his revenues are no longer growing particularly fast, but his profits are much healthier — and he gets to sleep in once in a while.

After joining Magicuts as a franchisee, Brian Luborsky acquired sole ownership of the discount haircutter in 1990. What to do for an encore? He pushed Magicuts into more retail chains, such as Zellers, and began operating higher-priced hair salons for more upscale clients such as Sears and The Bay. That growth helped Luborsky realize that chain haircutters have a big edge over independents when it comes to buying power, negotiating leases, and even training staff. With 90% of the $40-billion North American haircare business in the hands of mom-and-pop operators, he began to see an opportunity to build a continental colossus.

With the 1993 acquisition of Minneapolis-based MEI Salons, Luborsky's newly formed **Premier Salons International Inc.** became an international player. But MEI came with problems: despite owning such industry leaders as Maxim's, Essanelle, and Glemby Co., the US giant was bleeding red ink; sales had fallen to $200 million from a high of $300 million. As a result, Luborsky paid just US$30 million for the company, and threw himself into rejuvenating it, through shutdowns where necessary and with new products and improved customer service where possible. By the end of 1995 Premier operated more than 1,000 hair salons, 400 of them in Canada and 650 in the US. Premier's sales of $249 million represented five-year growth of 10,190%, good for first place on the 1996 PROFIT 100.

Besides standalone salons operating under a variety of names, Premier now operates salons for such diverse retailers as Sears, Wal-Mart, Holt Renfrew, and Neiman-Marcus, where haircuts can cost up to US$300. Luborsky says Premier's strength is its chameleon-like ability to blend in with the environment of the host retailer. "When we go into a store," he says, "we talk their language."

USEFUL TIPS AND LESSONS

Inspiring as they are, these stories provide only the merest hint of the myriad of histories, opportunities, strategies, and useful tips that underlie the complete lists. But even these few examples contain several useful lessons:

- **Success is a journey, not a destination.** None of these entrepreneurs had any idea where they would end up when they started out in their businesses. The road not taken isn't on any map, because if it were, someone else would already be there.
- **Quality service is key.** But the definition of quality may be different in every industry and every market niche.
- **Success can accrue in virtually any field of business endeavour.** High-tech firms such as Kita may seem like naturals for high growth, but who could have predicted the success of companies such as Premier in the haircare business, or of Accu-Rate in foreign exchange, surely the world's second-oldest profession?

THE PROFIT 100: AN OVERVIEW

To fully understand the dynamics of growth in today's economy, however, you have to dig a little deeper. Analysing some of the most recent PROFIT 100 rankings provides an in-depth glimpse into the new economy: who's succeeding, by how much, and in what areas. Before we can understand what makes Canada's newest business successes grow, it will help to know who they are.

Growth Rates

The PROFIT 100 is not about ordinary, everyday businesses. It is not a balanced cross-section of the Canadian economy. This is an elite group of companies ranked according to one criterion: average sales growth over the past five years. As the table below shows, their average five-year growth rate is exceptional, and it is a rate that has shown consistent growth.

But two changes in the survey tend to disguise the real growth in the following chart. First, in its initial three years, the survey tracked only fifty fast-growth companies. Thus the average growth rates for 1989-1991 are for fifty companies only, half the number used in later years. Second, in the first year of the survey, there was no minimum revenue requirement for the base year (1982). Twelve of the fifty companies in that survey had 1982 revenues of less than $100,000, creating much higher growth multiples than were seen in ensuing years when the survey adopted a base-year minimum level of $100,000 in sales.

Fast Facts: PROFIT 100 Average Growth Rates

YEAR	Average five-year growth rate
1989	820%*
1990	780%*
1991	790%*
1992	700%
1993	890%
1994	890%
1995	1,400%
1996	1,269%
1997	1,549%

* "fastest 50" companies only

What Do the PROFIT 100 Companies Do?

Over the nine years that PROFIT magazine has been studying Canada's Fastest-Growing Companies, certain patterns stand out. Without doubt, the most important is the sheer variety of companies and industries represented on the PROFIT 100.

Not all of Canada's top athletes are hockey players. And despite what many new-economy gurus might expect, not all of Canada's fastest-growing companies are computer companies. A look at the industries represented on the PROFIT 100 reveals a microcosm of the Canadian economy at its most diverse and energetic. For a country known as a hewer of wood and drawer of water, there are many unique and unexpected success stories represented on these lists. In 1997 alone, the PROFIT 100 included creators of tropically flavoured ice creams, three telemarketers, a microbrewery and a boutique winery, financial planners, system analysts, truckers, giftware wholesalers and retailers, producers and distributors of health-care products, a ginseng producer, a car-repair firm that expanded into final assembly of General Motors custom sports cars, real estate developers, printers, and a producer of hot tubs. The broad industry categories represented on the two most recent lists give some hint of the uniqueness of the companies involved and the diversity of their business plans.

Composition of the PROFIT 100

	1996	1997
Manufacturing	47	48
Business Services	28	26
Retail	9	4
Consumer Services	5	7
Distribution	7	7
Construction	3	2
Financial Services	1	4
Natural Resources	0	2
TECHNOLOGY DEVELOPMENT	34	38

MANUFACTURING: CANADA'S BEST-KEPT SECRET

Probably the single most important story on the PROFIT 100 is the dominance of manufacturing. Indeed, in 1995 manufacturers assumed a majority of 51% of the companies on the PROFIT 100. But even at 47% in 1996 and 48% in 1997, manufacturing remains surprisingly well represented on these lists. Of course this isn't General Motors-style heavy industry. And it doesn't mean union wages and double overtime for the companies' employees. These firms are by and large niche manufacturers, producing a narrow range of innovative, high-quality goods for very specialized markets.

In the past, manufacturers on the PROFIT 100 have produced goods such as helmet radios for snowmobilers, insulation for neon signs, medical-imaging equipment, geothermal heat pumps, psychological tests, T-shirts, rope, fibre-optics systems, and unmanned parachutes for US Army equipment drops. The 1996 PROFIT 100 included companies that produce skincare products, steel staircases, computer software, video-conferencing equipment, retail fixtures for stores such as Blockbuster Video, massively powerful parallel computers, bulk plastic-wrap dispensers, industrial robots, and electrical converters that turn battery power into household current which enables you to run a VCR in your car or a microwave oven on your boat. What's the connection? Generally, these are niches so obscure you've never heard of them, and small enough that the producers don't have to fight huge multinationals for market share. Their customers are demanding, want high quality, but are willing to pay for the privilege.

New Age Manufacturing

The label "manufacturing" is an increasingly unreliable indicator of what a company actually does. Today's manufacturers don't need assembly lines and dingy factories. PROFIT's list of manufacturers includes software developers, for instance. Few of these actually produce any tangible product. They usually contract out the physical production of the products they sell — computer diskettes or CD-ROMs, boxes and manuals. Their job is to write code, a task which has probably more of a traditional service orientation than most people associate with the term manufacturer. There is no assembly line, no electro-mechanical production equipment needing to be greased, no loading dock bursting with pallets of product awaiting shipment to distributors and retailers. Copying diskettes or stamping out CD-ROMs is the low-value part of the equation, a commodity industry in which a fast-growth company's chief weapon — uniqueness of product — takes second place to a manufacturer's ability to provide an agreed-upon level of quality at the lowest possible price.

Also counted as manufacturers are a few companies that have even less in common with traditional manufacturing than do today's software developers. These are companies such as **Kening Apparel** and **Thinkway Toys** (both of Markham, Ontario), that design consumer products actually produced by others, on contract, usually taking advantage of lower costs and extra capacity in factories in the Far East.

Kening Apparal (1995-96) produces quality casual men's clothing, primarily under the Quick Reflex label, which is sold in Canada and the US. Under President Ken Ng, it designs most of its fashions in Canada, and then has them produced at factories in China. The clothes are then shipped to North America for retail sale. Kening conducts all the functions of traditional manufacturers — market research, design, shipping, distribution — except for the actual assembly of the clothing. Again, that's because it can rent that capability from reliable specialists. It doesn't need the overhead, production problems or fixed costs associated with its own manufacturing line.

Thinkway Toys (1995) takes outsourcing a step further. Indeed, it may be one of the best examples of a new-economy company. One of its products is a plastic children's savings bank produced in the shape of the heads of several breeds of aliens from the television program "Star Trek." The characters — Klingon, Ferengi, Borg — were the products of fertile imaginations at Paramount Pictures in Hollywood. The banks themselves were produced, again on contract, in Chinese toy factories. Wherever they are sold in the world, the packages say "Made in China." But the true value-added step — that is, conceiving the idea of turning popular science-fiction characters into children's banks — was made in Canada. Thinking up the products, negotiating the licensing agreements, and designing the prototypes were the most important processes in actually creating the product line. And they took place just north of Toronto. Indeed, Thinkway's imagination and ability to execute has caught the eye of the best in the business. After receiving licences from Disney to produce banks and other lesser toy tie-ins for such movies as *The Lion King, Aladdin,* and *Beauty and the Beast,* Thinkway got the contract in 1995 to produce the sleeper hit of the year, the fifteen-inch-high Buzz Lightyear doll, based on the endearingly retro space ranger from Disney's animated blockbuster *Toy Story*.

Of course, there's nothing new about this form of outsourcing. For years, independent, anonymous contractors have been quietly manufacturing some of the world's best-known consumer products, from Coca-Cola to Pam cooking spray. In a global economy increasingly ruled by world product mandates and free trade, it is becoming clearer that the most important value in manufacturing lies not in producing the most widgets at the lowest cost, but in creating a track record for building brand names and creating successful new products.

In essence, then, the lines of traditional industry sectors are blurring. It's hard to tell where manufacturing ends and the service sector begins. Indeed, in many cases, what sets PROFIT 100 companies apart is their implicit understanding that niche manufacturing often has more in common with a traditional service industry than old-fashioned manufacturing. Today's best software developers are like business consultants; they even call their products "solutions." They know that their ability to listen to their customers' needs, and to be able to offer the after-sale service that their clients will require, is the key to making the sale in the first place.

McGill Multimedia of Windsor, Ontario (1996-97), produces interactive multimedia presentations for corporate clients such as Sears and General Motors, used primarily for marketing and staff training. Yes, they produce a tangible, physical product, but only after close collaboration with the client company. It's almost more a consulting contract than a manufacturing arrangement.

Similarly, **Eagle's Flight Creative Training Excellence Inc.** of Guelph, Ontario (1995-96), produces simulation games and training exercises, geared primarily to big corporations such as Air Canada, Disney, and Microsoft. Again, its product can be boxed and sold. Increasingly, however, Eagle's Flight's activities include supplying people to run those training exercises. Here again a manufacturer is slipping into a service role.

While hybrid businesses such as these make chart compilers' hair go grey, they point out yet another lesson to keep in mind. Whether they consider themselves manufacturing or service firms, today's growth companies share a commitment to communication with, and high-quality service to, their selected markets. Indeed, their most important asset isn't just the ability to conceive of or stamp out a good product, but to maintain strong relations with an ever-growing roster of clients.

THE TRIUMPH OF TECHNOLOGY

In the sixties' film *The Graduate,* a friendly neighbour pulls Dustin Hoffman aside to whisper some invaluable career advice in one word, "Plastics." Is there a turn-of-the-century equivalent to plastics? Of course there is, says the PROFIT 100. It's the computer. And it is becoming more dominant every day.

Aside from the increasingly vague category of manufacturing, the largest single category of companies on the PROFIT 100 each year stems from the sector that we broadly call technology development. This includes computer hardware manufacturers, software developers, systems integrators, and the odd company in biotechnology or telecommunications. In recent years technology companies have tended to account for between 33 % and 40 % of the PROFIT 100, which is good news for Canadian entrepreneurs any way you look at it. On the one hand, with companies such as graphics-software pioneer **Corel Corp.** (the first company to make the PROFIT 100 list six years in a row), connectivity-software designer **Hummingbird Communications, iStar Internet,** computer-aided manufacturing giant **Rand A. Technology Corp.**, printer-driver developer **GDT Softworks**, and video-conference systems producer **CBCI Telecom,** the PROFIT 100 offers proof that Canada is developing a growing, sustainable technology industry that is succeeding in world markets. And for those who prefer their glass half-empty, the fact that two-thirds of the PROFIT 100 list comprises low-tech or no-tech companies is also good news. It's proof that opportunities still abound in the more traditional niches that new-economy pundits tend to ignore.

Because of the growing number of technology niches, and the relative speed with which high-tech products reach world markets, tech companies are beginning to crowd the PROFIT 100. In 1997 there were thirty-eight technology development companies on the PROFIT 100 list. Throw in three telemarketers, three computer software and hardware retailers, a few consultants, and a printer and a cinematic special-effects firm that work almost exclusively with leading-edge technology, and it's arguable that high-tech firms now make up half the list of Canada's Fastest-Growing Companies.

With their often-enviable profit margins and economies of scale, tech firms have come to dominate the high end of the PROFIT 100, as is evident from 1997's top ten companies.

The Top 10 PROFIT 100 Companies in 1997

Oasis Technology	electronic funds transfer software
Shikatronics Inc.	computer memory
Hummingbird Communications Ltd.	Unix-PC connectivity software
The G.A.P Adventures Inc.	adventure travel
Iris Power Engineering Inc.	industrial-testing systems
Media Express Telemarketing Corp.	telemarketing
Brigdon Resources Ltd.	oil and gas production
Image Processing Systems Inc.	machine vision systems
Datalog Technology Inc.	drill site-monitoring software
Virtek Vision Corp.	machine-vision systems

That's three software developers, one producer of computer memory boards and three companies that combine hardware and software to produce industrial products companies — seven high-tech companies in the top ten. And with all the automation involved in outfitting today's high-tech call centre, there's a good case for considering **Media Express** (which sells insurance, credit cards, and other products by phone) a technology company as well.

Generally, technology companies look pretty formidable, and often incomprehensible, to outsiders. What mere mortal, for instance, could hope to duplicate the success of **Virtek** (1995-97), a $6-million-a-year manufacturer of laser-based machine-vision systems in Waterloo, Ontario? Spun out of the University of Waterloo's Pattern Analysis and Machine Intelligence Lab, Virtek now sells to such companies as Boeing, Lockheed, British Aerospace, and Eurocopter France.

Still, some of the PROFIT 100 companies have decidedly humble origins. **Gage Applied Sciences Inc.** (1995-97), a Montreal producer of computer accessories that replace any number of scientific measuring instruments, started out as a school project for President Muneeb Khalid. **Aurora Microsystems Distribution Inc.** (1996-97), a computer systems reseller in Copper Cliff, Ontario, was launched in 1987 by twenty-five-year-old physics graduate Kevin Fitzgerald. He had sold computers part-time during university and after six months of unemployment, decided to go into business for himself, figuring that Sudbury-area businesses and institutions needed a computer vendor who could be more sensitive to their needs. As with so many entrepreneurs, his first financial support was provided by credit cards and the bank of Dad.

Al Hildebrandt was selling staff-scheduling software to McDonald's Restaurants when he discovered a scheduling program being co-developed by the British Columbia Institute of Technology and a hospital in Kelowna, BC. The thirty-nine-year-old Grade 12 graduate saw a huge opportunity in helping hospitals manage their myriad of employees, specialties, shifts, union rules, and staff changes. He negotiated a technology-transfer agreement that allowed him to take over the product in return for cash upfront, royalties, and a continuing supply of updated product. Six years later his company, Kelowna-based **Total Care Technologies,** had revenues of $4.4 million, forty employees, and was selling to institutions in the US and Holland as well as across Canada.

Similarly, many PROFIT 100 technology all-stars started out with only a vague notion of what they would eventually end up doing. Like entrepreneurs in most industries, the founders of the PROFIT 100's high-tech firms had to take time to read the signals of the market place and find out where they could best add value. **Hummingbird Communications** started out as a computer-consulting firm before founders Barry Litwin and Fred Sorkin recognized a more secure niche (connectivity software) to see them through the recession they both anticipated. **Corel Corp.** started out selling desktop-publishing systems before coming to recognize the immense power of its graphics software CorelDraw.

While the technology behind many of these companies may be hard to understand, the reasons for their success are not. Much like winning companies in every other field, Canada's highest flyers in high-tech have won out because they knew their markets and identified a niche that no one else could fill as well.

CONSUMER BUSINESSES BEWARE

A second glance at the table on page 10 underscores another important characteristic of growth companies. Very few are solely active in consumer markets. For the five service companies on the 1996 list involved in consumer markets (think of lawn care, funeral homes or long-distance reselling), there were twenty-nine firms providing services to business. They included motivational training, computer and telecommunications consulting, telemarketing, trucking, industrial recycling, and oil-well monitoring. It only makes sense, of course, because business generally has much greater need for the sort of sophisticated, value-added services that fast-growth companies provide, and it's willing to pay more for them. Consumer services generally have to be sold one household at a time. In contrast, sales to business — especially blue-chip clients such as Stelco, Hydro-Québec, the Royal Bank, Boeing, and Microsoft, to name just a few of the companies that patronize PROFIT 100 firms — can result in multiple repeat sales to various corporate levels or branches, creating the foundations for fast and sustainable growth based on good relations with just a handful of key customers.

Retail, the traditional domain of the savvy independent entrepreneur, turns out to be a much less common route to fast growth. While Canada boasts many successful retailers, few of them are able to move beyond single store or regional operations. Retail, as they say, is detail. Reproducing a success formula that depends on close attention to a store's appearance, respect for the customer, and an intimate understanding of local markets is actually much tougher than manufacturing a consistently workable grapple-grommet or selling a package of services to businesses at a national or even international level.

Which is not to say that it can't be done. The 1996 PROFIT 100 list contained nine retailers (two of which were actually restaurant operations: **Humpty's Restaurants International**, a breakfast-style family restaurant chain; and coffee-shop franchisor **Comac Food Group**, whose growing chains include Grabbajabba and Company's Coming Bakery Cafes). Interestingly, four of the nine retailers (including both restaurant chains) hail from Calgary, a city normally better known for its oil and gas or even computer technology than its retail savvy. For a look at the challenges that confront any Canadian retailer who tries to grow by the stratospheric multiples enjoyed by the PROFIT 100, let's look at the story of the **Forzani Group**.

One Calgary retailer, **Forzani Group Ltd.** (1996), exemplifies the risks that ambitious retailers confront when trying to expand in today's relatively mature retail markets. The business was started in 1974 as a sports-shoe retailer, targeting local athletes who had previously been forced to go to the US to find their preferred specialty shoes. Under John Forzani, one of three Forzani brothers who played football in the 1970s for the Calgary Stampeders, the business grew through expansion and acquisition into a full-line purveyor of sporting goods. But it was only in 1994, with the acquisition of Provigo Inc.'s 180-store Sports Experts chain and the simultaneous opening of thirty-two new outlets, many of them football-field-sized superstores, that Forzani hit the big leagues of growth.

Sales quadrupled, but the company was sacked by high operating losses and a plummeting stock price. In the spring of 1997 Forzani announced a restructuring plan that included store closures and forgiveness of some of its debts — the end (for now) of its expansion phase. Still, John Forzani remained convinced he had made the right moves. He had acted to forestall the arrival in Canada of the new US sports superstores. While he failed to keep them out, he won at least one battle. In late 1996, US-based Sportmart, tired of losing money north of the border, announced it was closing all eleven Canadian stores, taking its ball and going home. In an industry that has seen US giants such as Office Depot, Wal-Mart, and Michael's push out homegrown Canadian competitors, it was a rare win — albeit a costly one — for the home side.

VALUE-ADDED DISTRIBUTION

With seven firms involved in various phases of the distribution chain in 1996, the PROFIT 100 underscores the importance of innovation as a growth tool. In the age of same-day couriers, retail-oriented warehouse clubs, electronic commerce, and increasingly closer ties between manufacturers, retailers, and end-users, most commentators have dismissed distributors as an endangered species. With the information swaps and direct-sales opportunities created by the Internet, goes the thinking, who needs the commission-swallowing middleman any more? The answer is that there will always be a future for intermediaries that add value. And the distributors on the PROFIT 100 include firms such as these.

IntelaTech Inc. (1995-97) is a Mississauga, Ontario, electronics distributor that started out as a manufacturer's rep, selling semiconductors and other high-tech electronic components to computer and telecom-equipment manufacturers such as Northern Telecom and IBM. Over time, however, it realized it had more in common with its customers than with the parts suppliers it represented. IntelaTech has since restructured itself as a value-added partner to its clients, helping them solve their production problems by sourcing growing numbers of parts from an increasing number of suppliers.

Similarly, **Maple Homes Canada Ltd.** of Richmond, BC (1996) doesn't produce anything itself. It sells quality wooden building products, such as Loewen Windows from Manitoba and Mercier Flooring of Quebec, to contractors and construction companies building upscale wood houses in Japan. Behind its rather bland self-description as a "building products consolidator," Maple Homes is really an innovative value-added partner to both manufacturer and contractor, helping expand sales for the Canadian suppliers even as it assists with customs clearance and quality control on the job site in Japan.

From software to sportswear, most PROFIT 100 companies share the link of unswerving commitment to providing value to a well-targeted customer group.

JOBS, JOBS, JOBS

It's almost too obvious to say, but too important not to point out. The diversity, ambition, and success of the PROFIT 100 have helped them deliver one thing that big business and governments apparently no longer can — jobs. As they grow, Canada's Fastest-Growing Companies are proving to be powerful engines of job creation, confirming the widespread notion that it is small- and medium-sized businesses that generate the most jobs in society today. The PROFIT 100 companies created 2,281 new jobs in 1993; 3,184 in 1994; 4,792 in 1995; and 4,089 in 1996. It's important to point out that these are net new jobs, not the results of mergers or acquisitions.

Nor are these simply the boring, low-wage McJobs that some pessimists claim would be produced in the global service economy. PROFIT 100 companies have a healthy appetite for experienced managers (usually to make up for the founders' lack of administrative experience), computer technicians, software developers, creative marketers, and skilled tradespeople. Nor are these people considered liabilities or mere units of production as they might be at some larger organizations. Miles Nadal, founder and CEO of **MDC Corp.**, a Toronto communications firm and three-time PROFIT 100 company, speaks for all fast-growth companies when he says, "Our quality people are our most important asset." (See Chapter 13 for more on PROFIT 100 entrepreneurs' relations with their employees.)

While PROFIT has never researched the average age of the employees of the PROFIT 100 companies, it would certainly skew young, the average probably being in the late twenties or early thirties. These are young companies, after all. In 1997 their average age was just ten years. In many cases, young people come with the technical skills growing companies need, especially in relation to technology. Further, young people tend to come cheaper than older ones, an important consideration for growing companies. Most important, young people tend to share the optimism, enthusiasm, and willingness to change that are the hallmark of their PROFIT 100 employers. "Because we have such a young team, we embrace new ideas and philosophies," says Vital Dumais, founder of contract-manufacturer **Triton Electronique**

Inc. (1994-96) of St. Eustache, Quebec. "Companies and management that have been around for twenty-five years tend to manage people and money the old way."

DISTRIBUTION OF THE PROFIT 100

When the government appoints new members to the Senate or the Supreme Court, geographic balance is of paramount consideration. When the National Hockey League selects players for its annual all-star game, it makes sure every team is represented.

The PROFIT 100 doesn't work that way. As a numbers-driven list, it suffers from none of the need for geographic correctness that afflicts government appointments, all-star teams or even such business awards as Entrepreneur of the Year. The PROFIT 100 represents the real world. In its rankings, each region or province stands or falls based solely on its ability to generate fast-growth companies. This means that the PROFIT 100 results paint a very interesting, and instructive, new map of Canada's economic landscape.

Coast to Coast: PROFIT 100 Ranking by Province (1995-97)

	1995	1996	1997
Atlantic Canada	0	0	4
Quebec	17	17	17
Ontario	45	52	53
Manitoba	3	1	3
Saskatchewan	2	1	0
Alberta	11	11	6
British Columbia	22	18	17

Distribution of the PROFIT 100 doesn't exactly reflect Canada's population patterns. Considering that British Columbia and Ontario respectively account for about 12% and 38% of the country's population, both provinces are clearly punching well above their weight class. The case of Quebec, with 25% of Canada's population but just 17% of its top growth companies, is less clear-cut. Although the PROFIT 100 survey is conducted by

PROFIT's ballot-distribution partners in French as well as English, PROFIT's status as an English-language publication undoubtedly skews the results somewhat. In recent years the magazine has entered into an alliance with Montreal-based newsmagazine *L'actualité* to increase participation among francophone entrepreneurs to reflect more closely Quebec's entrepreneurial activity. Of all the provinces only Alberta, which has a little more than 10% of Canada's population, traditionally places an equivalent number of companies on the PROFIT 100.

That the less industrialized provinces of Manitoba, Saskatchewan, and Atlantic Canada have been so under-represented in the survey helps demonstrate an inescapable insight into the nature of growth companies. They grow fastest in proximity to an existing industrial base. The bias, in other words, is not provincial but regional.

It makes sense, after all. We have already discovered that PROFIT 100 companies tend to develop close relationships with suppliers and customer groups. Many consider themselves business partners rather than mere purchasers or vendors of goods and services. Many, especially in high-tech industries, draw from the same talent pool, requiring that they locate close to the centre of the action. That's why closer observation of the 1996 PROFIT 100 reveals twenty-eight companies hailing from the Greater Toronto Area, with four more from the nearby Hamilton-Niagara area, and three others from the Kitchener-Waterloo-Guelph area. Similarly, thirteen of Quebec's seventeen PROFIT 100 companies hailed from the Montreal region and fifteen of BC's eighteen are located in Greater Vancouver. Of Alberta's eleven companies, nine came from Calgary and the other two from the Edmonton area. Nine companies hail from the Ottawa area (including one across the Ottawa River in Aylmer, Quebec).

But Canada's Fastest-Growing Companies are definitely not just a downtown crowd. Half of the Toronto-area companies come from outside the Metropolitan Toronto limits, from suburban cities such as Burlington, Mississauga, Richmond Hill, and Markham. The flight to better transportation and cheaper real estate is especially apparent in BC. Of the fifteen Vancouver-area companies on the 1996 PROFIT 100, only four are located in the crowded city of Vancouver itself. Four are in nearby Burnaby, three are in Richmond (close to the airport), two in Delta, and one each in Langley and Surrey. Clearly, Canada's Fastest-Growing Companies are not dependent on the downtown financial core so much as they prefer the wider-open spaces, cheaper rents, easier access to other new-economy, suburban-type companies, and a shorter drive to work.

Of course, outstanding growth companies can spring from diverse and unusual roots. It's a matter of odds. Out of 100 fast-growing companies, you'd expect a few to come out of home towns such as Antigonish, Nova Scotia, St. George, New Brunswick or Amherstburg, Ontario. It's a reminder that in the end, despite the importance of the right infrastructure and close customer ties, it's the vision, courage, and character of the individual entrepreneur that ultimately determines an organization's destiny.

THE PEOPLE BEHIND THE PROFIT 100

Four Roads to Success

Fred Sorkin arrived in Canada from Lithuania in 1976 at the age of thirty-eight with $150 in his pocket. Since he could barely speak English, potential employers weren't much impressed with his PhD in computer science, his master's degrees in mathematics and electronics, nor his recent position as chief designer for the Soviet Union's second-biggest computer company. For two months, Sorkin gathered scrap paper to survive. Twenty years later, as president and CEO of **Hummingbird Communications Ltd.** (1994-97), Sorkin was a world leader in computer technology and enjoyed an estimated net worth of $90 million. Today his company's name adorns Toronto's premier theatre complex, the Hummingbird Centre, known until 1996 as the O'Keefe Centre. Hummingbird's $5-million donation was Fred Sorkin's way of saying thanks.

Jeff Hunt was just nineteen when he dropped out of university to start a residential carpet-cleaning company. Having worked in carpet cleaning to pay his way through school, it was the only business he knew. Trouble was, he needed capital to buy equipment. With no experience, no savings, and no home to mortgage, the banks wouldn't touch him. Showing the creative side that would serve him so well in later years,

Hunt persuaded two friends from wealthy families to invest $6,500. Five other friends supplied free muscle in return for sweat equity in Hunt's new **Canway Ltd.** Seven years later in 1991, Canway first appeared on the PROFIT 100 as Canada's nineteenth-fastest-growing company, with sales of $3.4 million. In 1997, Canway made its sixth appearance on the list, with 1996 sales of $39.5 million — more than half of it generated in the United States. With a major US competitor having just declared bankruptcy, Hunt is now looking forward to accelerating Canway's US growth with the goal of becoming a $100-million company. He is thirty-two years old.

"I'm proud of my age," says sixty-four-year-old Sylvia Vogel. "It's not easy to get there." In fact, she says ten years ago people were asking why she hadn't retired yet. "They would never ask a man that." The reason she's never retired is she's now having too much fun. After working in her chemist husband's skincare business for fifteen years, in 1972 she jumped at the chance to start her own business to distribute an American skin-lightening product in Canada. Her company, **Canderm Pharma Inc.** (1996-97), had sales of half a million dollars a year by the mid-1980s, when her supplier was acquired by another firm which then refused to honour her contract. Feeling betrayed, she sued. Five years later, she agreed to an out-of-court settlement. In the meantime, she acquired new product lines, but her greatest coup was the 1991 launch of Neo-Strata. A pharmaceutical-based skin lotion aimed at baby boomers intending to fight growing older, Neo-Strata powered Canderm from sales of $350,000 in 1990 to $11 million in 1996. In that year Vogel also bought the Canadian rights to Pfizer's Bain de Soleil line of sunscreen products and launched Canderm's own R&D program to develop its own products. Obviously, it's not just baby boomers who know how to fight every step of the way.

Rob Bakshi was a Vancouver information systems consultant in 1986 when he teamed up with chief coroner Bob Galbraith to save lives. Galbraith was investigating a fatal collision of two police vehicles, and he wished he had some way to know what was going on in each car in the last ten or fifteen seconds. Bakshi saw the need for a black box of the sort used in planes to record speed, instrument levels, and scheduling. Together they started a company called **Silent Witness** to build those black boxes. The company went public to raise money in 1987, but Galbraith didn't want to quit his job. Bakshi was vice-president, but considered too young to run a public company. He resigned after a difference of opinion with the new president. Five years later, however, Bakshi was back, steering the floundering company into a new niche: tiny, vandal-proof TV cameras to monitor passenger behaviour on school buses and public transit. With Bakshi as president, Silent Witness is now targeting new commercial markets such as stores, banks, and gas stations. Its made-in-Canada closed-circuit cameras are now sold in twenty-two countries. With 1996 sales of $8.3 million, up 1200% in five years, "we've gained a lot of respect in the security market in a short time," says Bakshi. "We're now looked at as market leaders and innovators."

The Importance of Attitude

As these four stories indicate, there is no single career path for the people who start and run Canada's fast-growth companies. PROFIT 100 entrepreneurs are PhDs, MBAs, engineers, accountants, and high-school drop-outs. Some hit their stride only when they were nearing retirement age, while many are under thirty and using their youthful success to try to figure out what to do when they grow up. Most have been seasoned by working for other companies prior to joining the business that rocketed onto the PROFIT 100. But others got lucky on their first try. Some have known tough times and near failure, while others have been spoiled by rapid success. What they lack in shared background, however, PROFIT 100 entrepreneurs make up in one common characteristic: attitude.

You might say that business success today is not just affected by attitude. It depends on it. In 1995, St. Catharines, Ontario, academic and consultant Eugene Luczkiw surveyed forty entrepreneurs from the PROFIT 100 to find out more about today's successful businesspeople and what makes them tick. One of his biggest surprises came in his deceptively simple question, "Which of these three factors would you rank as most important to the growth of your enterprise: attitude, knowledge, or skills?"

Thirty-one out of forty respondents (77.5%) ranked attitude as number one. Just seven entrepreneurs cited knowledge first, and only two chose skills. In the excitement over the information economy and the rush to build knowledge-based organizations, it is intriguing to note that Canada's top growth firms consider attitude, not knowledge, to be the indispensable cornerstone of their success.

"How do you get a company to grow like crazy?" asks Premier Salons' Brian Luborsky. Darned if he knows, he says. But there's one Southern US saying (best recited, he says, with a slow Southern drawl) that sums up the attitude he believes it takes to succeed: "It's not the size of the dog in the fight, but the size of the fight in the dog."

For the record, here is a statistical breakdown of the 1997 PROFIT 100.

The People Behind the 1997 PROFIT 100

Number of women-owned and -run companies on the list:	4
Average age:	42
Percent with just a high-school education:	13
Percent who completed post-secondary education:	69
Percent of current PROFIT 100 CEOs who founded or co-founded the company they now head:	89
Percent of men who regularly wear a tie to work:	38
Average salary:	$196,000

CHERCHEZ LA FEMME

For many (perhaps half the population), the most dispiriting aspect of the PROFIT 100 is the shortage of women in its lofty ranks. In no single year has there been more than five female CEOs on the PROFIT 100. You can speculate endlessly on the reasons. While women are now starting businesses at a faster rate than men, the types of businesses they start (consulting, retail, and personal services, for example) are not the sort that commonly enjoy the wildfire expansion necessary to qualify for the PROFIT 100. Similarly, the sectors that comprise the biggest components of the PROFIT 100 — manufacturing and technology — are those that women have been least likely to go into in the past.

And then there are questions of personal management style. Many observers have argued that women are more concerned with a balanced lifestyle (or too busy running a family as well as a business) than in chasing down every opportunity in pursuit of unshackled growth. Women, say the pundits, are more likely to settle for a moderate rate of growth and a positive home life than to pursue growth for growth's sake. While awaiting further research on this topic, we will note these happy developments on the 1997 list.

Iris Power Engineering Inc. (1997) of Toronto was founded in 1990 by three male technicians and engineers in the research section at Ontario Hydro and a woman who had started out in the section as a secretary. In September 1996 the partners decided that management by consensus wasn't working and someone had to be in charge. They looked around to see which of them was most qualified and chose Resi Zarb, forty-eight, who by that time was already looking after marketing and finance. She believes that she brought consistency into the management of the company. "My biggest challenge will be keeping my three partners on track," she says. "They spin all over like free electrons, and that's what makes them good-idea guys."

Sylvia Vogel of **Canderm Pharma Inc.** (1996-97), a two-time PROFIT 100 winner, has another take on the subject of male versus female management styles. The founder and president of Montreal-based Canderm, she knows the disadvantages women face in the workplace. Before she started her own company in 1972, she spent fifteen years working for her husband's dermatological-products firm, which usually meant looking after her two young children by day and shipping product at night. "I was always the wife," she says. "I had total control of administration...[but] I was always described as giving him a hand. And I never thought it should be different." As she admits, she had grown up in a very traditional family and had no role models of businesswomen to look up to.

Even in her own business, she says, she had to deal with suppliers and others who considered her a figurehead or an easy mark. She proved them all wrong, acquiring the product lines (Neo-Strata and Bain de Soleil) that made her company successful. And she did it her way. Despite the problems she has faced, Vogel believes women actually have an edge in the so-called soft skills that are so important in small business. "Women have good intuition," she says. "I always hire management that knows more than me." As well, she adds, women "can admit to being emotional and nobody thinks that's strange. For example, I see my employees as being part of my family. I talk to them, I listen to their problems, and sometimes I even get involved in their personal lives. I don't think that's a common management technique these days, but it seems to work because they stick around, and they do their jobs very well." As the winner of a Canadian Woman Entrepreneur of the Year award as well as a two-time PROFIT 100 winner, she is now in a position to be the role model that was denied to her.

MONEY, MONEY, MONEY

One myth the PROFIT 100 *can* demolish is the notion that entrepreneurs need a lot of money to start a business with any potential. As we will discover in Chapter 11, some of Canada's top growth companies were founded on a shoestring. Jeff Hunt of Ottawa-based **Canway** enlisted a few friends to lend him money to buy carpet-cleaning equipment.

John Dobson, president of **Imports Inc.** in Antigonish, Nova Scotia, which operates six stores selling imported jewellery, handicrafts, and giftware, started out with a $2,000 loan from Dad. Like many others on the PROFIT 100, he accessed later capital needs by maxing out purchases and cash advances on an ever-growing number of credit cards. With sales of $1.4 million and a profit of $11,000, he now has no problem getting bank financing. But Dobson keeps a reminder close by of his early days. He has framed all his old credit cards and hung them on his office wall.

Many other PROFIT 100 companies were started by unemployed or moonlighting young people with little or no money. Many companies, from Imports Inc. to **Softkey Software Products Inc.,** now a US-based software giant, saved money by starting out in living rooms, garages or basements. The point, it seems, isn't really how much money you start out with, but how much you really want to get where you're going.

Toronto-based **High-Tech Cable Inc.**, number thirteen on the 1996 PROFIT 100, was founded by President Chris Koufatzis in 1990 to develop network designs and software for cable and telecommunications companies. When the banks laughed at the former Rogers Cable employee and his ideas, Koufatzis raised $100,000 by taking out a second mortgage on his house. That can be a risky strategy, but, as an immigrant from Greece, he figured he could afford it. "I came here with nothing, so if it didn't work, I figured I'd go back to Rogers. They'd take me back." Within five years High-Tech Cable had sales of $4.5 million, a staff of ninety, assets of $3 million and, he reported, "the banks are coming to me big-time."

REWARDS

Entrepreneurs don't do it for the money. The costs of building a growth business — the long hours, the sleepless nights, constant travel, worries about employees, the stress on family life — can't be paid for in any amount of cash. According to PROFIT magazine research, the average entrepreneur works about fifty hours a week, ten to twelve hours more than the average employee. But PROFIT 100 executives work longer still. Our PROFIT 100 surveys in 1992, 1993, and 1994 found that the CEOs of Canada's Fastest-Growing Companies worked sixty-two, sixty-one, and fifty-nine hours a week, respectively. While it appears that these CEOs are trying to cut back the workload, it is unlikely the average will come down much further. There is simply too much to do.

So why do they take this on, if not for the cash? The rewards of building your own business — the autonomy, the exhilaration of winning a new contract or beating out a competitor in a fair fight, the joy of hiring or of promoting a trusted employee, the ability to tell your bank to take a hike — these are the moments PROFIT 100 entrepreneurs treasure. As Brian Luborsky of **Premier Salons** notes, "I think most [entrepreneurs] would say that they do it partly for the money, but you can make money other ways. I mean, you can make money as an executive, and it's a lot safer. I think most entrepreneurs do it because of the opportunity and the interest, because it's fun to do. I don't know too many guys who run their own companies who say, 'It's really boring and I really hate it, but boy the money's good.' I hear a lot of dentists say it, or doctors, or lawyers, but not entrepreneurs."

Still, the rewards of running a successful business can add up. After a hard day's work, it's nice to drive home in the Lexus, the Jaguar or the '67 Mustang you always wanted. Or, like Ray Loewen, head of the billion-dollar **Loewen Group** of funeral-home operators (1993-95), it's convenient to have a 110-foot yacht in Vancouver harbour (complete with helipad) for the odd fishing trip or entertaining clients. And certainly, the reported salaries of the PROFIT 100 entrepreneurs don't include any gain in the value of their company shares over the years. Still, canny readers have already figured out that the high incomes of today's PROFIT 100 winners shouldn't overshadow the sacrifices many of them made through the early years of their businesses. Most of them have close personal experience of what it's like to live without a salary, taking only as much out of the company as they need to survive, sliding further into debt in order to make sure their loyal employees get paid every week. In many cases, it will take years for a salary of $150,000 or $200,000 to compensate for the personal and financial sacrifices these entrepreneurs have made over the years.

And if that doesn't pull on your heartstrings, consider these words from an entrepreneur and father of three on the PROFIT 100 after he paid himself an annual salary and bonus worth $450,000, "It doesn't matter how much you earn. There still isn't anything left at the end of the week. The taxes just kill you."

If PROFIT 100 companies represent a wide range of industries and business approaches, the people behind them reflect at least equal diversity. But in each of them there has been a spark, a flare, a sense of confidence, and a determination to do what must be done to right a wrong, solve a problem, or satisfy a customer. It is that persistent vision of a better way, along with the confidence that an individual's skill and effort can still make a difference in this complex world, that has created Canada's Fastest-Growing Companies. In the coming chapters, we will see what has shaped and sustained them.

CHAPTER TWO

DON'T JUST CREATE, INNOVATE

"It was either great wisdom or great stupidity to go ahead with a project that large . . . . We were pioneering, and it's tough when you're pioneering."

Allan Millman, president, Fantom
Technologies Inc.

Kerosene. The telephone. Basketball. The variable-pitch propeller. The pacemaker. The paint roller. The snowmobile. The aluminum hockey stick. Trivial Pursuit. Which of these products was *not* conceived in Canada or invented by Canadians?

The answer is the metal hockey stick. All the rest are truly Canadian innovations—brand-new ideas, superior extensions of previous products, or niche products to meet specialized needs. It's a short list (we didn't even mention standard time, the first television transmitter, retractable satellite radio antennas, insulin, or Balderdash), but it's an inspiring one. And it's proof that Canadians have always had a gift for problem solving and creativity.

To paraphrase the people who sell magazine subscriptions, innovation is the gift that keeps on giving. The ability to conceptualize and develop new solutions to nagging problems or customer needs is the single best hope for success in the world today, whether it be for an individual, a company or an entire society. As life speeds up, as people's problems become more complicated, as the competition for jobs, resources, and business opportunities intensifies, innovation is emerging as the key essential survival skill in business and life. Modern technology today allows almost everyone to follow the market leaders, or even go them one better. Only the ability to innovate competitively and continually will provide any sort of lasting edge.

Do the people who invented kerosene and standard time still have what it takes to succeed? Oh, yes. If the PROFIT 100 is any indication, innovation is as Canadian as maple syrup and double overtime.

Consider these innovative products from companies on the 1997 PROFIT 100 list of Canada's Fastest-Growing Companies:

- machine-vision systems that analyse used beer bottles to make sure the threads are unchipped and intact prior to refilling and capping (**Image Processing Systems Inc.**, Scarborough, Ontario);

- AC-DC inverters that enable household appliances to run off a car battery, allowing you to carry a TV or VCR in your car or boat (**Statpower Technologies Corp.**, Burnaby, BC);

- motorized carpet and vinyl-sheeting carousels for use in Home Depot and other warehouse stores (**Vidir Machine Ltd.**, Arborg, Manitoba);

- staff-scheduling software geared to the health-care industry in Canada and the United States (**Total Care Technologies Inc.**, Kelowna, BC);

- new processes for the preservation of fresh fruits, vegetables and flowers (**Pacific Asia Technologies Inc.**, Toronto);

- hardware and software to monitor the insulation condition of high-voltage motors, enabling heavy industries to avoid costly maintenance downtime and head off nasty repair bills (**Iris Power Engineering Inc.**, Toronto);

- mango-flavoured ice cream (**Tropical Treets/Caribbean Ice Cream Co. Ltd.**, Toronto);

- enclosure systems to house and hide the increasing numbers of phone lines, networking cables and power cords cluttering up today's offices (**Spider Manufacturing Inc.**, Kelowna, BC);

- retractable-roofed (à la SkyDome) swimming pool enclosures that allow year-round use of pools and solariums (**OpenAire Inc.**, Mississauga, Ontario); and

- hydraulically powered scaffolding systems that are safer, stronger, and much easier to move and set up than conventional work platforms (**Avant-Garde Engineering Inc.**, L'Assomption, Quebec).

The first thing to note is that none of these products is about to replace the telephone or basketball as a household appliance or international pastime. Innovations, after all, usually occur in incremental steps, not giant leaps. But more thoughtful consideration should generate substantially more respect for these innovating entrepreneurs. In an era when manufacturing is supposed to be on its last legs, they are all creating original, value-added finished products. At a time of increasing global competition, all are selling into international markets. In a country best known as an exporter of raw materials, they are creating much-needed manufacturing and service jobs by the score. And finally, none of these companies believes its product line is set. They are all reinvesting in research and product development, tweaking and poking their products continually to make sure that they are the best they can be.

In an economy still weighed down by unemployment and fears of recession, all the above companies posted five-year growth rates, from 1991 to 1996, in excess of 600%. It's a testament to the power of niche markets and to the ability of entrepreneurs to identify narrow markets where needs are going unmet and competition is just slack enough to allow new entrants a foothold. And the success of companies such as these reveals just an inkling of the broad spectrum of niches that is out there, awaiting the deft hand of the entrepreneur and innovator.

THE NICHE ECONOMY

We've all heard about the new economy that is changing our lives. It always seems to be associated with computers and telecommunications, science, and technology, and falling trade barriers. In fact, however, the most powerful element of the concept of the new economy may just be the raw potential it gives innovative products to transform niche markets and build substantial businesses. Sure, the new economy is a great place for PhDs to be selling products based on cloning or cold fusion. For most entrepreneurs, however, the new economy has one overarching significance. It's an economy whose affluence, diversity, and technological sophistication have resulted in an almost limitless supply of specialty markets, each waiting to be filled by new, quality products targeted directly to that niche. As the PROFIT 100 manufacturers above suggest, these products could be geared to consumers or business. They could be physical products you can see and touch, eat or use, or they could be intangible services. They could be sophisticated high-tech marvels or no-tech no-brainers. But the appetite for new specialty products has never been greater.

The evidence is all around us, though we don't even see it as that. Think about what you see in the aisles of any store you visit today. How many types of bicycles can you buy now? Jeans? Radios? (Sorry — stereos, CD players, boom boxes, scanners, and Walkmans.) A generation ago, North Americans ate spaghetti and meat balls or macaroni and cheese. Now we eat pasta in a dizzying variety of shapes and colours, augmented with more types of cheeses and sauces than grandma ever knew existed.

All this fragmentation represents the natural evolution of markets, from mass to niche. Today's customers and users demand choice, and today's entrepreneurs are the best available delivery vehicle. Since no one company can anticipate, let alone supply, all these emerging needs, the beneficiaries of market fragmentation are the sharp-eyed entrepreneurs who know individual markets and can move fast to supply the demands they see. While big companies are hiring focus groups to test their concepts or begging head office for development funds, free-ranging entrepreneurs are already out in the field selling, trusting their instincts and experience to guide them into and through their new niche. The best products start with a conviction, not a committee.

Of course, coming up with a new product doesn't assure success. Thousands of people have invented better mousetraps and waited in vain for the world to beat that path to their door. Successful product development is just one step in a long line of disciplines that an entrepreneur must master to create a successful and sustainable business. Most of these other factors — from distribution and marketing to hiring and financing — will be covered in later chapters. For now, however, developing the right product, one that is well targeted, innovative, and offers added value in its niche, is the first step in the entrepreneurial journey.

Let's say you get it right. You find a product that serves a niche better than anything else before it. What kind of difference can one successful product really make? In some cases, all the difference in the world. Let's look at the case of Allan Millman. He literally saved his company, and then transformed it utterly, by coming up with one product: a better vacuum cleaner.

• MARK OF THE FANTOM •

Allan Millman had a problem. As president of **Iona Appliances Inc.** in Welland, Ontario, he had risked his reputation and financial future to buy the company in 1984 after its former owner, a US multinational, decided that the Canadian manufacturer no longer fit its future plans. Millman believed in Iona — a plucky niche manufacturer if there ever was one — one of the last Canadian companies making household appliances such as hand-held vacuum cleaners, mixers, and electric can-openers. He managed to persuade a number of friends and contacts, including a former owner of the company, to back a Canadian buyout of the company.

But by the late 1980s, Iona was suffering from stagnant sales and increasing annual losses. The Canadian market, Millman realized, was just too small to support Iona's broad product line and need for innovation. Growth and security could come only by breaking into the huge, affluent US market. Trouble was, he didn't think any of Iona's current products — not even its best and brightest, the Dirt Raider hand vacuum or the Merlin rechargeable carpet cleaner — offered sufficient value or level of innovation to justify trying to crack the US market. What he needed was a killer product, something that could work better than anything else in its niche, something no one else was offering.

Millman was no stranger to innovation. A chemical engineer with an MBA, he headed new product development for a pharmaceutical division of Warner-Lambert Canada at the age of twenty-nine. He knew how tough it is to create and market an innovation. But he also knew an industry starved for new products when he saw it — the household vacuum-cleaner market.

Vacuum cleaners, Millman realized, hadn't changed in almost 100 years. They still whirled dust and dirt into little filter bags. And the bags were a pain. They get dirty and dusty. They have to be continually replaced. And the fuller they get, the more they reduce the airflow and the effectiveness of the vacuum cleaner itself. After almost a century, he figured, there had to be a better way.

Thus began Millman's long search for a better idea, a quest that took him to both sides of the Atlantic. Finally, a former director of Iona told Millman of a friend of his, a British inventor who had hit upon the idea he was looking for. The technology involved separating dirt from air by whirling it through two cyclone chambers; the dirt particles would come to rest in the plastic chambers. Vacuum users could see through the plastic chambers to know when they were full and needed to be emptied. In the meantime, the air flow continued to suck and swirl at full power, maintaining constant peak efficiency. This was the breakthrough technology Millman was looking for. He bought the rights to the system and started turning it into new products that busy US households couldn't do without.

Iona spent more than $350,000 developing and producing its first dual-cyclonic product in 1988, a carpet-cleaning machine called the Capture. "It was either great wisdom or great stupidity to go ahead with a project that large," Millman told PROFIT writer Michela Pasquali. "We were pioneering, and it's tough when you're pioneering." The Capture was sold primarily through Sears stores in the US and Canada and won a favourable review in *Consumer Reports* magazine. In 1991, Iona followed up with the Fantom, a dual-cyclonic vacuum cleaner with a gleaming, sci-fi look. By the end of Iona's 1992 fiscal year, total sales had reached a record $17.3 million, up 33% in a single year. The dual-cyclonic products now accounted for 44% of total company revenues, up from 17% in 1991. And US sales, mainly of the new floor-care machines, now accounted for one-third of total sales, more than double their share a year earlier. Iona had broken out of its Canadian-only ghetto with an exciting new product that was attracting major attention from US customers.

There was much more to be done. In 1993, Millman discontinued Iona's lines of kitchen appliances to concentrate on floor-care products.

Iona, which had been running in the red for years, wouldn't post a profit until fiscal 1995. Its marketing and distribution channels needed further fine-tuning. But Millman had completed much of the heavy work. He had recognized a market need, identified an appropriate concept, and turned it into a viable product. Iona was started on a growth track that would see it crack the $98-million mark by 1996. In 1997 it made its first appearance on the PROFIT 100 with a five-year growth rate of 658%. By that time, however, the company had changed its name to **Fantom Technologies Inc.**, a tribute to the power of a single product to turn a company around.

THE GOLDEN RULES OF INNOVATION

How do you find the right product? The experiences of the PROFIT 100 offer a few clues:

- **Know your market.** The only way to spot a new-product opportunity is to be close enough to a market to know what it needs next. Alan Millman of **Iona** spent years researching the vacuum-cleaner market, scanning for a technology that would truly be revolutionary.

- **Look for a sustainable advantage.** There's no point investing a lot of money in a new product that jealous competitors can duplicate (or improve on) in the blink of an eye. You need a sustainable competitive advantage that can get you a head start on the copycats. Iona's dual-cyclonic technology, for instance, was patentable.

- **Always remember who you're selling to.** Jim Crocker, CEO of **Virtek Vision Corp.** in Waterloo, Ontario, is selling laser-based computer vision systems, a high-tech product developed in the artificial intelligence labs at the University of Waterloo. Virtek sells to Boeing and other aerospace giants, and also to the top producers in two niche markets — the leather-goods industries and producers of prefabricated construction products such as roof trusses. It's easy to get carried away by the uniqueness of his products, says Crocker. But the secret to success is to forget the neat features and all the wonderful things the systems can do, and focus on the benefit to the customer.

- **Make sure this is something you can do.** Some companies run straight into a wall trying to develop a new product that turns out to be beyond their abilities. For instance, in the 1980s, developing a new business jet all but sunk the former Crown corporation Canadair. Billions in debt, the Montreal-based manufacturer had to be bailed out by Ottawa. It was later acquired by snowmobile-maker Bombardier Inc., which built a successful aerospace division on the back of the Canadair Challenger. It turned out to be a winning product after all, but was just too big a morsel for Canadair to digest by itself.

- **Don't scrimp on development.** Successful growth companies know that they have to invest generously in research and development if they expect to have a winning product and a lasting competitive advantage. Between 1987 and 1994, **Iona Appliances** poured $7 million into developing new products. That was a hefty amount for a company whose annual sales were only $20 million as recently as 1994. Proof of the importance of R&D? In 1997, the PROFIT 100 reported spending an average of 5.3% of revenues on R&D, a figure that has been increasing steadily over the nine years that PROFIT has been studying Canada's Fastest-Growing Companies.

- **Test, test, test.** The only thing worse than not having an innovative, superior product is releasing an innovative, superior product that turns out to have problems. Savvy companies test until they know that their products are ready for market, even if it means missing production or shipment deadlines. Software giant Microsoft is widely derided for almost never making its shipping dates, but that's because so much of its technology is new, and it considers quality so important. Asked the reasons for the success of his software development company, **KL Group** President Greg Kiessling offered a number of reasons, finishing up with "mostly, it's technical features and quality. We've tested better for bugs than anyone else."

- **Market the heck out of your product.** The best product in the world won't do you any good if you don't let the right people know it's out there. Or if you package it wrong. Or you charge too much. Or you don't back it up with appropriate distributor or customer support. At **Canway Corp.** in Ottawa, a six-time PROFIT

100 company, Founder and President Jeff Hunt offers a product that's a service: residential carpet and upholstery cleaning. As he constantly tries to tell his employees and franchisees across North America, offering a top-quality product is just a start. Delivering a superior product, he says, "is really a minimum expectation of the customer. You've done nothing special." Having created a quality product, he says, "you will have only dealt with 10% of what will make you successful."

- **Defend your product niche.** Your job isn't finished once a product is selling successfully. You have to continue to guard your turf. As Iona's Millman says, "we have defended our patents vigorously in the past, and we may have to do it again in the future." To keep the competition guessing, he adds, he intends to keep putting money and effort into new product development, so that as rivals do chase them, Fantom will always be out there, a lap ahead.

Clearly, there's a lot of work involved in these eight steps, but it can be done. Here's a look at one PROFIT 100 company that turned the rules of innovation into pure gold. **Corel Corp.** grew from a company based on one innovative product to become Canada's largest software company, and the first company ever to appear on the PROFIT 100 six years in a row.

The stunning success of **Corel Corp.**, the Ottawa-based graphics software giant, is firmly rooted in the first rule: "know your market." In fact, you could say that Corel doesn't just know its market, it owns it. Corel created its own market for PC graphics software with the 1989 release of CorelDraw, a product that has drawn rave reviews over the years, and continues to enjoy fierce loyalty from its best customers. Corel keeps its finger on the pulse of its market through CorelDraw users' magazines, annual Corel World conferences and other industry shows, and the Internet. With the later development of other innovative products — Corel Photo-Paint, CorelDream 3D, CorelXara, CorelCAD, Corel Ventura, Corel WordPerfect Suite, among them — Corel has grown from sales of US$10.6 million in 1989 (CorelDraw's first year) to US$334 million in 1996.

But when asked what he considers to be Corel's competitive advantage, President and CEO Michael Cowpland replies almost immediately, "the technology team that we have and the dynamic marketing team." His words are a testament to the rule of "don't just create, innovate." It's not enough just to create the best product out there; you have to continue to be creative in the value, service, and marketing you build around your product.

Witness Corel's launch of CorelDraw 7, the sixth annual update of its flagship graphics product. On October 8, 1996, illustrators, graphic designers, software enthusiasts, and media from around the world filled the Corel Centre, the new suburban hockey arena just outside Ottawa, to get a first look at the world's best computer illustrations. Corel Corp. had invited them to this black-tie event to witness the announcement of the winners of its seventh annual World Design Contest, which the company boldly dubbed "the Academy Awards of graphics." There were 4,800 entries from sixty countries, $3 million worth of prizes up for grabs, and the rules were simple: anyone could submit a piece of digital art, as long as they used one of Corel's products to create it. Corel went beyond — far beyond — simply releasing the latest upgrade to its key product and invented a new context in which to relate to the most important users of its most important product, a whole new creative environment, and a hierarchy of to-die-for cash and product awards for those who play the game. Now that's creating and innovating.

Of course, Corel's nine-digit revenues and the scale of its marketing ambitions may be beyond the reach of most entrepreneurial companies, but the same golden rules of innovation can be, and are being, followed by other savvy companies, whether or not they have their name on a $214-million hockey rink. Huge corporations or gutsy start-ups, Canada's Fastest-Growing Companies engage in a relentless quest not only to create or find the right product, but also to sustain the competitive advantages of service and value. It's all doable, even by individuals. Here's a look at another **PROFIT 100** company that went through all the phases of innovation, with varying amounts of self-awareness or even success. Yet it became a winner in the end because entrepreneur Gary McIntosh refused to give up, and despite all the setbacks and obstacles, managed to follow the golden rules of innovation.

• GDT SOFTWORKS: A CLASS BY ITSELF •

At the ripe old age of forty, Gary McIntosh retired from the Vancouver trucking company he had founded just five years earlier. Having proven himself a regular whiz-kid in the trucking business, he decided to settle down to devote more time to a growing family and to growing his personal investments.

Five years later, in 1984, Gary got the summons that would change his life. A long-time family friend in Toronto called to say he had a great business idea. Would Gary come East to take a look? It was the fourth or fifth time Terry had made such a request, and frankly, Gary was reluctant to get involved. But there was an urgency to the appeal that seemed different. Gary decided to fly out.

In Toronto, Terry and his friend David laid out their pitch. They were both fans of a brand new product called the Macintosh, a personal computer that combined powerful graphics capability with an intuitive operating system that was much easier to learn and use than the competing IBM PC. Although the Mac cost a little more than an IBM-compatible model, Terry and David believed that Apple had come up with a product that was so superior it could overcome that initial price differential.

Still, they saw a flaw. Apple users could only print their work out on Apple-brand printers, which were a little harder to find, slower to evolve new features, and more expensive than the competition. While it was clear that IBM's share of the PC market would always dwarf Apple's, Terry and David were convinced that more consumers would consider buying the Macintosh if they could use them with other brands of printers. All that was needed, they said, was a software product (known in the jargon as a printer driver) that would let Apple computers print to an IBM-compatible printer. If Gary could advance them the money, Terry and David said they could create the necessary software. With Gary's marketing and sales knowledge helping them tap this virgin market, they figured they could be rolling in revenues within a year.

Now Gary McIntosh was no techie — at that point, he had never even used a computer — but he had an instinct for business. And here was an opportunity that seemed to embody all the features an entrepreneur might dream of:

- **A chance to invest in a brand-new market.** Printer drivers were extremely novel. In fact, even regular printers as a product category were still achingly new. The business magazines of the day were filled with articles comparing the relative merits of daisy-wheels and the next big thing, dot-matrix printers. (In 1984, PROFIT magazine was still running ads for electric typewriters!)

- **A chance to link up with an international powerhouse.** Under the charismatic Steve Jobs, it was clear Apple was betting its company on the product. And Gary McIntosh (no relation), inspired by his colleagues' enthusiasm, shared their conviction that the Macintosh would be a winner. If he could convince Apple that these upstart Canadians could help it sell more computers, he could forge the productive, cooperative relationship with a market leader that any business, large or small, might envy.

- **Best of all, GDT faced no competition.** The very model of a modern market niche is a market opportunity so narrow or specialized that it provides relatively strong protection to any credible practitioner. As Terry and David pointed out, no one else seemed to have recognized this market need. With the right product, they could own the market before anyone else even knew it was there.

Won over, Gary agreed to kick in $40,000 to form a company and fund product development. Using the first initial of his own name and those of his two colleagues, he formed **GDT Softworks**. By the following year, however, things were looking very different. Terry and David, writing software whenever they could snatch a few moments away from their regular jobs (one was a municipal employee, the other a school principal) had fallen behind. The software wasn't finished and the project was seriously over budget. By that time Gary McIntosh had invested $80,000 in the venture and decided it was time to bail. Game over, he told the developers. Exercising his contractual rights, he asked them to send him the code he had paid for so he could determine if there was anything worth salvaging.

He took out a classified ad announcing he was looking for a Macintosh software programmer. The catch was that Gary would hire them only if they could prove that the project was feasible. A father and son programming team answered the ad and agreed to take a look at the unfinished software to see if there was a viable product lurking within.

They reported that it was doable. McIntosh signed them to a development contract and set out to conquer the Apple printer market.

From there, the story takes on the trappings of any traditional start-up. Production took longer than expected. Costs rose higher than McIntosh ever anticipated. His first employee was his wife, Donna, who came into the office to help with bookkeeping and administration while Gary tackled marketing and technical issues. Once GDT had a working product, marketing proved tougher than Gary ever thought. All of his efforts were concentrated in the US, but as a one-product company in an unproven market, the big national Macintosh parts distributors weren't much interested in dealing with GDT. As a lifelong trucker, Gary lacked the engineering degree or programming experience that might have lent him additional credibility in the highly turbulent software world. As McIntosh's capital began running low, banks and venture capitalists turned him down. Too risky a market, they said because the company was overly dependent on a single product. If Apple changed its proprietary systems, or if it stopped sharing insider technical information with GDT, McIntosh's dream would be extinguished.

But McIntosh had one thing going for him — the vision he began with. The product worked. As Gary, David, and Terry had foreseen, GDT's printer drivers were giving Apple users new power to use a wide range of competing printers from IBM, Epson, Canon, and so on. Its customers were saving money, and they were telling their friends. For computer buyers who intended to purchase a printer too, GDT's unique contribution made it easier for price-conscious consumers to justify paying the higher price for Apple's computer system now that they were no longer compelled to also buy its printers. "Was our software the reason that people bought a Mac?" asks McIntosh. "We don't know. No one has the figures." But he believes Apple shared GDT's conviction that it was helping promote and sell the Macintosh system in a world increasingly dominated by IBM clones.

Lacking professional distribution, Gary sold GDT's drivers through ads in US magazines such as *MacWorld* and *MacUser*, using a US postal box in nearby Blaine, Washington, to conceal his company's Canadian origins. Taking orders on GDT's toll-free 1-800 number, Gary and Donna would pack up the day's orders each evening and then drive them to nearby Point Roberts, Washington — the closest US border point. There, GDT could not only access the US postal system, but it could also dispatch orders via United Parcel Service, which was not operating regularly in Canada at the time, and charged much lower rates than the generally less competitive Canadian couriers.

It was a difficult time for the McIntoshes. As their dreams of early success faded, losses mounted. For five years, GDT failed to turn a profit. At one point, Gary had invested a total of $265,000 in the company. Although he had a few employees now to oversee production and shipping, he and Donna took no salaries, converting their investment into shareholder loans and living off accumulated savings. Slowly, however, their efforts bore fruit. Apple supported their endeavours. One by one, major US distributors such as Mac Warehouse came to understand the product and began carrying GDT's software for resale. By 1988, GDT's sales rose to $325,000, with its loss a manageable $36,000. A year later, sales rose 63% to $529,000, and losses fell to just $25,000. By 1990, sales jumped to $968,000 and the company recorded its first profit, a hefty $223,000.

It was a time of celebration and a time for change, as Gary McIntosh, exiting a winner again, retired from active management of the company and handed the mantle of president to his son Jim. By 1993, riding a Macintosh boom and a new product-packaging strategy, GDT recorded revenues of $9.1 million — good for a five-year growth of 2700%. It first appearance on the PROFIT 100 in 1994, in tenth place.

GDT qualified for the PROFIT 100 again in 1995 and 1996, becoming one of relatively few companies to make the list three years in a row. With a 95% share of the market it pioneered, says an amazed Gary McIntosh, "we never believed that the company would grow into what it is today." By 1997, with its five-year growth down to a "mere" 445%, GDT's string of PROFIT 100 appearances seemed at an end. But with a continuing commitment to innovative, one-of-a-kind products, Jim McIntosh is striving to follow his father's lead and keep the company moving into growing markets competitors haven't yet spotted. He's led GDT into wireless e-mail, and in April 1997 renamed the entire company Infowave Wireless Messaging Inc. Although the new corporate direction is clear, GDT will live on as the new company's Imaging division, and is now looking to penetrate Windows markets as well.

TWO LESSONS

Looking back, Gary McIntosh faced all the usual problems of an entrepreneur tackling new markets such as staking his ground, building a market, operating across borders, and struggling with cash flow. What finally fuelled his unexpected success was that simplest of business notions: a superior product. GDT's software is reliable, innovative, and unique. It breaks down hitherto unbreachable barriers in the computer industry and creates value for users and hardware manufacturers alike.

Having an innovative, superior product is undoubtedly the most important single component of business success today, but it's not the only one. And in some cases, as further chapters of this book will show, it's not a necessary condition for success at all. But Gary McIntosh's story offers the two most meaningful lessons for succeeding in today's market:

- You must offer unique or superior value to your market.

- Even with that, your success is not assured. You merely have a chance.

Without McIntosh's full complement of entrepreneurial skills — his ability to market, persevere, overcome challenges through hard work and singular creativity — that unique, high-quality product wouldn't have been worth the paper it came wrapped in. But combined with McIntosh's entrepreneurial skills, that printer driver built a company.

CHAMPIONS OF INNOVATION

How do you learn to innovate? On the job, in the trenches, under fire. The lesson of the PROFIT 100 is that niche opportunities are all around us. Sometimes it takes special circumstances to open your eyes to them. And sometimes no one else will share your vision. But the best innovators on the PROFIT 100 offer inspiring case studies of business formation and character building.

• HUMMINGBIRD COMMUNICATIONS LTD.:
BEST NICHE IN A STORM •

Founded in 1984 by Ottawa partners Fred Sorkin and Barry Litwin, **Hummingbird Communications** started out as a high-tech engineering consulting firm. Having made their names (and fortunes) by selling a previous high-tech company to Mitel Corp., where they briefly became senior executives, Sorkin and Litwin could now afford to hover on the fringes of technology, flitting from client to client like the hyperactive bird that was their namesake.

With multinational clients such as AT&T and British Telecom, you'd think the two partners were set for life. But that's not the way Sorkin saw things. As the 1980s drew on, the Lithuanian immigrant began to see worrying signs of the economic recession to come. He knew that consulting firms are often first to suffer in an economic slow-down as companies start cutting back on discretionary expenses. What he needed, he figured, was a tangible product that he could sell in good times and bad.

Using their background in computers, software, and engineering, Sorkin and Litwin went looking for a more secure line of work. Dismissing hardware as a dying sector, dominated by huge multinationals or small-scale clone producers scraping by on thin margins, they started looking for a solid software niche that would utilize their programming and marketing skills. It was Sorkin's reading of an article about an interesting but obscure new technology called PC X that caught their attention and changed their future.

PC X involved the convergence of two fast-growing and largely incompatible computer platforms: Unix (the high-powered multitasking operating system preferred by big corporations running computer networks), and the increasingly powerful personal computer. Five years earlier, researchers at MIT had developed an X Windows system that allowed computer users to access various applications running on different types of computers. But when Litwin looked into the market, he discovered that no one had put much effort into making X Windows reliable or easy to use. With users who wanted to run graphical Unix applications on their PCs paying $17,000 or more for specialized hardware configurations, Litwin and Sorkin realized they had an opportunity to create a much less expensive software solution that could blow the market wide open.

In 1991, Hummingbird released its first product, Exceed, which enabled stand-alone PC users to run Unix applications and cut and paste between PC and Unix documents. The system saved time and money. Instead of taking up space on scarce, expensive work stations, more users could work in Unix on their PCs, eliminating the need for extra workstations and reducing the traffic on corporate computer networks. Unix developers could even now take their work home with them or on the road, where Unix systems are traditionally scarce. Exceed represented a breakthrough in savings and convenience that "surpassed all other offerings at the time," says Lorraine Neal, Hummingbird's corporate affairs director.

Indeed, five years later Exceed was still around and stronger than ever, accounting for 54% of the PC X market, with more than four times the market share of its nearest competitor. While Hummingbird expects much of its growth in future to come from acquisitions, it isn't about to risk its Exceed franchise. With sales surpassing $100 million in 1996, Hummingbird spent $10 million on R&D, to make sure that its product retains its technological edge.

• HUMPTY'S RESTAURANTS INTERNATIONAL: KEEP YOUR EYES OPEN •

To find a product capable of supporting a successful growing business, you don't need to poke around for obscure corners of high-tech markets only a handful of people understand. Sometimes you just follow your nose ... or stomach.

Don Koenig was working for Zellers in Calgary when a relative called and asked if he and his wife Jan would like to buy into a restaurant that was up for sale in a nearby community. Somehow, the Koenigs let themselves be talked into it and soon they had food-service fever. When they sold the restaurant at a profit a year later, Don and Jan plowed their proceeds into three small soup-and-sandwich stores.

For years, Koenig had been a frustrated entrepreneur. Now that he had his own business, he hungered to make it grow. How did he do it? He found the right formula when he stopped thinking like a businessman and started thinking like a consumer. He had always been a lover of big breakfasts, and regretted the fact that it was so hard to get a good breakfast in Calgary restaurants. One day he put those two ideas together and had his growth formula. He converted one of his sandwich shops to Humpty's Egg Place and started serving hearty breakfasts of omelettes and pancakes and hash-brown potatoes. "Our menu was 95% breakfast," he says, and within a year sales were up 100%.

Long before McDonald's muscled into the breakfast market, Koenig added a second Humpty's restaurant in Calgary, then a third, and started receiving franchise inquiries from as far afield as Tampa and Halifax. He held off selling franchises for another five years, however, until he had two more restaurants operating profitably and had developed an operating bible and support system that would help outsiders duplicate his formula. In the meantime, Koenig also kept working on his product — the menu. One of his favourite innovations is the personalized omelette, which can be ordered, much like pizza or sundaes, with your choice of twenty-four different toppings or fillings (would you believe chili, peanut butter, and shrimp?). "No one has what we have for breakfast," Koenig crows. Over time, he expanded the non-breakfast menu to bring in crowds for lunch and dinner, and changed the name to **Humpty's Family Restaurants** to play down the scrambled-egg image. But the overall formula remained unchanged: low prices, big portions, and breakfast served twenty-four-hours a day.

By 1996 Humpty's Family Restaurants had forty locations across Western Canada (all but two franchised), sales (from two corporate stores and franchise fees) of $3.7 million, and 601% growth (good for 100th place on the 1996 PROFIT 100). With the Prairies saturated, Koenig plans to move into Ontario and the US. He admits those markets will be more competitive but insists that his breakfast focus will win out. "The rest of the day we do have competitors," he admits. "At lunch and dinner we'll hold our own, but we'll win out on breakfast."

Meanwhile, he's not above trying a little experimenting to move Humpty's beyond the breakfast niche. Recently he added a successful kids-eat-free promotion on Friday nights. "We get lots of young families out for that," says Koenig. The only problem is that "the franchisees sometimes don't like it because they have to take a Valium when it's over."

• VIRTEK VISION INTERNATIONAL INC.:
NARROW DOWN YOUR VISION •

Having a top-notch product is the beginning, but you have to know what to do with it once you've got it. That's a lesson learned by **Virtek Vision International Inc.** of Waterloo, Ontario, a PROFIT 100 company in 1995-97.

When heaven was handing out the brains, it gave a few extra grey cells to the founders of Virtek, the directors of the University of Waterloo's Pattern Analysis and Machine Intelligence Laboratory. They founded Virtek in 1986 as a contract research house to explore the commercial potential of machine vision, a complex visual-analysis and inspection system incorporating lasers, cameras, computers, and special software. Virtek developed some stunning capabilities, but the question was, what good was it? Who would pay for its pioneering laser-projection systems that could speed up production and virtually eliminate defects in precision manufacturing environments?

Virtek finally answered that question three months after hiring former management consultant and Harvard Business School graduate Norman Wright as president to bring business smarts to a company that had been dominated by engineers. Wright knew that Virtek had to start paying its way by selecting a niche or two in which to compete. After studying the technology, he came up with three quite different applications: manufacturing systems for the aerospace, construction, and leather-goods industries. After three months of getting his act together, Wright made his first sales call on Boeing Co. in Seattle. The aerospace giant, constantly looking for ways to shave costs and time, agreed to buy twelve laser-guided manufacturing systems worth $500,000. At last, said Wright, Virtek had a mission in life. "This was the real world calling."

From rented desks and makeshift work tables, using employees hired on the run, Virtek got its first order out the door on time, prompting Boeing to place a second order, twice the size of the first.

Wright went on to woo the makers of roof trusses and other precision-engineered, prefabricated residential construction materials. And Virtek also started selling to La-Z-Boy Canada and other leading leather-goods producers that use the laser-vision systems to analyse each individual hide and determine the best way to cut it to maximize yield and reduce waste. After just one complete year of selling product in earnest, Virtek boasted sales of $6 million in 1994, good for fifth place on the 1995 PROFIT 100. It also enjoyed a profit of $620,000. As Virtek's director of materials and contract administration told PROFIT writer John Harris, the company succeeded by selling not just its products but its employees. "It's our scientists on the client's shop floor talking to their scientists. There's a natural bonding."

But the following year the roof fell in for Virtek Vision. In 1995 Virtek sales fell to $4.1 million. The company lost $2.4 million and Norman Wright was gone. Picking up the pieces was CFO Rick Delogu who explained that the company had taken its eye off the ball technologically. "We underestimated how fast our competition could catch up," he said. "We took our lead for granted." He says Virtek's leaders learned a lesson, "always assume that your competitors are smarter than you think they are. Never get caught off guard." On the brighter side, he said, the competition would be good for Virtek. "It forces us to push our technology forward. If you're doing missionary selling and technology, it's easy to get tired or lazy if you're the only one in the game."

By 1996 Virtek appeared to be back on track, recording sales of $5.6 million and a loss of just $1.2 million, good for tenth spot on the PROFIT 100.

CONTINUOUS IMPROVEMENT

What makes businesses grow? In 1994 Statistics Canada published a survey based on its database of successful growing firms to find out what exactly it is that winning businesses do right. Its findings showed that "GSMEs (growing small- and medium-sized enterprises) are innovative in a broad sense.... A large percentage of GSMEs have adopted an aggressive strategy involving new products and technologies. A large portion focus their marketing efforts on introducing new products and/or penetrating new markets."

In addition, when researcher John Baldwin broke down his sample of 1,500 growing companies to find out what distinguishes the best performers from the less successful, he found that one factor stood out: "Innovative activities are the most important determinants of general success. That is, for a wide range of industries, they serve to discriminate between the more- and the less-successful firms better than any other variable," such as management, labour skills or quality of product. You don't have to tell that to Canada's Fastest-Growing Companies. They know that constant product innovation is the key to growth as well as to survival.

• BEACHCOMBER SPAS: HOT HOT TUBS •

One of the most long-term innovators on the PROFIT 100 is Keith Scott of Surrey, BC. Founded in 1978, his **Beachcomber Spas**, which qualified for the PROFIT 100 in 1992 and 1993, has been producing state-of-the-art hot tubs since long before they were cool.

Distributed today through seventy dealers across Canada, Scott's hot tubs have benefited from continuing innovation and creative thinking. As the hot-tub industry has grown in popularity and US-designed models have flooded over the border, Beachcomber has fought back with innovations that have made its hot tubs more functional, more comfortable, more affordable, and more energy efficient.

From the beginning, Scott has covered his hot tubs in western red cedar, for a long-lasting exterior and a beautiful wood shine. In 1980, Scott's wife Judy came up with a product that purifies the water in a hot tub, keeping it fresher longer. In 1983 Scott pioneered the "cab-forward" design that put the power source equipment outside the hot tub itself, creating more room in the hot tub for users' enjoyment and more room around the tub cavity for energy-saving insulation. The power supply itself was ingeniously packaged into a separate step that helps people climb into the tub.

In 1989 Beachcomber introduced new, easily interchangeable water jets for more therapeutic massages of the neck and back. Three years later, it added a compact hot tub for budget-conscious buyers. And in 1994 it introduced a programmable Energy Saver control that automatically manages hot tub heating and cleaning operations to save owners time and money.

And, of course, Beachcomber stands behind its product. It claims to have been the first in its industry to add a toll-free customer support line in 1982, and it selects all its dealers based on their ability to provide quality before- and after-sale service. If you're interested in a hot tub, your Beachcomber dealer will invite you in for a free pool party, in which you and your friends indulge in some hottubbing at the store afterhours. If that's not enough, Beachcomber even offers qualified purchasers a thirty-day in-home trial. If you don't like it, Beachcomber will take it back. Promotions like that are a necessary risk because most people are unfamiliar with how a hot tub works, how it will fit in in their home, how to take care of it, and how often they'll use it. Letting them get their feet wet, as it were, is Beachcomber's way of showing its faith in its wares, and letting the product sell itself. "We don't actually sell Beachcomber Hot Tubs," says Scott. "Instead, we help people learn how to buy one." And it backs its products with a service guarantee that's simple, straightforward, and watertight.

Scott claims that he picked up his values from his parents who ran a restaurant in New Westminster, BC, when he was growing up. Lesson One in business, he says, is to make sure your products and service are as good as you can possibly make them. If people don't feel good about your products, they won't come back. But if they fall in love with your quality and service, they'll tell their friends and relatives. For all other lessons, says Scott, see Lesson One.

INNOVATIVE DISTRIBUTION

"Our forte is marketing, not research."

Kevin O'Leary,
Softkey Software Products Inc.

Not everyone has it in them to design a better mousetrap, create a superior piece of software or even think up a superior new product. But never fear. One of the most subtle, yet essential, lessons of the PROFIT 100 is that opportunities can be found in the soft areas of distribution as well as in manufacturing, retailing or other higher-profile business sectors. The good news is that the cost of entering the distribution business is lower than that of most other industries. You don't need to put up your own plant and with any luck, you can use other people's warehouses and suppliers' cash.

But distribution has its own demands. Instead of requiring production skills and upfront capital, distribution demands extensive industry knowledge and a rigorous commitment to building relationships. Moreover, fast growth in distribution requires something more besides: the foresight and vision to identify a new link between manufacturer and end-user, and the skill to convince industry players that they can all win if they help you turn your concept into reality.

This is not a new idea. In fact, many of the most far-reaching changes overtaking business today are concentrated in the distribution sector. The stunning growth of Federal Express and other overnight courier services stems from business's and consumers' need to receive goods and documents faster than ever. Electronic data interchange is tying together manufacturers, suppliers and retailers in a virtual web of partnership and increased productivity. Catalogue marketers are shaking up traditional retail with quality goods and rapid service. While specialty retailers are threatening old-line department stores by offering unique selection and quality service, retail power centres are changing the suburban skyline with aircraft-hangar-sized warehouse stores that offer lower prices and a new definition of no frills. Finally, the rise of Internet retailers such as US book dealer Amazon.com hints at yet another retail revolution as shoppers prowl the infinite inventory of cyberspace before ordering on-line.

How are Canadian companies thriving on opportunities created by new trends in distribution? Consider the cases of three Vancouver-area companies in very different fields. All of them found success not so much in the product or service they created, but by the unique distribution strategy they invented or faithfully followed.

• A.G. PROFESSIONAL HAIRCARE PRODUCTS LTD.: AVOIDING THE MASS MERCHANTS •

Lotte Davis recalls lying awake at night back about 1990, eyes wide open as she thought about the trouble she and her husband John had gotten into. They had just started producing their own line of shampoos, conditioners, and other haircare products, and had invested their savings — plus $88,000 from a venture-capital firm — into a new lab. "It was a difficult time for us," recalls Lotte, "I just kept thinking, 'What have we done?'"

Not to worry. By sticking with care to its niche-distribution strategy, the Davises' company, **A.G. Professional Haircare Products Ltd.** of Burnaby, BC, has become one of the home-grown success stories of the haircare business.

John, a former hairdresser in Britain, and Lotte, whose background was in marketing and design, learned the tricks of the trade working for a haircare product manufacturer during the 1980s. While that firm ultimately failed, they remained convinced there was a market for a quality, Canadian line of hair products. They bought some thirty-two products in bulk from a generic manufacturer and starting pumping them into eight-ounce bottles in their basement at night and selling to salons by day, door-to-door. Unhappy with the quality of those products (it was probably the salt in the shampoo that most annoyed John), they resolved to make their own, even though, as Lotte admits today, "we had no money, no experience."

Investing in their lab, John and Lotte started selling their own products to the beauty salons of Vancouver, usually out of the back of their Nissan hatchback. They even did their own deliveries when they didn't have the cash on hand to pay a distributor and they knew a salon was waiting for an order. John would turn even that into an asset, however, parking his car out of sight of the shop and then alluding casually to the fact that his truck was parked just around the corner. That combination of service and chutzpah proved just right for the market. A.G. finished in fifth place on the 1996 PROFIT 100 with sales exceeding $7 million, up 5,400% over five years. Today John's hatchback has been replaced by a fleet of forty red-and-black company vans that distribute A.G.'s growing number of products across Canada.

All those products, however, still go to the same distribution channel — namely, small, mainly independent salons. A.G. has resisted the urge to go for the big score by expanding its distribution to major drugstore and food chains. In fact, it defines itself by its market niche. "We're only available from professional hairstylists," says John. "We can't be purchased at regular retail."

The Davises' thinking is simple. Haircare products aren't exactly a growth industry in the mass market these days. National brands are fighting for market share tooth and nail, and finding new shelf space in the local drugstore is next to impossible. To go mass market would expose A.G.'s products to unruly, price-driven competition that could spell the end of a small, quality line without a lot of money to spend on advertising or in-store promotion. You can't buy A.G. products at Shoppers' Drug Mart, and you probably never will.

The result, though, is that A.G. takes good care of its retailers. Unlike most haircare producers, A.G. maintains its own sales staff. That cuts costs, says John Davis, and allows A.G. to monitor customer service levels more closely and jump on marketing opportunities faster. When the Davises noted that their large rivals were lax about promoting in-store retail, for instance, they added attractive display units and posters to their marketing mix. "Initially we had an advantage in not being in the industry," says Lotte. "We didn't know how other people did things. We just went ahead and did what we thought made sense. If we'd been more traditional, I think we would have had a harder time making a niche for ourselves."

The Davises emphasize competitive pricing, little extras such as Christmas gift packages that generate incremental sales for salons, and radio and print advertising that supports local salons by pointing out that they're the only stores that sell the products. A.G. also produces two-ounce samples for salons to sell or give away. Enclosed with the package is a brochure that offers hair tips and answers ten common questions about the difference between buying hair products at a professional's salon or at the corner drugstore. "The salon's name is on the brochure under the shrink-wrap," says John. "It promotes our products and makes the salon look good."

LESSON: YOUR DISTRIBUTION CHANNEL IS YOUR MARKET NICHE.

It must receive as much attention in your business plan as the development of your products or services themselves. Choosing the right distribution strategy will be a key determinant of your ultimate success or failure.

A.G.'s experiences demonstrate that your choice of distribution channel will be one of the most important business decisions you make. It may even determine whether or not you have a business. It's essential that your marketing strategy match the distribution network that's best for you. And as John and Lotte Davis's success indicates, you have to keep working that channel, giving your distribution partners the extra care and attention that builds long-term loyalty and sales. By avoiding the mass merchants and creating a new level of value-added service, A.G. became one of the top three salon brands in Western Canada, head and shoulders above the rest of the competition.

• MAPLE HOMES CANADA LTD.: THE JAPANESE CONNECTION •

When Brad Grindler left his home in Vancouver to teach English in Japan, he had a plan. He wasn't going because he wasn't ready to settle down, or even because there weren't many good jobs in British Columbia in the mid-1980s. He was engaging in market intelligence.

Coming from a family with its own commercial fishing operations in BC, Grindler had always intended to start his own business. In foreseeing that Japan would offer a host of trading opportunities, he was ahead of his time. When he studied international business at the BC Institute of Technology in the early eighties, he was the only kid in the class.

Grindler spent eight years in Japan, teaching English to support himself at first while he learned the language, and then branching out. First he got involved with a company importing seafood from Canada, but soon discovered a less volatile niche. He teamed up with a Canadian friend in the construction business to begin importing wood building products from Canada, impressing Japanese builders with his knowledge of Japanese culture and customs. When he returned to Canada in 1993, he had contacts on both sides of the Pacific and a company that was already known for quality products and personal service.

That company was **Maple Homes Canada Ltd.**, now headquartered in Richmond, BC. Grindler describes his firm as a "building-products consolidator," but that tends to obscure the creativity involved in what he does. Maple Homes represents thirty of Canada's highest-quality wood building-products manufacturers, makers of everything from doors and kitchen cabinets to windows and mouldings. Representing firms such as Loewen Windows of Manitoba, BC's Merit Kitchens, and Mercier Flooring in Quebec, Grindler is taking advantage of a little Far East realpolitik. Home construction is one of the few industries in which the Japanese government, eager to upgrade the domestic stock, is actively encouraging imports. While a Canadian log home is beyond the reach of most Japanese, affluent consumers don't mind paying $400,000 or more for the quality, stability, and energy efficiency associated with the best Canadian building products. But maintaining that reputation for quality isn't easy. Grindler has to vet his suppliers carefully and try to anticipate his customers' every need. "The Japanese are very particular about the products they use," he says. "Their expectations are high and the service required to maintain their business is demanding."

Between 1990 and 1995 Grindler's attention to quality and service paid off. Maple Homes' sales jumped from $115,464 to $8.7 million — a five-year growth rate of 7,409% that earned his company second place on the 1996 PROFIT 100. Grindler's feat is all the more amazing when you consider he did it with a staff of just seven.

Besides its close contacts with Japanese builders, Maple Homes' edge comes from its ability to consolidate shipments. By packing three, five or ten different products into a container, it can minimize freight costs by filling every cubic inch, and also reduce the chance of accidental damage. While Grindler is facing increasing competition in his niche now, he is confident that his experience will hold him in good stead. "When we started we had very few competitors. We were at the head of the pack, so we developed good relationships and had the support of government agencies. We built up a knowledge of what's required in that market." He was also hoping that that experience and his contacts with Canadian suppliers and trade officials would help him in his latest quest — tackling markets in Eastern Europe.

Maple Homes could be the model of a New Age company. It is global in scope, small in size, quick to act, and burning with ambition. What makes it most interesting, though, is that it produces nothing tangible and consumes almost nothing. It's a pure service company that exists simply because Brad Grindler saw an opportunity to bring together two different sets of buyers and sellers who might otherwise never have met. It's a true win-win situation. He introduces innovation and competition into one market just as he creates new revenue opportunities in the other. That's what adding value is all about. And Maple Homes' success proves that value can result as much from an innovative service as from a product.

LESSON: THE DISTRIBUTION GAP

Even as international trade is taking off, many supply lines are inefficient at best. Finding new ways to help companies increase exports or source new products is a growth industry in itself. And if you can help cut costs out of the distribution process, you can add value for everyone involved — including your own business.

• COST-LESS EXPRESS LTD.: THE ALLIGATOR BIRD STRATEGY •

One of the more unusual companies ever to grace the PROFIT 100, Cost-Less Express Ltd. carved out a market you'll never find in any business school textbook. And that is precisely what makes it an essential study for anyone interested in the future of growth markets and business opportunity.

Like some fidgety, fast-reacting bird that hangs around an alligator hoping to grab a few leftovers from between the giant reptile's teeth, Calvin Johnson built his business scavenging sales from Costco Warehouse Canada, the retail giant disguised as a warehouse club. Johnson, a high-school graduate now in his late twenties, started out as just another young man with a pick-up truck doing odd delivery and moving jobs. He did a lot of work helping consumers bring home big, bulky items such as furniture from the local Costco store (now PriceCostco). With his eye for marketing, he soon noticed that the no-frills warehouse store was losing sales to other furniture dealers such as The Brick simply because they offered delivery and Costco didn't. "So I went to Costco and said 'Hey, I can do that for you,'" says Johnson. "And they said fine." In October 1989 he launched his own company, Cost-Less Express Ltd., to serve Costco customers with the warehouse giant's unofficial sanction.

As he got close to Costco, Johnson spotted another opportunity. In the evenings he noticed a lot of shoppers in business attire coming to Costco to buy business supplies. These, he figured, were affluent and busy people who might prefer to pay him a bit extra to deliver those supplies if it gave them an extra evening free. So he got out his typewriter and typed up a primitive catalogue listing Costco's office supplies, adding a small margin to Costco prices to reflect his delivery fee. He photocopied his makeshift catalogue and passed it around town without seeking Costco's blessing first, based presumably on the time-honoured entrepreneurial maxim that it's easier to ask forgiveness than permission. After all, he figured, if this worked, Costco would benefit from the incremental sales as much as he would, if not more.

As it turned out, Johnson had found himself a valuable niche. Within six years, Cost-Less Express had grown to nine employees and sales of more than $3 million, good for twelfth place on the 1996 PROFIT 100. (The following year, Cost-Less placed just out of the money in 102nd spot.)

Johnson's big break came when he moved out of the suburbs and started soliciting business downtown, from home-based businesses, law firms and even government departments. Here he was selling a price advantage as well as convenience. Even with Johnson's mark-up, Costco's prices were much lower than those of established downtown office-supply dealers. Busy entrepreneurs, lawyers, and managers could use him to obtain suburban warehouse prices without ever leaving downtown. (He also saves them the $40 annual fee they would have to pay to become Costco members and shop there themselves.) In 1996 Johnson had 3,000 regular clients and distributed between them around 80,000 catalogues at a time, each promoting more than 2,500 items ranging from software and printer paper to soft drinks and toilet paper. Still, some things don't change. To keep his flyers from looking too professional and thus expensive, Johnson still does the layout himself rather than hand it to a graphic artist.

Besides making the PROFIT 100, Johnson achieved another breakthrough in 1996. He finally moved the business out of his home and into a real office, and he signed his first contract with Costco, becoming its official catalogue and delivery partner. Today his staff answer the phone by saying, "Cost-Less Express, Your PriceCostco Connection." His business continues to benefit, however, from customers' uncertainty whether or not it is part of Costco. For instance, Johnson has few problems collecting receivables within ten days because most customers don't want to mess with a US$19-billion international giant.

Like the alligator bird continually at risk flitting about the alligator's jaws, Johnson knows his company's long-term future is uncertain. It depends on the continuing goodwill of the host company, Costco. In 1993 Costco merged with Price Club, a lookalike warehouse-store chain that offers catalogues in some US locations. Indeed, several Costco stores in the US have started offering delivery now too. Johnson hasn't pushed the point with Costco, so he doesn't know what the future holds. If worse comes to worst, however, he is sure there are other niches to explore. For now, he is enjoying the challenge of growing his business and his own character. "This is better than business school," he says, "and way more fun."

In one sense, there's nothing new about Johnson's niche — a gypsy company that depends entirely on the crumbs left behind by a much larger, more established business. Just think of the hot-dog vendors who set up their carts outside sports stadiums on game day. But Cost-Less stands out not just for its growth record, but for Johnson's ability to spot a gap in the distribution chain that he could fill better than the multinational corporation that created it.

LESSON: ASK THE RIGHT QUESTION

As new business formats alter old buying habits, new entrepreneurial opportunities are being created right alongside them. From new retail formats to on-line commerce, distribution channels to consumers and business are undergoing revolutionary change. As entrepreneurs like Calvin Johnson are proving, there are many ways to bring products and buyers together. The only limit is your ability to see and ask, "what if?"

THE SOFTKEY STORY: THE CAMPBELL SOUP OF SOFTWARE

A.G., Cost-Less, and Maple Homes all demonstrate some of the opportunities created by new and emerging distribution channels. But there is one **PROFIT 100** company that prospered by inventing its own distribution channel. When it comes to shaking up established markets with an innovative distribution concept, **Softkey Software** wrote the book.

Softkey started in 1983 in the garage of the home of Kevin O'Leary, a Toronto marketer-turned-TV-producer-turned-entrepreneur. When he found a primitive charting program that would help him put more attractive and informative computer graphics on screen during hockey broadcasts, O'Leary jumped into the software business. He saw an opportunity to sell graph- and chart-making software to the exploding new market for personal computers.

Quitting his day job, O'Leary teamed up with John Freeman, a Suncor executive who had written a graphics program as a way to create better sales charts. Together they sat down to adapt the software (dubbed KeyChart) to work with the hottest product of the day — the brand new IBM PC. "We were writing the program at night and selling during the day," O'Leary recalls.

But, as many inventors have discovered, getting distribution for a single, unproven product is tough. O'Leary was forced to find an alternative to conventional retail — selling the program to manufacturers of computer printers and plotters for bundling with their hardware. After all, it was software such as this that helped separate the PC from its arch-rival at the time, the stand-alone word processor. The new Softkey Software Products was on its way — slowly. "We started in my garage," says O'Leary. "Then we took over the basement, then the kitchen, and then a bedroom upstairs."

Soon Softkey was developing other programs, including a mailing-list product called KeyMailer, and selling through US computer-product catalogues. Gaining strength and confidence, it also acquired the rights to programs for such specific industries as auto-body shops, hotels, and retailers. But that was a mistake, says O'Leary. "We didn't realize how difficult support would be." When a system failed, clients needed immediate aid. Softkey spent hundreds of thousands of dollars flying in support people to bail out troubled clients.

Through this period, KeyChart and KeyMailer were selling steadily to consumers and small business. That's when O'Leary realized that perhaps the future belonged not to high-margin specialty software, with its distribution challenges and support problems, but to low-priced products for the mass market. At a time when few software companies had the capacity to design or sell more than one product, O'Leary resolved to market a whole line of software. O'Leary had learned about brand management in his earlier work with Standard Brands, and he brought his consumer-marketing expertise to bear in this new industry. To create awareness and critical mass, the software titles would all sell under a single brand name: Softkey.

The problem was finding the right products and the right way to reach a mass market. O'Leary discounted the idea of Softkey creating its own programs. "Our forte is marketing, not research," he said. R&D accounts for the high cost of most software, and you can pour a bundle into new software development only to find at the end that you have a program that doesn't do what you wanted, has too many bugs, or has just been made obsolete by a bunch of teenagers working in a garage in California. On the other hand, once you have a completed program, the economics become very attractive. "The marvel of software is that it costs you so little to manufacture, and the returns are so high," says O'Leary.

His breakthrough was hitting on the idea of licensing proven software products whose development has been paid for by someone else. That way, Softkey could eliminate the R&D risk, become a low-price leader and still enjoy the industry's traditional high margins.

O'Leary set out to convince professional software developers to license him their products, a tough sell even in the mid-eighties. O'Leary's tactic was to identify a top-selling software program, usually number two or three in a market, and then try to convince the publisher it was missing a whole new market. He would tell the company that its $200 word-processing package, while a good value for many businesses, was too expensive for home users and most small firms. He asked them to license their product to Softkey. It would sell it under its own name — unaltered except to remove the developer's name and identifying marks — for $39.95. That would open up a huge, untapped market to the original developer and pay off in a 10% royalty. O'Leary promised there would be little risk of eroding the developer's original market. For one thing, no one would know they were supplying to Softkey. Best of all, few corporate buyers would buy the Softkey version over the originals, he said. They would be sniffing at the brand as too obscure and the price as too low.

It sounded too good to be true. Moreover, it meant a big cultural change for an industry that had gotten used to demanding high prices from deep-pocketed corporate customers. Many developers were understandably suspicious. But O'Leary kept plugging away, slowly signing up brand-name software products and producing bigger and bigger mail-order catalogues of Softkey Software. "I told everyone we wanted to be the Campbell Soup or Harlequin Romance of software," says O'Leary. "People would buy the title because they trust the brand."

As it gathered more titles, ranging from spell-checkers and forms software to surprisingly complex computer-aided design, Softkey moved into retail — but not through the traditional and expensive computer-dealer chains. O'Leary took his racks of popularly priced software into retail chains such as Radio Shack and W. H. Smith in Canada, and Wal-Mart and Circuit City in the US. As he concluded in 1992, a few years before the rest of the world caught on, "Marketing software is not about technology. It's about facings, market share, distribution, and brand management. Software has become just another commodity."

The result was electrifying. In 1986 Softkey had ten employees and sales of $375,000. By 1991 it had 250 employees and sales of $36.9 million. That 9,738% growth rate was enough to put Softkey in first place on the 1992 PROFIT 100. The following year, Softkey's retail channels expanded and it licensed a new program of fonts for a hot new operating system called Windows 3.1. Its 1992 sales ballooned to $61 million, placing Softkey second on the 1993 PROFIT 100 — the best back-to-back finishes in the survey's nine-year history.

By that time, software publishers were flooding Softkey with products they wanted it to distribute. In April 1992 alone it received 280 programs to review. Needing to upgrade its marketing and logistical skills as US retail channels became more and more important, Softkey hired US marketing muscle and moved its publishing division to Boca Raton, Florida. It was determined to live up to its bold new slogan: "Changing the way America buys software."

Softkey kept the identity of its software suppliers strictly confidential, but in 1992 PROFIT ferreted out one developer to confirm that O'Leary's original plan was actually working. The company was Form-Gen Corp. of Bolton, Ontario, then one of North America's leaders in software for making business forms. It had licensed its flagship product, FormGen, to Softkey for four years, along with a few lesser titles. Then-President Randy MacLean admitted that Softkey's $39.95 Key Form Designer Plus was a faithful duplicate of the $279 FormGen, and updated as regularly as the original program.

MacLean said he had been sceptical when Softkey first approached him about licensing FormGen, but O'Leary's persistence made him a believer. After four years of partnering he came to call it "one of the best deals we ever made." If there had to be a low-priced rival in the forms market, he said, "we would much rather be competing with ourselves."

Softkey foresaw, and perhaps in some small way hastened, the shake-out that overtook much of the software industry in the mid-1990s. Its post-KeyChart strategy was entirely based on rising above the one-product ghetto and becoming a brand leader to enable it to survive the software price crash O'Leary knew had to come. Survival and growth, however, required more cash than Kevin O'Leary or Softkey's early revenues could provide. In 1987 venture capitalist Michael Perik directed a $500,000 investment in Softkey. In 1989 he joined the company as chairman bringing financial and strategic smarts to complement O'Leary's sales skills. Perik saw Softkey as the vehicle to accomplish his vision: a "merchant bank" of software companies.

His strategy was simple. High-tech firms have two things in common: a desperate need for cash, and trouble raising it. As a public company since 1986, Softkey offered a vehicle for promising software companies to team up and gain the clout needed to attract investors and clients. By 1992 Softkey had already made two major acquisitions, primarily by issuing shares instead of cash. "Instead of three small businesses, we have one medium-sized business that has a capacity to finance itself," Perik noted in 1992. "Our critical mass makes it easier to grow."

Indeed, 1993 was Softkey's last year as one of Canada's Fastest-Growing Companies — because it went on to become one of America's fastest-growing companies. That year, Perik and O'Leary completed a three-way merger that had industry heads spinning, uniting with consumer software developer Spinnaker Software Corp. and WordStar International Inc., the former word-processing leader that was shoved aside by WordPerfect. The company that resulted from that US$244-million merger boasted 150 titles and was based in Cambridge, Massachusetts. But it was called Softkey International, and running the show were Perik and O'Leary.

Again, Softkey was ahead of its time. Seeing how giants like Microsoft were chewing up the business-software category, it set its sights on the home category, which included games, educational, and novelty software. The key to gaining the clout to find shelf space with such general retailers as Wal-Mart and Toys R Us was to get bigger still.

In the next sixteen months they snapped up five more companies in deals valued at US$70 million, funded mostly by issuing more stock. In October 1995 Softkey raised US$350 million on the bond market. It used the proceeds to buy Minnesota Education Computer Corp., producer of Oregon Trail and other educational titles. And on the same day, October 30, it launched a hostile US$600-million takeover bid for The Learning Co. of Fremont, California, the developer of such hot-selling children's software titles as Reader Rabbit. Once the dust had settled in 1996, Softkey (now renamed The Learning Co.) had become "the largest educational software company in the world," announced Perik, "with a broad selection of high-quality titles and a distribution system in retail, OEM, international and direct response unmatched by any competitor."

Industry analysts credited Softkey with a coup, theorizing that bigger volumes meant better distribution, lower costs, and more control of pricing. As the magazine *PC Week* said in an upbeat profile of Softkey in November 1995, "He who grabs the most shelf space wins." Concluded the writer (apparently unaware of Softkey's Canadian origins), "The East Coast tough guys want to shoulder you off the shelf."

LESSON: SHIFT YOUR PARADIGM

The business lessons from Softkey are many and varied, from marketing and finance to the importance of vision, partnership, and sheer ambition. But the key breakthrough came more than ten years ago when Kevin O'Leary saw a chance to change the distribution pattern of software, from a high-cost model targeting business customers to a mass consumer one. He dared to try to change the way software was sold, and persevered long enough to succeed. In the 1990s we would call this "a paradigm shift." Then and now, it was a remarkable insight. It is an inspiring example of the way entrepreneurs and innovators can bring new value to established industries when they have a new idea and the commitment to carry it to fruition.

• FANTOM TECHNOLOGIES: A COBWEB-FREE DISTRIBUTION STRATEGY •

When **Iona Appliances** (now **Fantom Technologies**) saw its new dual-cyclonic Fantom vacuum cleaner jump off the shelves in its first year of sale at Sears stores in the United States and Canada (see Chapter 2), Allan Millman could have been forgiven for thinking the worst was over. Unfortunately, he still had as big a job ahead of him in reinventing his distribution channel as he had just reinventing the vacuum cleaner.

Within a few years of the introduction of the Capture dry carpet cleaner in 1988, sales began to falter. This was partly due to Iona's focusing its attention on the new Fantom vacuum cleaner which came out in 1991, and partly to the renewed recession of the early nineties. But when Fantom sales stalled after a couple of years, Millman realized he needed a new sales model. Changes in the department-store industry had created a less than ideal environment for selling his product.

As the retail wars heated up in the early nineties, Millman had seen store after store cut back its sales staff. Discounters like Wal-Mart in the US and Zellers in Canada were eating up market share without any sales associates doing much other than manning cash registers. That worked fine if you were selling brand-name commodities, but it represented a setback for higher-priced products such as Millman's dual-cyclonic cleaning products, because their features and benefits really required some explanation. "The people who bought the product just loved it, but we weren't achieving the kind of sales growth we needed,"

Millman told PROFIT's Michela Pasquali. "We were on the secret list. We had a great product, but nobody knew about it."

How do you sell the benefits of a revolutionary but kind of complicated consumer product? In 1993 Millman hit on a new strategy almost un-Canadian in its boldness: the thirty-minute infomercial. He called it "a television advertising format which lends itself, better than any other, to demonstrating the product's features and benefits while, at the same time, providing an opportunity to achieve immediate payback on invested dollars."

By now it should be evident that Allan Millman doesn't do things halfway. He hired one of America's most experienced infomercial companies, Iowa-based Hawthorne Communications, headed up by chairman Tim Hawthorne, regarded by some as the father of the modern infomercial.

Iona agreed to spend $300,000 to produce a thirty-minute infomercial featuring an on-air host and taped testimonials from satisfied customers. Broadcast several times a week in markets across the US and Canada starting in October 1993, it included a 1-800 number for consumers who couldn't wait to get to a store.

The odds were steep. According to Washington, DC marketing firm NIMA International, only one infomercial in twenty pays off. And, as Millman knew going in, the most successful infomercial pitches were for cosmetics, exercise equipment, and self-help books, tapes, and courses. In direct-response TV, vacuum cleaners were an unproven product.

But Iona's debut performance exceeded all expectations. Once consumers could actually see what kind of benefits the Fantom offered, Iona's operators were no longer standing by. They were run off their feet taking orders for Fantoms at US$250 (plus $19.95 shipping and handling). The whirling dirt particles, the scientific mumbo-jumbo, the folksy anecdotes all did their job. In 1994 Iona spent $3.4 million on media and generated direct orders worth $9.1 million — almost half the company's total sales that year. "The average successful infomercial delivers $1.70 of sales for every dollar of advertising spent," says Millman. "We've delivered an average of $3." A good thing too, because sales through Iona's retail channels fell 34%.

By 1996 Iona's sales pitch was as slick as any on television. In one infomercial, one satisfied user said she had pulled enough hair out of her carpet to make another dog. Another woman said her husband was convinced that the Fantom had come delivered with dirt already in it from the factory, since it sucked up so much dirt so fast the very first time it was put to work on the household carpets. Among the benefits that manage to slip out in the half-hour story were no more hassles installing or removing vacuum-cleaner bags; you can actually see how much dirt it's picking up at any given time; you always know when the transparent plastic canister is full; it's two units in one (an upright vacuum or a cleaning wand, using the detachable handle as an extension that lets you clean drapes or keyboards); a clean exhaust system that doesn't blow half the dust, dirt, pollen, and mould back into the house (in fact, its filtration system is certified as being able to remove 99.7% of all particles passing through it). If users have any questions or problems, there's a 1-800 customer-service number printed right on the side of the machine. Probably best of all for harried housewives, though, was one vignette featuring a man who so enjoys watching the dirt collect inside his Fantom that he won't let his wife vacuum any more. He insists on doing it every day. Who could resist a pitch like that?

"The infomercial put us on the map in the US," says Millman. "It gave us an opportunity to tell a complicated story in thirty minutes." And while it created a new direct-ordering channel for the Fantom, the infomercial has another side-benefit. Now that consumers had a better idea what it could do, its success spurred other retailers such as Kmart, J.C. Penney, and the Home Shopping Network to stock Iona's products.

LESSON: FIND DISTRIBUTION METHODS THAT FIT YOUR SALES NEEDS

The Fantom's new status as TV star put Iona in a whole new league. Sales soared from $20.5 million in fiscal 1994, to $59.4 million in 1995, and $98 million in 1996. For the fiscal year ended June 30, 1997, sales were expected to almost double again, to close to $180 million. For a company that used to be dependent on the Canadian market, Iona (renamed Fantom Technologies) now generates more than 95% of its revenues in the US. By 1997 Iona employed 400 people, up from just 137 four years earlier.

By 1996 Fantom Technologies was spending less on infomercials. In part, it found the cost of TV time in the US was growing too expensive. Equally, however, Fantom didn't need that channel as much any more. Infomercials had succeeded in raising the Fantom's profile so significantly that major retailers, from Montgomery Ward to Target Stores, Caldor, and Service Merchandise had all begun selling the product. Millman knew it was time to emphasize retail again. But he will keep investing in infomercials as a key distribution vehicle for the direct-response sales they generate and the awareness they create. "As seen on TV" is an old line that still has star power.

Clearly, developing a better mousetrap is not the only way to succeed in business. Finding a new way to get that mousetrap to market may be equally promising, and probably easier. As the barrage of manufacturers' new products increases, as international markets converge, and as new distribution channels emerge — from new forms of retail to electronic commerce — innovative entrepreneurs are discovering that a little creativity in distribution can take them a long way.

MARKET-DRIVEN DIVERSIFICATION

"You've got to do things from a position of strength."

Mark Skapinker, Delrina Corp.

The moment comes in the life of every business. "C'mon," says someone (or perhaps it's just a little voice in your head), "Your company makes apple sauce. You should really get into apple juice now. It's going to be big!"

For entrepreneurs who want their companies to grow, the temptation to expand and diversify is exceedingly strong. Sure, you know that most of the great busts in Canadian business came from overzealous expansion into industries the owners didn't understand. And yet, didn't Simpsons and Eaton's run into trouble for sticking too long to a once-successful strategy? Besides, no one wants to be a one-trick pony. And surely diversification, to the extent that it insulates you from some potential market downturn, is a sound defensive strategy?

There's no right answer to these questions. Diversification into new markets and new products is the key expansion tactic of successful growth companies. And yet, it's also the point where many businesses go off the rails. In a regular feature called "Post Mortem," PROFIT magazine studies business failures to find out what went wrong. Time after time, the answer is lack of focus. Businesses such as Stratford Software's Suzy on-line service, Queen Street Camera, Multitech Warehouse Direct, and The Steals People all eventually failed because they attempted ambitious expansions for which either they or their target markets just weren't ready.

In contrast to the above companies, the PROFIT 100 have largely succeeded at expanding successfully. They have done so because, for the most part, they have taken a strategic approach to diversification. They study their proposed markets carefully and weigh the pros and cons before committing, and make sure they have some financial cushion in place in case things turn sour too soon. Most importantly, however, they pay attention to all the signals their market is sending them. They know that expansion will turn out best when it is driven by the forces of the market, not by chance opportunities that crop up or an impatient voice in the back of your head.

In fact, you could make the case that much of the success of PROFIT 100 companies stems from their ability to follow the dictates of the market. Problems at Eaton's and Simpsons didn't flow so much from their inability to change — they switched around internal systems and marketing strategies almost as fast as the mannequins in their show windows changed clothes. Quite simply, the big retailers lost touch with their markets, and no longer knew how to respond effectively when customers started deserting them for more stylish boutiques or lower-priced discount stores.

FOLLOWING THE MARKET'S LEAD

What does market-driven expansion mean? It means knowing your market, tracking its signals, and understanding when to stick with your business plan and when to throw it out in order to go in the same direction as your customers are heading. Over the years, some of the brightest lights on the PROFIT 100 have chalked up incredible growth records because they have followed their market's lead instead of blithely keeping on in the same direction and expecting the market to follow them.

The number one company of 1995 (it was fourth in 1996) was **Alex Informatics Inc.** of Lachine, Quebec, a producer of high-performance parallel computers, a kind of economy-model supercomputer made by aligning conventional PC processors so they can solve massive computing problems in parallel. Founded by corporate tax lawyer Marc Labrosse, Alex started off as a custom software business that tackled specialized programming jobs for demanding clients such as Hydro-Québec. One contract, to compute the environmental impact of a new dam on a Quebec river, defied the processing power of any conventional computer, so Alex wrote software for a French brand of parallel computer that could handle the job. Seeing all sorts of applications for parallel computers, they started distributing the French line. Over time Alex also developed its own hardware production capacity, and dropped the French line to sell its own product, the AVX.

Alex penetrated markets as diverse as Boeing (which used its computers to drive a system to process radar signals from the US Air Force's AWACS surveillance planes), university research departments, and the Institute for Marine Dynamics in Newfoundland, which used an AVX to simulate a ship's movement at sea — saving the time and expense of building a scale model and towing it through the water.

As more companies such as IBM jumped into the parallel-computing market, however, Alex had to change again. Once hardware becomes commoditized, the money is in software, so Alex is now returning to being a software company again. It is developing software systems that turn its computers into high-powered media servers, which can provide video content to a multiple users over high-capacity networks. What's that mean? Alex's Libra media server pioneered a distance-learning trial in Trois-Rivières that saw fifty economics students access multimedia lessons over their cable TV. A French hotel chain now offers guests movies and other video on demand using an Alex media server. No more coming in late or waiting around; your favourite movie now starts whenever you're ready. Plus, the server provides VCR-like controls — pause, fast-forward, rewind — that put the viewer in charge of the show.

And in late 1996, Alex beat out giants such as Philips and Sun Microsystems to win a $5-million contract to supply France's new Bibliothèque Nationale in Paris with a digital library system. Its two media servers will let up to 1,000 users at a time access historic films, photos and sound recordings from France's national archives. In May 1997, the Canadian Advanced Technology Association named Alex Canada's Information Technology Innovator of the Year — all because it knew how to follow its market.

Accu-Rate Foreign Exchange, the number one company in 1994, started out as a spin-off of an Ottawa rare-coin dealership. When customers started asking President Paul Davis, a habitual world traveller, if he could exchange their foreign currency, he sensed a market opportunity. By 1994, Accu-Rate had recorded five-year sales growth of 19,000% — while the original coin dealership plodded along far behind.

ISG Technologies Ltd. in Mississauga, Ontario, was a three-time PROFIT 100 company that finished as high as number three in 1993. A pioneer in 3-D imaging, ISG originally set out to sell flight simulators. Michael Greenberg, a neurosurgeon, was brought in to consult on setting up a medical-imaging division. He identified a huge market niche for computer workstations that would provide 3-D computer scans of people's insides. He was so persuasive that the company moved into medical imaging full time, and made Greenberg president.

Philip Services Inc. of Hamilton, Ontario, a four-time PROFIT 100 company that finished as high as sixth in 1995, started out as a trucking firm hauling away waste materials from Stelco. Founders Allan and Philip Fracassi were smart enough to see that instead of paying to dump the waste at landfills, they could recycle much of that material and turn it into a profit centre. They applied that principle to become Canada's largest industrial recycler, and have now expanded further into other maintenance and engineering services for large industrial clients.

These companies and many others succeeded because their key strength turned out to be not just knowing how to produce a good product or service, but in understanding their market. They changed direction over the years because they recognized their markets were going in a different direction than they had expected, and they knew enough to follow their customers instead of trying to push things through their own way.

Of course, not all expansion is strategically driven. When **Shikatronics Inc.** of La Prarie, Québec, first began selling to Mexico's computer industry, it did so only because one of its finest employees, a native of Mexico, decided to return home in 1995. Reluctant to lose a good employee, President Alnoor Sheriff created a job for him, to try to crack open the Mexican market. By early 1997, Mexico was generating sales of $500,000 a month.

TIP: MAKE EDUCATED GUESSES

Never dismiss the power of serendipity or opportunism. But don't mistake it for strategy, either. The best "gambles" are still the ones that you have researched and studied to the point where you've reduced the risk as much as possible.

RULES OF MARKET-DRIVEN DIVERSIFICATION

Heed What Your Market Is Telling You

Market forces are always sending you a message. Sometimes competitors' actions or customers' demands will be pulling you into new areas of endeavour. But just as often the market may be pushing and prodding you to get out of the market you're in, or at least start doing things differently.

That was clearly the case at **Cooke Aquaculture Inc.**, number sixty-two on the 1997 profit 100 (unless otherwise cited, all the companies in this section hail from the 1997 list). Cooke, one of the new breed of salmon-farming operations along New Brunswick's rugged Bay of Fundy shore, started in 1987 as a harvester of adult salmon. Things looked promising. Salmon prices then averaged $6 a pound.

With the recession coming on and world competition increasing, however, salmon prices tumbled. The Cooke family, father Gifford, a marine mechanic, and his sons Glenn, a fish broker, and Michael, a civil engineer, saw the writing on the wall. The market was telling them they had to get more efficient or pack it in. Their solution was to become more vertically integrated, to control their costs better, and capture more of the value in each salmon for themselves. The happy result is that Cooke's diversification move helped sales boom 965% between 1991 and 1996, even as salmon prices dropped in half.

Of course, sometimes market signals are more positive. In Markham, Ontario, **L.E. Cherry & Associates** is a mail-order computer dealer operating under the name **Computer Buyer's Warehouse Direct**. Founder Lorne Cherry started the company as a marketing consultant. But as a longtime computer buff, he found that the advertising agencies he was dealing with kept asking him what he knew about the latest computer equipment and what it could do. He took the hint and opened up a business to sell high-end Macintosh clone computers and equipment geared to a graphic-arts market. It wasn't a "blind swing," Cherry insists. He spent six months thinking through the decision to switch strategies, and composed a new business plan for the operation. "I still have it and follow it, although it is constantly in flux," he says. "In the computer industry we wake up every day and things are different."

Establish Feedback Mechanisms

To read your market, you have to make an effort to stay in touch. New York pop marketing guru Faith Popcorn believes entrepreneurs should be in touch with 150 customers a year to ensure they know what's going on in their industry and which way their markets are headed.

PROFIT 100 companies are developing these two-way information streams. Toronto-based **Tropical Treets** offers a toll-free phone number to facilitate comments, questions, and complaints from consumers of its Chubby soft drinks. **Just Kid'n Children's Wear** hires a team of telemarketers a few times a year to call customers to tell them what's new at the store and listen for feedback. **Datalog Technology Inc.** of Calgary stresses face-to-face communication with its clients — 5,000 oil executives around the world. That creates opportunities for selling and for listening. **KL Group** and other software developers use trade shows and customer-support lines to find out the problems customers are having and where they would like to see the company go next.

Ottawa-based **Fulcrum Technologies Inc.** encourages feedback loops with customers, subscribes to market studies, and even commissions its own market research to try to understand where its niche, information-retrieval software, is heading next. But CEO Eric Goodwin insists that this all adds up to data, not direction. Successful technology, he says, "starts on vision, not listening to customers."

Leverage Your Existing Resources

To diversify successfully, you must first know what your business's most important assets are. Could it be your customer list? Your patents? Your understanding of technology, or your ability to produce at a lower cost than rivals? Successful strategic expansion begins with finding out what you're good at, and using those assets — animal, vegetable, mineral or intangible — as your springboard into new profit centres.

In Arborg, Manitoba, **Vidir Machine Ltd.** hit the big time with a motorized display rack that holds rolls of carpet and vinyl tile. Its acceptance by wholesalers and warehouse retailers such as Home Depot opened networks of opportunity for selling related new products. Thus its carpet-cutting machines are found in carpet-jobbers' warehouses, and it is working on getting its motorized shelving carousels into retail stores for storing and displaying lawnmowers, lawn tractors, bicycles, and other bulky items. So far, most retailers don't know what a shelving carousel can do for them, in terms of maximizing selling space by getting bulky items off the floor, but Vidir is working on that. President Ray Dueck says, "We let them know there's a need they didn't know they had."

Similarly, when **Philip Services** moved into recycling and then into industrial services, it was making use of its most important asset: its ability to work with and understand the needs of major heavy-industry clients. And when Lorne Cherry moved from consulting to computer retailing, he changed only the product he was selling. The target market, at least at first, remained the same, because it was his knowledge of that market and his credibility there that created the opportunity in the first place.

Add Value for Your Customers

PROFIT 100 entrepreneurs know that they're in business to help their customers thrive. By creating value for their customers first, they ensure themselves a sustainable future.

One of the canniest of PROFIT 100 diversifiers is **Magnotta Winery Corp.** of Vaughan, Ontario, just north of Toronto. Started in the mid-1980s to sell grape juice to home-based winemakers, Magnotta has slowly branched out to provide one-stop shopping to consumers looking for better value in their beer, wine, and spirits. "As far as we know, Magnotta is the only liquor manufacturer in Canada that has become triple licensed, for wine, beer, and distilled products," says founder Gabe Magnotta.

It was Magnotta's predecessor company, Festa Juice Co., that kicked off the diversification strategy. While Festa thrived through the 1980s selling imported juice to amateur winemakers, Gabe and his wife Rossana feared the end was nigh. Their target market, second-generation Italian, Portuguese, and Greek immigrants, was steadily shrinking. To reduce the risk, they decided to expand into winemaking itself. They acquired a winery in Blenheim, Ontario, and moved it to a bland-looking industrial park in Vaughan.

The move could have been fatal, because Ontario's Liquor Control Board — the government's virtual monopoly on retail liquor sales in the province — promptly cancelled the winery's listing on its shelves, citing a shortage of shelf space. "We were very upset," recalls Magnotta. "We had put our life savings into this." But that setback helped refine Magnotta's unique niche. The company discovered that provincial regulations allowed them to add a retail outlet beside its winery. They did, and passed the savings on to their customers. Where Gabe Magnotta had counted on receiving $2 from the LCBO for a bottle of wine that would sell for $6 at retail, he concluded he could now sell at $3.95 and still net $2.50! At that price, he admits, "everyone assumed it was plonk." The saving grace was an in-store tasting bar that allowed consumers to try before they bought. The result was, according to Gabe, that consumers who came to buy two bottles left with two cases.

Magnotta's success has spurred a number of expansion thrusts, including the acquisition of three vineyards in Ontario and Chile to assure a secure supply of grapes. But the most eye-popping initiatives have been Magnotta's move into beer and spirits. In 1996 it introduced "True North," an all natural lager, produced in a new $1-million brewery. The point again was one-stop shopping. As Gabe Magnotta told PROFIT writer Richard Wright, "I have to offer a diverse selection to attract the customers. I have to be a mini-LCBO." Again, value is the key. A case of True North sells for $5 less than most microbrews. The launch proved such a hit, Magnotta had to limit sales to one case per customer.

But that's not the end of it. In early 1997 Magnotta opened a distillery to convert the leftover grape skins, stems, and seeds into distilled spirits. The result was grappa, a traditional Italian eau-de-vie, and "ice grappa," Magnotta's take on the craze for icewine. With more than a hundred products now (including gin, vodka, and bottled water), stores in Mississauga, Scarborough, Niagara, and Kitchener, Ontario, and a new winery opened in mid-1997 on busy Highway 400 just north of Toronto, the Magnottas are looking to continued growth for their integrated alternative to the LCBO. "I've got a lot of new ideas up my sleeve," says Magnotta.

Add Value for Yourself

It is important to move in directions that cut costs or replace expensive inputs. While Magnotta's ongoing diversification has been targeted at increasing value to customers until they had no choice but to flock to Magnotta's store for award-winning products and below-retail prices, the expansion created value for Magnotta as well. Its extended product lines helped fill the production channels and created economies of scale. As CFO Fulvio De Angelis says, "once you have the infrastructure in place, suppliers, trucks, and a customer base, it's not that much of a leap" into other products.

Cooke Aquaculture Inc. moved in a similar direction with its vertical-integration strategy. In fact, it found that producing more of its services and supplies in-house not only reduced costs but created new profit centres, because it could sell these services to others.

In 1988 Cooke opened its own hatchery, to free itself of its dependence on larger corporations and government ponds, and has since opened a second hatchery. More recently, Cooke set up its own teams to vaccinate its salmon — one at a time — to protect them from diseases sweeping the Bay of Fundy. In doing so, it repatriated work that was being performed by teams from Norway, and now it performs the same services for other hatcheries in the Maritimes and in nearby Maine. And in 1996 Cooke started making its own giant nets — which can cost up to $8,000 each — that pen adult salmon as they mature in the ocean. Now it's even selling nets to competitors.

"Any successful business in the Maritimes has to be integrated," says CEO Glenn Cooke. "In the Maritimes you don't have a lot of choices as to where you buy goods and services. Because volumes are smaller, the competition is less so the cost of services and supplies we buy is higher." But by supplying yourself, he notes, you can keep the cash in the company. And by selling surplus production to competitors, you generate your own profit centres — as well as making customers out of competitors. In 1996, $3 million of Cooke's $19 million in sales came from spin-off businesses.

But Cooke also created value for itself by climbing up the value chain. Why not? "We can add value by filleting or steaking," says Cooke. Where whole salmon sells for less than $3 a pound, smoked salmon goes for $12. Cooke acquired a processing plant in 1992 to gut and clean the fish, and then invested $100,000 more in 1995 to produce steaks and fillets. Cooke has also built its own distribution network of 150 customers throughout Canada and the US, helping push its "True North" line of products (no relation to Magnotta's beer) into major restaurant chains and retailers. It recently built a new $1-million processing plant to produce even more products, from smoked, frozen fish kebobs to salmon burgers. "Within five years 60 to 70% of what we sell will be in some kind of added-value form," Cooke vows.

Don't Push the Envelope

When expansions fail, there's usually a reason. Often, it's because a company decides to stake its future on a brand new product or service that markets just haven't asked for and simply aren't ready for. There's often only a thin line between market-leading vision (that's when you win) and sheer ignorance of the market (that's what people say when you lose). In general, markets don't like leaps of faith.

Consider Echo Lake, a revolutionary software product produced by four-time PROFIT 100 company **Delrina Corp.** of Toronto in 1995. Echo Lake wasn't anything like the forms or fax software that Delrina made its name on. It was an attempt to turn consumers on to the new multimedia power of CD-ROMs. It was created as a multimedia scrapbook or photo album, in which whole families could record their thoughts and impressions of the past, a diary in words and in pictures (photos could be scanned in electronically at Black's camera stores). To prompt your memories, the CD offered 2,000 thought-provoking questions ("Who was your best friend in second grade?") and an eclectic collection of photos and sound and video clips of important events of the recent past. The system was based on the metaphor of a fondly remembered cottage to which a family returns year after year. It was just as weird as it sounds.

Nonetheless, Echo Lake got rave reviews. "As a practical, graceful, and easy-to-use tool, Echo Lake is one of the most effective multimedia CD-ROMs to come down the pike in a while," gushed *Computer Shopper* magazine. *Multimedia World* said, "The features are impressive, but the visual metaphors, the seamless integration of multimedia tools, and the elegant interface will knock your socks off."

Consumers said no thanks. Delrina had tried to create a new paradigm, a whole new type of software. At the same time, it was appealing to a whole new market, and using a new distribution system. Delrina broke all the above rules. It had bitten off too much, and the product, launched with much fanfare, was quietly set on the back burner in the summer of 1995 when Delrina was acquired by US software giant Symantec Corp.

Reduce Your Risk: Test, Test, Test

No matter how confident you are that a new initiative will succeed, only someone who's gotten tired of eating bets everything on a single horse. The essence of entrepreneurship is reducing risks, not taking them, so be sure that your diversification efforts are well researched and well backed financially. Investing in new products or strategies is like playing the stock market. If you're not prepared to lose your entire investment, you shouldn't be playing the game.

How do you do it? Keith Scott at **Beachcomber Spas** (1992-93) in Surrey, BC, tries out new ideas at just a few of his 100 dealers across Canada. If it doesn't work, there's little money at risk and scant harm done. Most dealers and consumers never even know about it.

PROFIT 100 **Yogen Früz World-Wide Inc.**, the Toronto-based company that has become the world's largest frozen-yogurt franchisor, spends nearly $400,000 a year developing new products. It's not just new flavours, says Aaron Serruya, one of three brothers running the company. Yogen Früz is always looking at new categories of products, such as non-fat and low-fat ice cream. Before introducing a new product into a market place, Yogen Früz asks the master franchisor in each country to test it in its stores. "Just because it works in Canada doesn't mean it will sell in Venezuela," says Serruya. "Through tests with master franchisors we get a very good feeling about what will work where."

Yogen Früz also learned an important lesson about the limits of diversification when it came up with its own ice cream a few years ago. The product was supported by $350,000 worth of advertising, but accounted in the end for just 3% of sales, less than a quarter of the target of 12% to 15%. "It was a flop," admits Serruya. "The public couldn't get their brain around a yogurt company making ice cream." A few years later, Yogen Früz re-entered the market the right way. It bought Bresler's, a sixty-two-year-old US ice cream company with good name recognition. Bresler's stands may sell Yogen Früz frozen yogurt now, but at least, says Serruya, "it's not Yogen Früz trying to be ice cream."

PROFIT 100 How do you decide when to take a strategic leap into new markets? **Delrina Corp.** then-President Mark Skapinker offered his answer in a PROFIT interview just after the Toronto software developer had announced its decision to sell out to US-based Symantec Corp. "You've got to do things from a position of strength," said Skapinker. "You have to understand that if you're not taking risks, you're not running a business; you can't grow without taking risks all the way along. The only way to make good decisions and safe decisions is to make risky decisions. If we hadn't gone all out with Winfax (a fax program for Windows), we wouldn't be where we are now [1994 revenues were $100 million].

"And that's true for the way we ask people to make decisions in running the business," Skapinker continues. "If they think, gee, should I do this marketing program, because it's a bit risky, and who knows if it will succeed, I still want them to do it. The issue is how to not make the same mistake over and over, and how to take reasonable risks. I think you take risks that allow you to measure the results of them, so that if they are successful you can actually use them on the other side. You find a balance between safe and risky, between investment and cash cow."

Do Your Homework

What sinks most new expansions and initiatives? Failure to sweat the details. To launch a new initiative you must have money in place, experienced, capable people who know the market, and a long-term strategy that helps you set goals and objectives for the new project. Unfortunately, like high school students with spring fever, few expansion-oriented businesses do all their homework on time.

PROFIT 100 Similarly, Grant Reynolds of Mississauga, Ontario-based **Auto Control Medical Inc.** (1994-97) admitted to "not doing extensive enough market research before committing to a product." He admits Auto Control tends to do its own market research, since the experts don't come cheap. But there are a lot of potential medical and diagnostic products to choose from. "We're doing at least five or six at a time, we could be looking at 100 briefly and 15 to 20 with any kind of focus." Friends have warned Reynolds that amateurs engaged in market research usually hear only what they want to hear, so he tries to keep that in mind as he wrestles with decisions that experts could make if they didn't cost so much.

PROFIT 100 At **CC Petroleum Inc.** of Downsview, Ontario (1996), a petroleum transporter and wholesaler, President Cal Christiansen admitted to a similar sin, when they bought a company a few years ago without checking its books out thoroughly. He got some nasty surprises "and lost a lot of money." His assessment: "I was too anxious. Always do your homework," he says. "Never want something that badly."

In the end, your expansion attempt will be only as successful as it fits with your organization's infrastructure, expertise, and long-term objectives. While **Chai-Na-Ta Corp.** (1996-97) of Langley, BC, is a grower of North American ginseng for export to China, where it is regarded as the miracle root, and where the North American variety is actually prized above the Asian product for its contributions to long-term strength and vitality. While Chai-Na-Ta is engaged in a number of different initiatives to expand its ginseng markets and product lines, President Gerry Gill says patience and caution are key. Asked to name his top strength as a manager, Gill suggested it was his ability to focus on the long-term amid the never-ending pressures for more growth and diversification. "We have kept our management focus on what we wanted to do when there are so many opportunities coming up every day. We identify projects and stick to them. We constantly review our objectives with management and track the results regularly." Ginseng may strengthen the body, but it also seems to lend clarity to the mind.

CHAPTER FIVE

KNOW
YOUR
CUSTOMER

"Having the best product is not enough to bring people back."

Kelly Cahill, Just Kid'n Children's Wear.

A New York television executive who commuted regularly to his network's production offices in Los Angeles once found a pithy way to describe his audience and, perhaps unintentionally, his own attitude to the people who paid his salary. "The public," he said, "is what we fly over." Few business organizations today can afford the luxury of such a bird's-eye view of their market. It's a perspective more suited to a monopoly than to a competitive market, but then what else was the broadcasting scene twenty years ago, when just three US networks controlled more than 90% of American television?

Today, buffeted by new US networks, nationally delivered superstations and cable networks, pay TV, video rentals and, yes, the Internet, the once arrogant television giants are fighting for their lives. No longer can they take their customers for granted. Now they have to duke it out for viewer loyalty, feet firmly on the ground, market by market, just like everybody else in business today. As advancing technology and increasing competition turn every market into a niche market, companies that fail to respect and to intimately get to know their customers are courting disaster.

When they set out to fill a niche, businesses implicitly accept the idea that they are no longer just "producing a product," but also serving a specialized market. As they try to define themselves, some companies will retain the idea that their specialty is product, that they produce the best database software in the world or sell the best children's jackets in town. More often, however, as managers review their organization's strengths and weaknesses, they discover that their real strength lies not just in knowing all about their product, but in understanding the market that wants it. It's an important epiphany, and one that usually leads to a straighter path to success.

PROFIT 101. Knowing your customer isn't just good business. It can be the difference between success and failure, even if you're a little guy up against big, experienced competition.

On a visit to Florida in the mid-1980s, Torontonians Aaron and Michael Serruya took note of the latest trend in US fun food: frozen yogurt. Low in fat and often mixed with real fruit, frozen yogurt was starting to rival ice cream as the favoured cool dessert, and Aaron and Michael, aged twenty and twenty-one at the time, wondered how the trend might fare in Canada's colder climate. They didn't have long to wonder. Soon after, a major US retailer of frozen yogurt came north, opening 100 stores on city streets across Canada. Its formula had worked in the States, and the company had no reason to believe it wouldn't succeed equally well in Canada.

Today, just two of those 100 stores are still operating. The big expansion was a bust. And it wasn't because Canadians don't like frozen yogurt.

Aaron Serruya believes he saw the company's mistake from the beginning. It neglected the impact of a long, cold winter. For a local frozen-dessert chain to work, he realized, it couldn't locate its outlets in outdoor street locations. "It would have to be mall-driven. Because the only way to survive in winter would be to be in malls, where the best month of the year is December."

With seed capital from their family, Aaron, now thirty-one, and Michael, thirty-two, started their own yogurt outlet in Toronto's

Promenade Mall. They called their product **Yogen Früz**, to capitalize, as Häagen-Dazs did, on the allure of a vaguely European-sounding connection to what was actually a North American product. Expanding craftily through malls and franchises inside doughnut shops, rather than opening their own free-standing outlets, Yogen Früz has now grown to more than 225 Canadian outlets. And just three of them, in downtown Toronto, Vancouver's Robson Street, and near the company's head office in Markham, Ontario, are actually located at streetside.

With sales of $30 million for fiscal 1996, Yogen Früz is one of Canada's most successful food-service companies and the world's largest franchisor of frozen-yogurt outlets. With franchises in the Middle East, Asia, and South America, requests from potential franchisees arrive daily. The ruling Serruyas (who now include brother Simon, 26) say their success stems equally from a good product — they spend $400,000 a year developing new products — and top locations. While their US rival was snapping up high-traffic street locations, Yogen Früz concentrated on premium mall sites. "People try to emulate us, but we have the best locations tied up," says Aaron. "As long as we pay our rent on time, we'll be there forever." As Yogen Früz's success demonstrates, a little customer insight goes a long way.

Understanding the needs of the market, as opposed to knowing how to turn out a specific product, provides a clear direction for future product offerings, enhancements, and updates. It helps a company grow from a product to a business. But it's a process that never ends. As companies begin diversifying or expanding their product lines to meet more of the needs of their chosen customers, they have to work harder to get to know their clients and understand their needs, or else surrender their niche to someone else who will.

Over the years, few Canadian retailers have progressed far on the PROFIT 100. In the first place, Canada is generally considered to have too many stores already. Witness the restructuring that has already begun with big chains such as Simpsons, Woolworth's, Woodwards, Consumers Distributing, and Eaton's. And secondly, most of the growth in retail is in the superstore formats imported from the United States by giants such as Wal-Mart, Price Club/Costco, and Home Depot.

But the biggest barrier to go-go growth in retail may be that success is generally harder to duplicate in retailing than in many other businesses. In manufacturing, growth often means ramping up production, producing the same thing, only more often. In software, the economies of scale go through the roof. Retail, however, is a people business. It's tricky enough to get right the first time, without trying to duplicate your achievement in other locations. Many notable retailing winners such as McDonald's have succeeded by creating a standardized operational bible whose insistence on detailed precision virtually eliminates freedom of action on the part of the hourly staff. In fact many retailers, such as Toronto's Honest Ed Mirvish, have never tried to expand beyond the single outlet, because they just didn't want the 1,001 headaches of trying to make lightning strike twice.

One exception to this rule, however, is a young, aggressive retailer of upscale, mainly unisex, children's fashions called **Just Kid'n Children's Wear Ltd.** in Langley, BC (1996-97). Run by the brother and sister team of Kelly Cahill and Colleen Hazelwood, by the end of 1996 Just Kid'n had seven stores and sales of $1.9 million, up from just $230,000 five years earlier. The explanation for this growth was Just Kid'n's in-depth and ever-growing knowledge of its customer base.

The business started based on Hazelwood's insights into the "echo boom," the junior baby boom touched off in the mid-'80s as baby boomers finally decided it was time to have kids of their own. From her own experience as a mother of four, she knew it was hard to find quality, hard-wearing clothes in the designs and sizes she needed, and she knew many mothers felt the same way. Having sewn all her life, she began designing the clothing she wanted to be able to buy for her own kids, and felt there would be a market on a commercial basis. Baby boomers, as a rule, are having fewer children than their parents did, and they're having them later in life, which means that they are willing to spend more on them to make sure their clothes are more rugged or more fashionable. She persuaded her brother Kelly, who was working in sales and marketing for an international food company, to bring his management expertise to the business. Together, they came up with a plan for a company that would make and sell its own fashions, eliminating distributors' commissions, and long production delays. Cahill quit his job to get involved in **Just Kid'n**, and brother and sister each own half the company.

Today, Cahill can tell you exactly who his customers are: 90% are women; 70% are parents, 30% are grandparents, relatives, and friends. Their age is 25 to 45, and they tend to have mid to high incomes. Hazelwood still designs the clothes, which are produced by a team of seamstresses in Langley, but quality clothing alone doesn't account for the business's success, says Cahill. "We have a uniqueness factor, but that's not enough. That's the mistake so many people make, thinking that if you build it they will come. You still need good service. Having the best product is not enough to bring people back."

Cahill's solution was to put his marketing dollars into developing a database that would let the company build one-on-one relationships with its customers. "With relationship marketing, rather than selling to the masses, we're selling to the individual," he says. "You build a relationship with the customer, who will have a good feeling about us and want to come back and shop again and again."

Like many retailers, Just Kid'n offers a bonus club that any customer can join. Using its point of sale technology, Just Kid'n registers every sale to club members. Once a customer's sales hit $300, she get $30 off her next purchase. "That brings people back," says Cahill. "But just as important, it gives us information on customers that we can manipulate to use for marketing."

In fact, the heart of Just Kid'n is its database of over 100,000 customers, for which it is always finding new uses. Identifying the top twenty customers of the month at each store, for instance, enables store managers to send out handwritten thank-you cards with a coupon good for a 10% discount on any purchase made in the next thirty days. Occasionally, Just Kid'n searches its database for the names of all first-time purchasers, then hires its telemarketing team to call and thank them, and then offer them a discount coupon. More recently, Cahill has experimented with a cooperative program with other retailers targeting children with birthdays coming up. Just Kid'n would send out a birthday card to children listed as having a birthday in the next month. Each card would include invitations to visit Just Kid'n and other participating retailers for a free gift. Anyone who visits all the participants would then qualify to win a free birthday party. "The goodwill does generate new business," says Cahill. "If Little Johnny comes in and wins a prize, he brings ten or fifteen other kids who aren't necessarily customers, but we hope they will be."

The owners also encourage their sales staff to keep in touch with their customers by phone whenever possible. "I'm amazed at how many customers and staff know each others' names," says Cahill. The result is pure gold. According to Cahill, more than 80% of his business is repeat. And much of the rest, he says, stems from these repeat customers who tell their friends about the product and service they've received at Just Kid'n.

LESSON: LOW-COST MARKETING

The best part of Just Kid'n's relationship-marketing effort is that it doesn't have to cost a lot. Cahill estimates his costs at less than 1% of sales; he pays for it out of incidental funds that might otherwise be spent on occasional media advertising. As long as you keep collecting and updating names, a database can continue to perform for you, year-round. The only limit is your ability to come up with relevant and imaginative uses for your list, and that depends mainly on your ability to think up legitimate excuses for contacting your customers, and new, value-laden reasons why they should come back to your business.

HOW TO GET THE INSIDE TRACK ON CUSTOMERS

A business that truly understands what drives its customers can begin to create a relationship with them that can provide lasting benefit to both parties. Increasingly, successful companies are building two-way relationships that bring them closer to their customers at the same time as they create new sales or marketing opportunities.

How do you know what your customers want? PROFIT 100 entrepreneurs, in general, follow three paths to enlightenment:

1. **They know their industry because they have been involved in it for years** — sometimes as a customer, usually as a supplier. By watching it develop and grow, they know what their customers are looking for, and how other players are meeting their needs — or not.

"I've never forgotten what it was like to be a truck driver myself, and I've hired the right people who do the same," says Kieran O'Briain of **Kee Transport Group** (1996-97). Mississauga, Ontario-based Kee grew 2,000% in five years by supplying better-qualified and motivated drivers to corporate trucking fleets. "Most of the people who work in our office were truck drivers, or worked at trucking companies for years," says O'Briain. "The guys who deal with drivers have all driven a truck."

"We've stayed pretty focused on what people need," says **KL Group**'s Greg Kiessling. "We focus on products that we think a lot of people will use." Kiessling, and co-founder Ed Lycklama, came by their first market insights the easy way. They themselves were exactly the sort of computer programmers that their first products — programming software that makes Unix programs easier and faster to create — were aimed at. Today, as markets splinter and KL's founders spend more time managing and planning than programming, it's tougher staying in touch with their market. So they make sure KL receives and analyses as much customer feedback as possible, through hiring sales and support people who are customer-focused, meeting potential users face-to-face at trade shows or listening to complaints and suggestions on its customer-support lines. Kiessling says customers aren't very good at telling you what products they want next, but careful listening or reading between the lines offers directions to go in. Based on the feedback KL encourages, he says, "we have a good track of guessing what they want next."

2. **They hire the best people from within the industry** to provide a continual influx of new ideas and front-line perspectives.

At Montreal-based **Lemire & Habrich Consultants Inc.**, for instance, a dealer and consultant in CAD/CAM software, President Alex Habrich believes in doing what you know. All of the firm's sales people and consultants understand the software and know how to use it, he says. In fact, 20% of the company's revenues come from actual design work done for clients who need to outsource to overcome capacity bottlenecks or meet some pressing deadline. Says Habrich, "Our slogan is we use what we sell and we sell what we use."

3. **They maintain strong links to customers and encourage continual feedback.** Customer support lines help companies such as **KL Group** or **GDT Softworks** stay in constant contact with customers and identify emerging market needs. Even non-tech companies like **Tropical Treets** (1996), a Toronto food processor and importer, are creating new feedback links with customers. The labels on its line of "Chubby" soft drinks imported from Trinidad contain a message asking consumers to offer their comments and suggestions by calling 1-888-4CHUBBY.

Getting to know your customers' needs can have an added benefit. Because you've taken the time to understand them better than your competitors have, you have an opportunity to bring them unique forms of added value. Smart marketers try to do both at once: enhance their reputation in their target markets at the same time as they're getting to know these markets better.

That's a key reason that Joe Robertson's **Arcona Health Inc.** of St. Catharines, Ontario, holds regular seminars for its customers. Arcona is a national distributor of dental supplies. It's not exactly a high-growth industry, and indeed Arcona offers few products that its rivals don't. But Arcona grew 637% from 1990 to 1995, mainly by carving its own niche in service, marketing, and getting to know its customers.

"We have started sponsoring seminars for thirty to 100 dentists or hygienists at a time," says Robertson, a former merchant banker with no dental experience, who always wanted to run his own company. Arcona has its own conference facility in Vancouver, and rents space in other cities. Seminar topics may involve new medical techniques or presentations on new products; some are free, while others that feature well-known figures in the dental community cost attendees up to $450 each. All fees go to the speakers. "We're not doing it to make money," says Robertson. "It helps us to differentiate ourselves and be seen as adding value in the eyes of our customers."

It doesn't even have to be difficult. **FirstService Corp.** of Toronto, a five-time PROFIT 100 company, is now a $170-million company. It has grown mostly by acquiring various companies involved in business and consumer services, from house painting to building maintenance.

Founder and President Jay Hennick, a trained corporate lawyer in mergers and acquisitions, used the simplest trick in the book when he was pondering new acquisitions. Prior to acquiring a painting company, for instance, he went out to a shopping mall by himself to chat up consumers and find out what they thought about house painting in general and the work done by students. "Before we acquired the lawn-care division I sat in shopping malls in Toronto and Montreal, because that's where the two key markets of our business is, just to talk to people," says Hennick. "I was the crazy guy sitting in the middle of the mall drinking coffee asking women what they thought of lawn care — what was their general view of the environmental issues, for example. I do that quite a bit. I talk to everybody that will talk to me about service."

Whatever your mechanism for generating customer insights, putting yourself in your clients' shoes may be the most important job in business. After all, you're successful only as long as you're solving your customers' problems or making them happier.

CHAPTER SIX

PROFIT IN PARTNERSHIPS

"I am a firm believer that you can take two ideas from two individuals and what you get is much greater than from each of those two minds. One plus one does not equal two."

Robert Murray, MSM Transportation Inc.

It's one of the enduring images of business — the entrepreneur as solo artist. Lone Wolf. Renegade. It's also one of the Big Lies of our time.

Myth, legend, and general human laziness have combined to paint a potentially misleading picture of successful entrepreneurs as feisty, independent renegades who tread solitary paths, shunning convention and thumbing their noses at established industry players. The truth is quite different. As the PROFIT 100 proves, some of the most successful growth companies in Canada have been founded by teams, two or more entrepreneurs who have worked together, pooling their knowledge, contacts, and financial resources to build a solid foundation for their new business. And as these companies grow, the best of them emerge from their start-up shell to take a respectful place in their industries, drawing on contacts, strategic partnerships, joint ventures, and alliances to increase their expertise, extend their reach, and crack new markets.

The myths arise naturally from the way successful businesses tend to evolve, from team start-ups to CEO-driven (one-individual) corporations. Everyone knows Bill Gates and Microsoft, but few remember Gates's co-founder, Paul Allen (now a billionaire in his own right and the owner of Ticketmaster and the Portland Trailblazers, among other assets).

In Canada, some of our most famous fortunes have been founded by partners. Very often they were family members working together: the now estranged McCain brothers or the Reichmanns, for instance. But as a company grows bigger, two things tend to happen. One partner adjusts to growth more readily than the others, or perhaps just shows more interest; meanwhile, a new group of professional managers, hired to bring financial and administrative stability to the organization, makes the lesser partners increasingly dispensable. Witness the eventual breakup of the team of Conrad and Monty Black, or of Roy Thomson and his onetime right-hand man, Jack Kent Cooke. But the fact remains that in a business's early stage, when it is searching for direction, unsure of its strategy, lacking in experienced management, and suffering regular financial peril, two, three or four heads — not to mention phone books, sets of eyes, and wallets — are much more effective than one.

The same principle applies once a company has achieved a certain size or reputation in its industry. Sure, a maverick company can try to go it alone, bulling its way into new markets based on the appeal of a superior product, better service or lower price. But it is much easier, and usually less costly, to form associations with other organizations, to solve common problems and explore new opportunities. Indeed, the lesson of the PROFIT 100 is that the best growth companies carefully and strategically build strong relationships in their industry. They learn quickly that levering their own resources by forming good relations and strategic alliances with larger, more established organizations — gatekeepers, suppliers, distributors, and customers — is the short cut to fast and more healthy growth.

TEAMWORK AND PARTNERSHIPS

Giving the boots to the notion that entrepreneurs are the Greta ("I want to be alone") Garbos of the business world, thirty-eight companies on the 1997 PROFIT 100 were founded by teams of two or more entrepreneurs. About half of those were family start-ups, usually involving brothers or husband and wife teams, and in at least one case, a brother and sister. Of those that began with non-related teams, most were colleagues who had met while working in the industry, sometimes for the same company, and sometimes for competitors. Either way, the aspiring partners realized they had three things in common:

1. dissatisfaction with the current state of their chosen industry;

2. a desire to produce a good or a service better than anyone else was doing; and

3. the common-sense notion that it would be easier to succeed together than separately.

Just look at some of the results.

• ALL IN THE FAMILY •

After five years of running a grape juice business for home winemakers, Gabe Magnotta gave it up. He and his partner just weren't seeing eye to eye. But rather than set out on his own, as some people might do after a disappointing partnership experience, Magnotta teamed up in another juice-making venture with his wife, Rossana. The match proved made in heaven. With her background as a chemist and lab technologist, she brought the technical smarts to the new company, Festa Juice, that Gabe lacked with his background as a supply teacher. Between the two of them, they built Festa into a major player. In 1990, when they could see growth tapering off in the juice market as their core target audience of European immigrants grew older, and the next generation proved more interested in buying wine than making it, they managed a deft move into winemaking. By 1996 **Magnotta Winery Corp.** had sales of $11.3 million and a listing on the Toronto Stock Exchange. Chairman and President Gabe Magnotta attributes the growth largely to his wife's sense of order and discipline. "I'm a pro-crastinator," he says. "I'm messy and not organized like my wife. My strength is in new directions and products, not organizational skills." He admits he and Rossana argue quite a bit, "because we're both head-strong," but there's no arguing with their success, "We're doing it for common goals."

• "ONLY ONE PERSON COULD BE THE MAD SCIENTIST" •

When PROFIT asked thirty-three-year-old Kyu Lee of **Queue Systems Inc.** of Markham, Ontario, to name the smartest thing he'd ever done for his business, he didn't hesitate before saying, "Going into business with my brother." Kyu and his brother, Alex, then eighteen, launched their computer consulting firm in Kyu's apartment in 1989. They thought they would start when they were young and had nothing to lose. Through close attention to customer needs and coming up with imaginative tech-nological solutions, losing was not an option. By 1996 Queue had forty employees and sales of $3.5 million. Kyu says they owe it all to teamwork, "I know that a big part of my success is him, and vice versa."

Early on Kyu, a computer-sciences grad, and Alex, an engineer, real-ized that their skills were too similar. The company didn't need two techies; but it did need a marketer and strategist. As Kyu told PROFIT writer Michael G. Crawford, "only one person could be the mad scientist." He went out and started selling, helping Queue move from the small busi-nesses they had originally targeted to such blue-chip clients as Bell Sygma and Deloitte & Touche. Still, he continued to include his younger broth-er in every decision. "When I describe this to people, they think this is the most inefficient management style," he says. "But I may make twenty decisions in a day and to consult Alex on all of them might take five min-utes in total."

• ONE PLUS ONE DOES NOT EQUAL TWO •

When Robert Murray and Mike McCarron formed **MSM Transporta-tion Inc.** in 1989, they knew they were combining two types of manage-ment expertise, plus two very different personalities. McCarron, the company's managing partner and primary marketer, is boisterous and outgoing, passionate and, as he admits, impulsive. Murray, MSM's president, trained originally as a credit manager and comes across as quiet, thoughtful and more of a long-term thinker. Oil and water? Of course.

But Murray says the duo's strength lies in the fact they can disagree, argue feverishly, work it out, and then move on. With two partners who share a similar vision for the company, if not the same temperament, Murray says debate becomes a positive force that generates new ideas and better decisions. In an industry notorious for its lack of marketing or financial skills, MSM benefits from both. "I have seen a lot of companies have great difficulty because of a lack of understanding or skills in other areas of business," notes Murray. "My partner makes me much more effective and, I believe, much better at what I do," because they question each other's assumptions and strategies.

• TO BOLDLY GROW •

Another team start-up is **Tescor Energy Services Inc.** of North York, Ontario, an energy performance contractor that helps schools, hospitals, government institutions and business reduce energy costs by redesigning their heating, lighting, water and air-conditioning systems. President and CEO Tom Tamblyn founded the company in 1979, and still owns 80% of it, but he has given minority shareholdings to his most trusted lieutenants, chief administrative officer Gary Johnson and chief operating officer Mario Iusi.

Johnson describes Tamblyn's strength as personal integrity and insightful strategic thinking, with a good intuitive sense of what's happening in the market. Iusi, says Johnson, combines an understanding of systems with a focused operational bent, while Johnson himself deals with the heart of the organization, reviewing and assessing the possibilities and potential relationships in a strategic way. "We're more self-aware than the stereotypical engineering firm," says Johnson. "We deal with feelings and relationships. We're part psychologists."

Together, says Johnson, the three partners make a team worthy of the Starship Enterprise. Not Captain Kirk's ship, where one guy was always in charge, but more like the ship in "Star Trek: The Next Generation," where three people shared the bridge. "Tom is like Jean-Luc Picard and Mario is like Riker, the make-it-happen guy," says Johnson. He compares himself to ship's counsellor Deanna Troi, "who always wants to know how people are feeling." With those distinctions recognized and understood, he says, "our management team can work more intimately and share risk and vulnerabilities with each other, play to each other's strengths and fill in for each other's weaknesses." Based on Tescor's results, Johnson's assertions appear logical. Tescor has grown at warp speed, with sales reaching $30.7 million in 1996, up from $3.6 million in 1991.

Tips for Teamwork and Partnerships

What lessons can you derive from the varied partnership experiences of PROFIT 100 management?

- **Two heads really are better than one.** Business is getting simply too complex for one person to know everything he or she needs to run an organization effectively. A company that wants to grow needs to tap diverse sources of expertise as early in the process as possible.

- **Even if you start up as a solo operation, it's never too late to get some help.** Bringing in a partner at a later stage can help you overcome financial problems, relieve administrative headaches, master a new skill or penetrate new markets. Sure, employees can also provide much of that. But depending on the financing of the deal, partners could cost you less up front if they are buying a stake in the company, rather than demanding to be paid a full salary every two weeks. Plus, new partners will be more motivated to succeed than the average employee when they see the prospect of increasing the value of their equity as the company grows.

- **Getting along is key, but being able to disagree and even fight, without breaking up your team, is even more important.** Ideally, you should enjoy your partners' company, but in reality all you need is respect for their ability and commitment. Most crucial is your team's ability to disagree and then reach a quick and bloodless resolution. It's unrealistic to expect that all partners will agree all the time — make sure you have a mechanism for bringing disputes to an end, arriving at a solution and then moving on.

  Everyone in your team has to be prepared to compromise, or it isn't a team at all. Consider an appropriate business version of the marriage counsellor's classic advice to troubled clients: Never go to sleep angry. It'll only get worse in the morning.

• **Encourage specialization.** While two people with equal skills and interests might consider themselves a perfect team, consider what would happen to a line-up of baseball players who could all hit but not field. All they could count on was one good inning, assuming they got to bat first. As the Lee brothers at **Queue Systems** learned, teams thrive on complementary activities, skills, attitudes and expertise. If you don't have these to start, you will have to acquire them, through either internal development or external recruitment.

Most in need of this sort of help is the stereotypical visionary entrepreneur who founds a company based on a wonderful product or remarkable market insight, but lacks the patience or skill to look after day-to-day operations. The only way these people can grow their businesses safely is to surround themselves with strong administrative or financial people who enjoy looking after the little things, and have the clout, confidence or equity investment to be able to say "no" to the entrepreneur once in a while.

• **Teams offer a tactical advantage because they can access more resources.** When times were tough in the early days of **MSM Transportation**, the partners had to reach into their savings to reinvest in the company, a sacrifice neither could have made by himself. When **Excell Store Fixtures** (1996) needed additional funds to finance its new manufacturing operation, it took on a new partner who was flush with cash after recently selling his own business (see Chapter 10). By spreading the risk or passing the hat, partners bring added financial stability to a young operation, not to mention expanded access to other financial sources, product ideas or potential customers.

• **Draw up procedures for the splitting up of the partnership.** If your relationship goes south, a buy-sell agreement or similar negotiated contract will help your team work its way through the rubble and out the other side. As with a marriage contract, lawyers advise drawing up such provisions early in the partnership, when goodwill is probably at its height and the amount of money at stake is likely at a minimum. While many people find it difficult to conceive of ending a partnership just when it's getting started, knowing that the process is there will provide focus to later discussions and perhaps even help head off potential disagreements.

- **Even if you don't have formal partners, draw on the power of teamwork anyway.** Any entrepreneur has colleagues, associates and friends that might be called on to take semi-official responsibility for the company's welfare.

At Les Systèmes Zenon Inc., a systems integrator in Longueuil, Quebec, co-founders and partners Eric Bourbeau and Chad Loeven set up "the Friends of Zenon," a group of advisors who consult on strategy and help head off any problems they see looming. "It's like a board of directors," says Bourbeau. The voluntary, unpaid board includes experts in related technology fields, the company's lawyer, an accountant, and a venture capitalist who has seen it all before. "We're very cautious and don't want to lose our focus," Bourbeau explains. "Before we take any potentially risky decisions we go to those guys and we check everything out. That way we have enough qualified people around us to make sure we rarely do anything stupid."

JOINT VENTURES AND STRATEGIC ALLIANCES

Probably no management tool since the electronic spreadsheet has attracted as much fanfare as the joint venture or strategic alliance. From lofty high-tech firms collaborating on bold new operating systems to local retailers tentatively planning their first joint promotion, more and more companies are extending their reach and bypassing their weaknesses by teaming up with other organizations with similar interests or goals. Indeed, the federal government has given business alliances its seal of approval as most favoured economic development mechanism. In 1996 Industry Canada dug into its depleted coffers to invest $1.8 million in the Canadian Business Networks Coalition, a non-profit consortium of businesses and trade organizations dedicated to uniting companies in specific industries to help them solve common problems such as R&D or cracking new markets.

The trouble with joint ventures and strategic alliances, however, is the difficulty of sustaining them over time. Corporate objectives change, priorities shift, people move on, misunderstandings develop. It takes a strong management group with cause and commitment to make formal business relationships work over time. Like a partnership within a business or a marriage, success requires shared objectives, agreements on operating standards and ethical principles, good faith regarding the sharing of costs, opportunities and information, and faith in the concept that if all the participants in an alliance don't win, the exercise has been a failure.

Despite the odds against success, however, joint ventures and strategic alliances remain the key offensive weapon of fast-growth companies. Through these they can develop better products, stretch their marketing dollars, reach more customers, obtain more feedback on their products or services, provide better customer service and extend their operations around the block or around the world. Indeed, when you look at the export successes on the PROFIT 100, you see that many of them are founded on the concept of joint ventures and strategic alliances.

The reasons for these symbiotic relationships is clear. The PROFIT 100 have succeeded primarily because they have identified a clear need on the part of their clients. These companies' dynamic growth is the natural result of their ability to wriggle into the client's operation and simply make themselves, their products or their services indispensable. Ideally, they get so close to their associates that their interests become intertwined. By growing their business they help their cohorts, and vice versa.

All-Star Alliances

As examples of innovative and value-added alliances, look at three PROFIT 100 all-stars, all of them number one companies from recent years.

Softkey Software Products Inc. (1992) succeeded because it created mutually beneficial associations with second-tier software developers. President Kevin O'Leary persuaded them that allowing Softkey to repackage their software under its own brand name and sell the products at discount prices through mass merchandisers could generate incremental royalty revenues without affecting their target markets at all. The cooperation of those proprietary software packages gave Softkey access to a full spectrum of software products at virtually no cost, which it used to blast open new software distribution channels through retailers ranging from bookstore chains to Radio Shack. In turn, that retail dominance has helped Softkey, which later moved to Massachusetts and is now known as The Learning Co., grow by acquisition of "real" software developers to become the biggest publisher of educational software in the world.

Premier Salons International Inc. (1996) became a $250-million company through the magic of quality service, franchising and trusted affiliations. While few Canadians know the company by that name, many would recognize it by its brand-name retail chain, Magicuts. But the majority of Premier's 1,100 outlets operate under other names — such as The Bay, Wal-Mart, Sears, Holt Renfrew, Macy's and Neiman-Marcus. Premier has grown by proving it can run capable and profitable hair salons in department stores across North America, at prices ranging from $8 to $400 per cut. The big stores have long since farmed out their specialty departments such as pharmacies, optical or haircare, knowing they couldn't run them as efficiently as the experts. Through sophisticated recruiting techniques, extensive employee training and significant economies of scale, Premier prides itself on a chameleon-like ability to adapt to the needs of its various hosts and supply appropriate value to all clients, whether they're paying $8 at Zellers or a small fortune at Saks in New York. To make sure Premier stays on good terms with the associates that can make or break it, President Brian Luborsky stresses close relations and intimate understanding of their customer service needs. In fact, some salons at US Sears stores have sought ISO 9000 certification as a sign of their commitment to quality, and to maintaining their alliance with America's retailing icon.

Oasis Technology Ltd. (1997) doesn't sell commodities. Like many technology companies today, it sells sophisticated electronic solutions to its clients — specifically, electronic funds-transfer systems geared to banks and retailers. When founders Ashraf Dimitri and Sunny Siu launched Oasis in 1989, they targeted a hitherto overlooked niche, the financial institutions that couldn't afford the proprietary electronic banking systems then being developed for affluent North American banks. They developed an "open-system" product that could run on Unix and ordinary PCs as well as high-powered computer workstations, opening up a new market for cash-short or technologically underpowered institutions. Oasis's first sale was to a bank in Jamaica, but it wasn't easy. Dimitri spent eight months in the capital of Kingston building and testing the system. Its products now are totally "scalable" — computer jargon for being adaptable to big organizations and small. "We have customers running on 486 technology managing five ATMs," Dimitri told PROFIT associate editor Jennifer Myers. "We also have clients running on IBM Solutions managing close to 50,000 terminals."

But client relationships aren't the only kind Oasis thrives on. It built its sales to $13.4 million by affiliating with hardware vendors such as NCR and Hewlett Packard. It was the best kind of association: win-win. Oasis gave these hardware manufacturers a chance to bid on contracts in an industry hitherto dominated by a few giants with proprietary systems that were incompatible with any others. And in turn, these manufacturers helped Oasis make the leap into new markets such as Guatemala, Bolivia, Venezuela and Saudi Arabia. "When we hooked up with people like NCR, they kept saying 'We have a need here, and here, and here,'" says Dimitri. These contacts resulted in instant credibility and global reach. Oasis is one of only two PROFIT 100 firms that have managed to crack the ranks of Canada's Fastest-Growing Companies without actually generating any revenues in Canada — a tribute to the power of strategic alliances.

Changing the Face of Business

As stories such as Softkey's, Premier's and Oasis's suggest, strategic alliances not only offer new opportunities to ambitious businesses, but they can change the way business is conducted. At one time, big firms such as NCR or Sears might have laughed at the idea that they needed the help of small suppliers or recent start-ups to serve their customers or crack new markets. Now big and small players alike recognize how much they need each other. The advantages of small firms — innovation and precise focus — are becoming recognized as important assets in a world where business and technology are changing so fast that no one organization has all the answers any more.

"In today's environment, all companies, large and small, must work in partnership with others to succeed," says Francesco Bellini, president of Montreal-based **BioChem Pharma Inc.** (1995). "The explosion of knowledge and technology means that no one company has all of the expertise, technology or money to succeed alone."

FIVE KINDS OF STRATEGIC ALLIANCES

What types of associations most often lead to success? Canada's Fastest-Growing Companies seem most adept at forming five kinds of strategic alliances:

1. Bringing buyers and sellers together.
2. Solving problems for customers.
3. Technology and R&D alliances.
4. Adding value for dealers.
5. Teaming up with competitors.

Five Kinds of Strategic Alliances

Bring Buyers and Sellers Together

With so many products and services to choose from, it's a miracle whenever buyers and sellers make the perfect connection. In fact, buyers and sellers alike will eagerly embrace anyone who can help them connect, forming a promising partnership based on mutual assistance.

Maple Homes Canada Ltd. (1996) of Richmond, BC, cracked foreign markets for Canadian building materials not by coming up with its own unique products, but by forming close relationships with the very best Canadian suppliers of wood building products such as support beams, cupboards and windows. In return for their assurances of quality, President Brad Grindler was able to help them expand into the Japanese home-building market because he had already developed relationships there. He spent eight years in Japan, first teaching English and then moving into business, all with the goal of getting to know the language, the culture and the market. That knowledge alone, he knew, could create a sustainable business advantage as Japanese builders upgrade their housing stock and provide higher quality products for discriminating high-end buyers.

PROFIT 100 Linking existing marketers with new customers doesn't have to be an exercise in transoceanic diplomacy. Calvin Johnson of **Cost-Less Express Ltd.** (1996) in Burnaby, BC, helped expand the market for Costco warehouse stores in Vancouver by starting a catalogue ordering and delivery system for downtown clients who wanted warehouse prices but couldn't afford the time to head to the suburbs for them. For years, his chief business tools were a photocopier and a pick-up truck, as well as his ability to capitalize on a market gap no one else had sensed. Call this a one-sided win-win relationship: after five years Johnson finally got his first contract allowing him to represent Costco *officially*.

Solve Problems for Customers

One PROFIT 100 entrepreneur whose company was later acquired by a US multinational had a simple formula for success, "My customer's problem is my problem." In six words he crystallized the challenge for marketers everywhere. To identify completely with the customer, and by doing so, ensure that the customer identifies with you.

PROFIT 100 There are many ways to accomplish this goal. Obviously, quality customer service is the key way of establishing respect and trust, the twin pillars of any relationship. In Hamilton, Ontario, **Philip Services Inc.** (1995-97) managed the transition from industrial recycler to a broader service company meeting the varied operational needs of big industrial clients. Philip (formerly Philip Environmental Inc.) started out recycling industrial by-products, specifically, the metal and sand left over from steel-manufacturing in Hamilton's big steel mills. Its motto is "one industry's waste is another industry's raw material."

In the environmentally sensitive 1980s Philip saw that business as a huge growth industry and expanded into a range of environmental services such as waste collection and landfill management. Over time, however, founders Allen and Philip Fracassi realized that the more important niche in the long run was to emphasize its expertise in metal recycling for industrial plants across North America. And the relationships it created with big industrial players helped it recognize the broader niche of performing a wider variety of services for North American factories. Chemical producers, oil refiners, steelmakers, and car assemblers were all demanding more and more tightly managed processes in their plants, from waste disposal and general maintenance to instrumentation and electrical services. As Philip built its reputation as a problem solver in industrial environments, it realized this was the business of the future.

Here's one example of how Philip solves problems and creates value for clients. Car manufacturers use up to twenty pounds of paint on each car they build, two-thirds of which never finds its way to the car and ends up as sludge in landfill. Philip's Paint Services Group eliminated the generation of paint sludge by creating a new process within the carmakers' self-contained "paint booths." A solvent continuously dissolves and captures the "overspray," which is returned to a Philip recycling facility. Philip then recovers the solvent and the paint emulsion, which is returned to the carmakers' for reuse, while the paint solids are recycled for use in a variety of industrial products such as fillers and adhesives. At Ford's Michigan truck plant, where Philip's technology was introduced, the new system reduced waste and improved painting efficiency. By 1997, Philip's system was operating in more than twenty assembly and parts-manufacturing plants across North America.

Philip has now turned away from the environmental business for good, moving into industrial services, where it has the opportunity to build on its knowledge of industrial infrastructure and its reputation for turning clients' problems into opportunities.

IntelaTech Inc. of Mississauga, Ontario, (1995-97) also managed a bit of a transition, from a manufacturers' rep for electronic components to a new-style value-added supplier that includes sourcing-consulting and contract manufacturing in its armoury. "We help customers compete in their own market place," says President and founder Michael Ruscigno. "We provide added value to strategic customers by giving them what they were looking for, but more importantly, giving them what they were not aware that they could get."

Rather than simply supplying clients with, say, semiconductors, IntelaTech has tried to move up the value scale by helping clients such as Bell, IBM and Nortel source whole subassemblies or even find ways to subcontract manufacturing in Canada. Like Philip, IntelaTech knows that big industrial customers are outsourcing more of the functions they used to do internally, and working hard to reduce the number of suppliers they deal with. IntelaTech's strategy, like Philip's, is geared to making sure it survives the shakeout by becoming an indispensable part of the client's strategy.

Ruscigno admits that the semiconductors, circuit boards, and other components his company represents aren't much different from those of its competitors. IntelaTech's competitive advantage, he says, "is that we understand our clients' business in terms of their products and their customers. We spend a lot of time understanding their benefits and features, so we can show how our parts make their products more competitive in the market place. We make IntelaTech part of the customers' team."

You don't have to be heavy into industrial maintenance services or high-tech electronics to build strong relationships by solving clients' problems. Many PROFIT 100 companies add value for their key customers through educational seminars as well.

Another Mississauga-based PROFIT 100 company is **Auto Control Medical** (1994-97), which distributes medical products for home use such as blood-glucose meters, blood-pressure monitors, and ear thermometers. Most of these products are designed to be easy for consumers to use, but since pharmacies account for 90% of the company's sales, there is still a training and basic familiarization component required. Auto Control Medical looks after that by providing training to pharmacists to help them better understand the products, and thus sell more of them. In an industry where distributors, manufacturers, and retailers are often nickeling-and-diming each other to death, Auto Control stands out by thinking of its retailers' health first.

Technology and R&D Alliances

Joint ventures and strategic alliances are especially effective when you are trying to develop or market an absolutely groundbreaking product — something so new your own customers have no idea what to do with it, or so new that even you're not sure if it's going to pay off. It's a way of spreading the risk by finding compatible associates with the development skills or marketing orientation needed to get a product off the ground.

BioChem Pharma Inc. of Montreal (1995) was one of the pioneers of strategic alliances in the global pharmaceutical industry. It entered into an alliance with global giant Glaxo in 1990 to develop a drug called 3TC, one of the first successful anti-HIV treatments. Approved for sale in the US in late 1995, within a year 3TC was being marketed by Glaxo around the world. "Ours was one of the early relationships of this kind," says President Francesco Bellini. "In fact, many people thought we were crazy. But no one is laughing today. Our partnership has been very successful."

Today BioChem works with research labs and experienced pharmaceutical distributors around the world on various projects, ranging from basic science to testing to marketing. "We have always worked on a collaborative basis with outside partners to optimize our resources and access complementary technology," says Bellini. "Partnership is second nature to BioChem." In recent years it has particularly expanded its research associations with business and university researchers. That allows BioChem to play to its strengths, developing commercial uses for other people's basic science. "Academic scientists play a key role in determining gene function, developing an understanding of particular disease processes, and identifying new biological targets," says Bellini. "Armed with this knowledge, our scientists can then make more effective and safer drugs." To raise funds for this development, he notes, BioChem will be affiliating more extensively in future with financial institutions and other sources of funds to ensure that technology developed in Canada can also be commercialized in this country.

Clearly, alliances of this kind require entrepreneurs to understand precisely what their company's strengths are. Then, too, they have to be able to demonstrate that expertise effectively to all potential partners. One company that scores on both counts is **McGill Multimedia Inc.** (1996-97) of Windsor, Ontario. "Powered by Partnerships" is the slogan of this multimedia company, which uses the latest communications technology to create cutting-edge interactive presentations — think marketing demonstrations and training programs — for clients such as Chrysler, General Motors, Toyota, Newcourt Credit Group, and the Canadian Forest Service.

McGill's alliances are not just with clients, but also with suppliers it feels will continue to pioneer new technologies. Its associates include Dutch electronics giant Philips Consumer Electronics, whose interactive CD-i system flopped in retail markets but lived on in institutional applications — thanks mainly to third-party content developers such as McGill Multimedia.

McGill produced interactive CD-i programs for trade show kiosks to introduce car buyers to the merits of Lexus's new LX450, for instance, and also prepared a CD-i training program for steelmaker Dofasco Inc. incorporating video, graphics, and text to make training more comprehensive, interactive, and effective.

McGill is also developing Internet-based content using servers made by Digital Equipment Corp., and was named an Oracle Corp. Business Alliance Partner for its work with the US-based software company's Internet applications. When potential users ask these big manufacturers how they can get the most from their products, the manufacturers usually refer them to their most trusted developer partners — companies like McGill.

Add Value for Dealers

Many manufacturers are wholly dependent on a network of distributors or dealers to actually sell their product to their customers, whether they are businesses or consumers. In most industries, that means dealers and suppliers have traditionally been at each other's throats. One of them is obsessed with costs (invariably too high), delivery (usually late), and sales support (or lack of same), while the other is constantly fretting over why its products aren't flying off the shelf faster.

One of the most promising trends in business over the past few years has been the efforts of companies on both sides of this fence to make peace with each other. Despite all the potential for disagreement and dispute, dealers and principals are recognizing that their best hope for survival and growth is to find ways to overcome mutual distrust and work together.

The pioneer in this field is Keith Scott, owner of **A.J. Leisure Group** in Surrey, BC, which operates as **Beachcomber Spas**. Canada's largest hot-tub producer, Beachcomber qualified for the PROFIT 100 in 1991 with sales of $9 million, which have since ballooned to $25 million. Yet if Scott's plan to set up international dealerships bears fruit, Beachcomber could well crack the PROFIT 100 again.

Scott didn't start out as an enlightened associate. For the first years of his business, which began in 1977, he admits he was the typical manufacturer, fighting his dealers for every dollar. "I'd push them, and they'd push back," he told PROFIT's Richard Wright in 1992. "The basis was antagonistic." Finally, however, he realized that approach wasn't getting him anywhere. It was time to team up. In 1989, Scott hand-picked one retailer from each geographic region of Canada to join a Beachcomber advisory council. "Not necessarily the top sellers," Scott says. "I was looking for the ideas men, and the best team players." Four times a year, Scott brings these reps to Vancouver on his own tab. Then Beachcomber's top staff and their dealers sit down to discuss common problems and new opportunities in what Scott insists be a high-spirited, free-for-all. The scrum gives Beachcomber new product and marketing ideas to work on while the retailers return home to communicate the decisions made at the meeting to other dealers in their region. As one participant from Red Deer, Alberta, told PROFIT, "one dealer off in the wilderness never had much impact. Now we're really talking to the people who make the decisions, and we are getting things done."

Once a year, Beachcomber puts on the big event, an annual convention of its 100 dealers across Canada. Many of them carry hot tubs as a sideline to their main business of selling fireplace equipment, swimming pools or patio furniture, but Scott takes them all under his wing. Product previews and feedback sessions are all on the agenda, but the main emphasis is high-powered entertainment and education with the likes of Jay Conrad Levinson, the author of *Guerrilla Marketing*. The point is to share ideas, motivate, strengthen the links and learn together. Says Scott, "It's like a good marriage. It gets better every year." In a way, the relationship he is forging is more like that of a franchisor helping franchisees than the typical manufacturer and dealer, but Scott puts it down to an investment. "Most businesses are just trying to sell products to their dealers. I'm trying to show them how to build a business."

Creating a productive two-way relationship with your dealers can be tough on the old ego. "A lot of people try to protect their product," says Scott, by deflecting criticism or ignoring feedback. Scott encourages his retailers to point out quality problems that the factory doesn't catch. "We believe we build the best quality spa in the world, but they helped us face the truth within ourselves," he says. "They helped us recognize that we have to control the quality better." Among the improvements inspired by dealer complaints, Beachcomber has changed the way its taps operate, switched the types of screws it uses, and simplified the controls to make them easier to operate. As Scott notes, every change in a manufacturing process is a big deal, but he recognizes his products, and his business, are the better for the feedback. "You have to be prepared to listen, you have to be prepared to change."

Team Up with Competitors

We all know that business is becoming more competitive every year: more entrepreneurs are competing for niche markets, customers are increasingly fickle as they chase added benefits and lower prices, margins are shrinking. And yet, there's a counter-trend happening, in which respected competitors turn to each other more often for mutual self-help. The key driver is the customers' ever-increasing expectations of quality service. If you as a supplier are ever caught short and can't meet your customer's requirement, what do you do? If you have prepared the groundwork by setting up a trusting relationship with one or more of your competitors, you let a rival in on the action in order to preserve your long-term reputation as a reliable supplier of your customer's needs — whatever it takes.

Leetwo Metal Inc. (1996) in Pointe-Claire, Québec, produces sheet-metal products, primarily for casings of high-tech gadgets such as electronic games and airport X-ray machines. President Mike Lee worked as plant manager at a similar company before founding Leetwo in 1989. His reason for leaving was that he felt he was doing all the work while the owners were working less and less; his boss was always calling him from the car or racquetball club. Cleverly, however, the then-thirty-year-old Lee didn't make a fuss. He left the company quietly and stayed on good terms with this former boss. Which was a good thing, since on occasion he turns to his former employer to help him out with a contract to meet a customer's needs when Leetwo just can't get it all done. "I believe in cooperating or collaborating with competitors when possible," he says. For instance, he and a competitor have a mutual customer in Northern Telecom. If the competitor is out of a part, Leetwo has often been asked to supply it. Leetwo could refuse, but Lee sees it strategically, as helping out Northern Telecom as much as his rival. Besides, he knows that competitor would do the same for him.

Sometimes it makes sense to anticipate new competitors and strike up a relationship before they're even in the market. After all, if you can convince a new market player to piggyback on your product or services, you help them meet their goals while expanding your own opportunities. Brian Edwards, president of **MPact Immedia Corp.** (1995-97) in Montreal followed this strategy in his business, the fast-moving world of electronic commerce. MPact has proprietary technology to help companies convert paper-based transactional documents such as invoices, cheques and bills into a much more efficient electronic system. So far, however, the world of electronic commerce has resisted standardization, and there are still new players with new ideas entering the field. Among the most-feared competitors are the chartered banks, whose financial infrastructure and sheer size would help them dominate the industry.

When Edwards realized the Royal Bank of Canada was eyeing his market, he decided on a pre-emptive strike. He managed to convince the bank that MPact's software was the system of choice, and that the bank itself should market it as its preferred electronic commerce solution. As a result, the two companies formed a joint venture to establish Can-Act, a system that allows customers to make recurring business payments to governments, utilities or trading associates electronically. In 1996 one Bay Street analyst estimated that Can-Act could add $20 million or more to MPact's revenues over the next five years.

"There are more competitors coming in, and we're trying to partner with them," says Edwards. "They can use our technology to get in quickly." The benefit for MPact is twofold: not only do these new competitors adopt its system instead of someone else's, but they then become adjuncts of its own sales force, marketing MPact's system to their own clients. And MPact's alliances list is pretty impressive, including as it does US-based NationsBank, Citibank and Bank of America.

The Export Edge in Technology

MPact Immedia's success with offshore associates (foreign sales now account for 50% of company revenues, up from nada in 1991) points up the often overlooked benefit of alliances—the leverage factor that can make home-grown companies into dynamic world traders. Find the right affiliate, and you too can see your electronic commerce network flogged in Britain, your children's fashions selling in Asia, or your oil-well-monitoring system used at drill sites all over the world.

In 1996, a record sixty-five PROFIT 100 companies were involved in exporting, and in 1997, the number dropped only slightly to sixty-one. While a few companies made their international forays entirely through their own sales efforts (Ottawa's **Corel Corp.**, for instance, takes pride in the fact that its entire global sales team is safely ensconced in Ottawa), there's no doubt that most PROFIT 100 firms use bigger, international associates to crack open world markets. It makes sense. Why invent the wheel when you can use someone else's? In fact, the experience that so many PROFIT 100 companies gained forging synergistic relationships with other alliances has undoubtedly helped lead to their global success as well. Once you're used to dealing with big corporate clients in Canada, it becomes an almost seamless transition to deal with other branches or divisions of those corporations in other countries or even worldwide. Thus, the PROFIT 100's propensity for joint ventures from the beginning helps sow the seeds for their success in foreign markets.

One of the best examples of this leverage at work can be seen in the success of **Oasis Technology Ltd.**, the number one company on the 1997 PROFIT 100. The North York developer of electronic funds-transfer software owes its five-year growth rate of 10,114% to the relationships it established as a trusted solutions provider for globally minded financial institutions. "We do business in forty-five countries," says President Ashraf Dimitri. "We're everywhere."

Oasis developed the first affordable electronic-banking systems that let financial institutions run ATM networks on existing computer networks, instead of on costly proprietary systems from a handful of manufacturers. After it made its first big sale to a bank in Jamaica, Oasis began signing up distributors to market its products worldwide. (Canada was never really a prospect because Oasis was targeting a generally less affluent or technologically sophisticated market than the blue-chip Canadian banks.) But some of its greatest coups came from less formal partners, such as the hardware makers whose systems Oasis software ran on, and the banks that were impressed by Oasis's ability to meet their needs. "Our industry is based almost exclusively on credibility and references," says

Dimitri. "We've had significant customers adopt our software, which gives us major credibility."

Consider the case of Citicorp, the US$32-billion behemoth which is America's biggest bank and probably the most globally minded. (It's also the world's biggest supplier of credit cards.) After Oasis installed its IST/Switch system at a Citicorp office in Saudi Arabia, an impressed executive suggested Dimitri talk to the bank's regional office in Singapore, which was a global mandate for tracking down potential new software for Citicorp's use. Two years later Oasis was named an official software supplier to Citicorp, creating a vast new market and further fuelling the company's reputation. "It gave us money, but it also pushed our credibility factor tremendously," says Dimitri.

Calgary-based **Datalog Technology Inc.** (1996-97) used the same principle to boost its overseas sales from 0 to 60% of revenues between 1991 and 1996. Datalog offers software-based oil-well-monitoring services that help oil companies check on the production and drilling status of their oil and gas wells. "We don't do traditional marketing," says President Ian Underdown. "We develop relationships." By proving itself in the Canadian oil patch, Datalog won fans in transnational companies such as Shell, Chevron and Amoco. As a result, they transferred the technology themselves to their drilling operations in other countries. Today, Underdown says 99% of Datalog's foreign work comes from repeat orders. "If we do work for Amoco in Romania we'll do it for Amoco in Colombia," he says.

Hummingbird Communications Ltd. (1994-97) of North York, Ontario, followed a similar course, although much more deliberately and strategically. When the connectivity-software developer went looking for distributors in the all-important US market, it specifically selected smaller niche players rather than large national distributors. Why? Hummingbird wanted to establish a long-term relationship with its resellers, and it knew the best way to create a strategic alliance was to make sure that its business was of significant size to warrant its associate's full attention. That way, Hummingbird's success could create a massive new opportunity for the right distributor, as opposed to being a blip on the sales charts of a major national company. "This was an extremely important decision that has since paid dividends for Hummingbird and for the companies it chose to become its distribution partners," says marketing services director Larry Rudolf. "With one exception, the four distributors have since transformed their businesses into multimillion-dollar concerns, largely founded on the Hummingbird business."

The Export Edge in Non-Technology

Relationships count for just as much in non-technology industries, and perhaps even more, since profit margins are a lot lower in most other industries than they are in the software business.

In Langley, BC, children's clothes producer and retailer **Just Kid'n Children's Wear** has built a $2-million business selling their durable, upscale fashions in seven mall boutiques. But now that business is poised to take a leap, President Kelly Cahill says he has received many calls from overseas retailers wanting to carry Just Kid'n's lines. He has always turned down these offers. Recently, however, he found an affiliate he liked: a $4-billion Singapore mail-order company. He created ten mix and match items for the catalogue giant's April 1997 flyer, which could be the beginning of a new business for Just Kid'n, but Cahill was hedging his bets. He marketed those clothes under a new name, "Dare to be Different," so that its success or failure would not affect his own plans to eventually expand his retail chain in Asia.

Between their enthusiastic suppliers and well-satisfied multinational clients, Canada's Fastest-Growing Companies are learning the payoff from solid foreign joint ventures and strategic alliances: It's a small world after all.

TEN TIPS FOR JOINT VENTURES
AND STRATEGIC ALLIANCES

Successful business alliances are like standing on one foot: easier to start than to maintain. Here are ten tips from Canada's Fastest-Growing Companies on developing and nurturing the most productive joint ventures and strategic alliances possible.

1. **Do your homework:** Assess your organization's strengths and weaknesses. Know where you want to go, and then identify the areas where you need help. Research the market to learn who can help you reach your goals.

2. **Think win-win:** Before you propose an alliance or joint project to another organization, ask yourself, What's in it for them?

3. **Feel out potential partners:** Make sure your potential associates share your values and level of commitment. As a number of PROFIT 100 entrepreneurs commented, you should also *like* your associates. After one strategic alliance fizzled because he had chosen an incompatible affiliate, Tom Tamblyn of **Tescor Energy Services** in North York, Ontario, learned his lesson. Today potential alliance associates have to go through an intensive two-way, two-day interview to determine if there is a good fit both strategically and operationally.

4. **Put the best available person on the project:** Your associates and allies deserve quick access to the relevant decision makers.

5. **Put it in writing:** Spell out your mutual expectations and responsibilities in a contract. Determine allocation of costs. Both sides should obtain legal advice.

6. **Set measurable objectives and realistic deadlines:** Nothing spoils a partnership faster than a perception that one side is letting the other down. Both sides need ways of determining that the other associate is doing its share of the work.

7. **Stay in touch:** Keep open lines of communication with your partners. They can be formal (regular reports) or informal ("let's meet for coffee").

8. **Keep tabs:** Use regular feedback sessions to review the project's progress. Is it meeting the goals of both parties? If not, how can you fix things?

9. **Do it right:** Your associates expect you to give a joint project your best shot. If you can't, let them know. Internally, your goal should be to make your associate the real winner; that will help you snare more joint projects in future.

10. **Exit stage left:** Before forming an alliance, determine how either side can get out.

MASS APPEAL: FORGING CONSUMER RELATIONSHIPS

Clearly, the most productive relationships in business are those between business-to-business associates that are reasonably well matched. But how can companies create relationships with partners with whom they have almost nothing in common? In other words, can you also have close or productive relationships with your customers when they are consumers?

According to the evidence of the PROFIT 100, the answer is an emphatic yes. Building relationships with a more scattered group of individual consumers requires a different set of tactics, but the strategy is the same: to expand your customers' vision of you and increase your perceived ability to solve their problems. To make a relationship work, you have to offer something of value to remind your customers how important they are to you.

Accomplishing this with consumers who are scattered across a city or even a continent requires different tools than dealing with a small group of business associates. Basically, you have to use the media to magnify your voice and your "touch." Behind the newsletters, Web sites and mailings, however, your interest has to be sincere and thoughtful, or the benefits of close customer relations will be lost.

Here's how a number of 1997 PROFIT 100 companies strive to maintain enhanced relationships with their consumer customers.

PROFIT 100 Magnotta Winery Corp. of Vaughan, Ontario, has built an integrated wine empire outside of the cozy protected world of Ontario's Liquor Control Board. While its products have won hundreds of industry awards, they can only be bought at Magnotta's five Southern Ontario stores, and Magnotta's limited advertising budget ensures it remains one of the industry's best-kept secrets. As a result, founders Gabe and Rossana Magnotta have to get the most out of every customer who finds his or her way to a Magnotta outlet.

To do that, Magnotta offers tours of its winery and, for customers of its Festa Juice operation, demonstrations on how to make your own. It also sends out between 100,000 and 200,000 newsletters several times a year, letting customers know about new events at Magnotta, new products and the latest awards they've won. Gabe and Rossana are front and centre as the main characters in the newsletter, touring their newly acquired winery in Chile, or opining about the healthful effects of red wine or their latest spat with the LCBO. In a world of anonymous, corporate-run businesses, the Magnottas convey an image of real people who are sincerely interested in their customers and are eager to share their experiences building a company that has grown from sales of $2 million in 1991 to $11 million in 1996.

To create closer ties, Magnotta offers other services to its customers, letting them know about upcoming price discounts and providing recipes that combine Magnotta products with various seasonal foods. Rossana herself oversees a special promotion for customers of Festa Juice. She encourages them to enter their home-made wines into local wine-tasting competitions, promising that all winners will receive cash (up to $100) and a commemorative certificate from Magnotta.

South of the Border runs six gift stores in malls in Atlantic Canada. President John Dobson discovered early on that advertising didn't do much to help sell his imported jewelry, textiles and wood carvings. His target market is the loyal customers who come into the store ten to twelve times a year, spending $500 or more annually. "We want loyal customers buying here more often," he says, so he stresses community values — donating to the local firefighters or the church bazaar, for instance — and in-store service. "Our game plan has been to have the best customer service in our industry," says Dobson. "There is no gift store that would give cash refunds, and we do. We offer free gift-wrapping, year-round. Last year we spent $50,000 on gift wrap. It costs, but we'll be around next year and other retailers won't."

Yogen Früz World-Wide Inc. is more a franchisor and manufacturer than a retailer; its nearly 3,000 frozen-yogurt outlets worldwide are primarily franchisee-owned. But Yogen-Früz has just started trying to build worldwide brand recognition and a closer relationship with its retail customers. Its primary tool is the Internet. Yogenfruz.com offers consumers information about frozen yogurt, the history of Yogen Früz, store locations and the company's various frozen desserts. It also includes a face-to-face introduction to Fruzer, the company's cone-headed mascot, and an interactive name-that-dessert game. Players are eligible to win prizes such as T-shirts, but more importantly, the act of registering to win a prize allows Yogen Früz to learn more about its customers' names, countries, ages and incomes — and to compile a database that is the first step toward relationship marketing.

With the greying of North America, **Priva Inc.** of Anjou, Quebec, has a hot product, but it's one that no one likes to talk about. Priva makes reusable adult-incontinence products, "diapers" geared to senior citizens and the handicapped. In the past, its marketing has remained very low key — brochures in doctors' offices, that sort of thing. There was certainly no question of trying to build a relationship with a group of customers who don't particularly like using Priva's products and don't want anyone to know that they do.

When Priva placed its sales brochures in urologists' offices, for instance, uptake was slow; no one wanted to be seen even picking up the brochure. Once Priva moved them into the doctors' washrooms, however, the brochures began to move. According to President David Horowitz, they had to be replenished every second day.

To gain mass attention, Horowitz realized, Priva's marketing had to be geared to a different audience. It decided to create a community of its users' caregivers, the people who look after their sick and elderly loved ones. In early 1997 Horowitz launched the first annual Priva National Caregiver Award in the US, his biggest market. The aim is to draw attention to the efforts of the twenty million Americans who look after sick or elderly adults every day, and position Priva as a caring leader in the sector. To ensure media coverage, Priva lined up Abigail Van Buren — better known as syndicated advice columnist Dear Abby — to join the five-person judging panel, which includes health-care experts and Horowitz himself. Winning caregivers in each state will win a day at a spa (plus professional care for their patients while they're away). The national winner gets a seven-day cruise to relax and renew themselves while their loved one receives professional nursing care. "The life of a caregiver is rough," says Horowitz. "We hope to inspire and educate others about the significant role of caregivers throughout the United States, while applauding their service above self."

It's classic relationship building, turning a fragmented market into a community. With Priva's products newly being distributed by such mainstream retailers as Montgomery Ward and the Spiegel catalogue, Horowitz feels he's on the verge of a breakthrough. The key could be his ability to sustain the spirit of community and position Priva as not just a professional in the growing home-care field, but as an organization that understands its customers and truly cares. Even if most caregivers will never win anything more than a warm and fuzzy feeling that someone understands and appreciates the work they do, Priva is giving something back — which is the key to relationship building anywhere, anytime.

CHAPTER SEVEN

HARNESS TECHNOLOGY

"I'm going to be so far ahead of my competitors — I'll even be ahead of most of my customers."

Jack Ramnauth,
Dwarf Courier (1993) Ltd.

For the past twenty years, businesses have poured billions into new technology designed to speed up their assembly lines, trim their product-development costs, and improve administrative efficiency. And yet productivity statistics show there's been precious little to show for it. "Where are the productivity gains?" ask the economists. Nobody knows. The best guess is that businesses invested in technology that wasn't ready, or wasn't appropriate for the job at hand, and they spent too much time and money automating old and inefficient systems instead of using technology to define new ways of doing business.

For many of Canada's Fastest-Growing Companies, those mistakes belong to other people. Indeed, many firms made the **PROFIT 100** list year after year precisely because they have harnessed technology in new ways that have generated significant

competitive advantages. And we are not talking high-tech manufacturers or software developers here, but old-fashioned manufacturers and service companies that have found technology a
valuable tool not just for doing business better, but redefining
their business.

• S&P DATA CORP. : ANSWERING THE CALL •

You're selling concert tickets (or books or cars, or offering tourist information) on the Internet. People come to your Web site, browse your
pages, read about your product benefits and look at the pictures.
They're perfect sales prospects. They're in the mood and ready to be
hooked, but if you can't get them to pick up the phone and call, you've
probably lost them. They'll surf on by to somewhere else, perhaps never
to return.

It's a problem for anyone trying to sell on the Web. How do you
make contact with the increasing number of shopping cybersurfers? A 1-
800 number helps, by cutting out the cost of a call. But it doesn't do anything to twist the browser's arm to actually get in touch and start asking
questions. And if the Internet user is using the household phone line for
surfing, they can't call you now anyway; you have to hope they'll write
your number down and call you once they're finished exploring the Net.

Enter net.Vectoring, the solution to these problems and the marketing world's latest attempt to marry the phone and the Internet. Users
type their own phone number into the appropriate field on their screen,
and within thirty seconds *you* call *them*. If the line is busy (say, if it's
hooked up to the Web), the "predictive dialler" will keep calling until it
gets through. When the customer picks up the phone he or she will be
greeted by a live customer service rep who will amiably enquire about
the user's needs and then try to close a sale or send more information.

Science fiction or marketing reality? Net.Vectoring is up and running on telemarketing systems created by **S&P Data Corp.** of North
York, Ontario, a four-time **PROFIT 100** company (1994-97) that has
become one of Canada's biggest telemarketing firms thanks to its
aggressive approach to technology. "Our competitive edge is informa-
tion-based technology," says founder Dan Plashkes, thirty-seven, who
first wrote out his plan for a full-service telemarketing company as a
business-school project. In 1996 S&P posted revenues of $28.7 million,

and boasted a client list that included such *Fortune 500* names as McDonald's, American Express, Compaq and Mercedes-Benz.

More and more, customer service is delivered through telemarketing, whether it be "outbound" calls to find out how you're enjoying your new car, or "inbound" service when you call to request a catalogue. As specialists, telemarketers have to be able to perform these tasks more efficiently than their clients, without sacrificing customer care or product knowledge. Training is a big part of that, but technology is the key. In 1995 S&P invested more than 8% of sales in research and development as part of its continuing commitment to upgrade its systems and become Canada's most technologically advanced call-centre company.

To meet its technology goals, S&P has partnered with its key suppliers. Bell Canada and Northern Telecom have helped it install cutting-edge call-routing networks, while S&P worked with a software partner to develop its own predictive-dialling system. It was one of the first programs of its kind to incorporate computer-telephone integration and skills-based routing. Among the leading-edge features are "outbound" calls that are dialled by computer, which boosts productivity an estimated 300%, since live operators come on the line only when the computer has determined that a live person (not a machine) has answered the phone. (Busy numbers or no-answers are stored and called on a later shift.) Since S&P's call-centre operators are representing two or more client companies on any given shift, the computer prompts the customer rep by displaying detailed scripts on-screen. It may also display historical data on the customer at the other end of the line, so reps can understand their needs or concerns faster and more effectively. And to keep customer service levels high, the system routes all calls, inbound or outbound, to the best-qualified customer rep, not just the first one to become available. Where possible, a call from a particular customer (say, someone calling about their Cantel cellular phone account) will even be routed to the same service rep who helped the customer last time she called. With technology like this, S&P can offer more efficient and personalized service than all but the most sophisticated general marketers — a key reason why S&P grew 2,090% between 1991 and 1996.

Now S&P is actively embracing the potential of the Internet. And recently, through an alliance with Intel and Genesys, S&P announced a new software-based service that will marry telemarketing with the fast-growing world of videoconferencing. S&P is creating a multimedia call centre, so that people dialling in for service using their video-equipped computers will be able to send and receive visual data as well as plain old speech.

Investing in technology, says S&P founder Plashkes, has helped his company meet its goal of becoming each of its clients' trusted ally. S&P doesn't just do as good a job as clients' own customer reps would do, it goes them one better by searching for new ways to help the clients reach their markets and build their brands. "We're becoming greater partners," he says. "They don't just hand us an assignment and that's it. We provide added value on top of our call-centre services."

TECHNOLOGY STRATEGIES

S&P's ongoing commitment to technology underscores a common theme among fast-growth companies — their dedication to staying not only up to date on technology, but moving to the very forefront of change. While many businesses see advancing technology as a threat, savvy entrepreneurs know that technology represents untold opportunity, not just to improve output or customer service, but to gain a beat on the competition. S&P's experience hints at four of the common factors that unite fast-growth companies as they deal with technology:

1. **They're keenly interested in technology.** Not for technology's sake alone, but for the advancements it can bring in areas that the company cares most about, such as production efficiency, product quality, turnaround time, personal productivity, etc.

2. **They are not afraid to spend money.** Even when S&P was a $10 to $15-million company, it was spending $2 million to $3 million a year on new technology. It replaced its computer systems and routing networks as often as four times a year to make sure clients were receiving the best service possible.

3. **They don't try to do it all themselves.** They learn from partners and leverage their technology investments. From the beginning, S&P has worked closely with equipment manufacturers such as Nortel or software companies such as Genesys to find out what's new, and then work with these suppliers to develop even better applications more closely targeted to their needs.

4. **Technology investments must advance the company's strategy.**
It is S&P's commitment to provide high-quality, informed, personalized service — thus reassuring clients they can leave their telemarketing requirements to S&P for years to come — that has driven its investment in database technology and system design. And it is Plashkes's personal conviction that the Internet will eventually have a major impact on the telemarketing business that has led S&P to pursue such new tools as direct voice-Web connectivity and interactive videoconferencing. "You've always got to meet new market needs," he says. At S&P, "we're always twelve to eighteen months ahead of the market."

Technology, they say, is just a tool, but think what Michelangelo could do with a chisel in his hands. Here's another example of how PROFIT 100 companies have used technology to carve out new niches or even reshape their business.

• DWARF COURIER: IN THE DRIVER'S SEAT •

Its slogan is "When time is short, count on Dwarf," but Richmond, BC-based **Dwarf Courier Ltd.** (1993) thinks big. The two-time PROFIT 100 winner has become a dominant player in its market, and official courier of the Vancouver Canucks hockey-team, by emphasizing fast and reliable service. And recently it laid the groundwork for a campaign to go province-wide by investing in technology that would enable it to offer faster and better service than ever.

From 1989 to 1994, Dwarf's sales grew from $770,000 to $6.8 million. Its staff jumped from three employees to fifty-two. When Dwarf made the 1995 PROFIT 100, President Jack Ramnauth got a call from a local Richmond company that specialized in electronic dispatching for taxi fleets. Was he interested in exploring the opportunities for satellite tracking in the courier business? Not likely. Ramnauth ignored his calls for months.

Over time, however, he realized things were getting out of hand. As Dwarf's volumes grew, so did employee stress levels. The same-day courier business is a hothouse atmosphere at the best of times, but Ramnauth felt control slipping away. Competition was increasing, customers were demanding faster service, and dispatchers and drivers were constantly berating each other.

Ramnauth was no stranger to technology. He had overseen the 1991 conversion of his office systems from paper-based forms to electronic document processing, a move that helped the company double sales within a year. But the company was now three times larger again, and needed help. In late 1995, Ramnauth sat down with the persistent salesman from Direct Dispatch Systems to see what high-tech communications could do for him.

Eighteen months and $800,000 later, Dwarf was reborn. Ramnauth equipped his 110 delivery trucks with the latest mobile technology that puts head office in closer touch with its drivers and helps them get their work done faster. For a year, Ramnauth put sales and marketing on hold while he worked on the upgrade. He knew service levels were slipping and feared that any new clients they did win wouldn't last very long. But when the system was completed on June 1, 1997, Ramnauth was convinced it would give Dwarf an edge on every courier firm in town, making it the most advanced local courier in the country.

The key to Dwarf's new system is a multifunctional hand-held computer given to each driver. Drivers take the "hand-held" to every pickup and drop-off, using it to scan in the bar code for each parcel so that it's logged into the system as soon as it's picked up. That way, dispatchers or salespeople at Dwarf's office can track the parcel's progress through its system. They know where it's going, when it's supposed to get there and what truck it's on now. When recipients sign for their packages, they sign right on the computer screen, giving Dwarf an instant record of every delivery. From now on, when clients call with the perennial complaint that their parcel never arrived, Dwarf knows either where it is now, or who signed for it.

When the drivers return to their trucks, they dock the hand-held into a "hot shoe" that radios the information directly to Dwarf on its own personal frequency. Plugging in the computer also engages the satellite-tracking mechanism. An antenna atop the truck beams a signal up to three orbiting satellites, which transmits the information back to Dwarf's computers. That allows the system to triangulate the position of each truck to within a few metres. A click of the mouse on Jack Ramnauth's desk enables him to call up a map of Richmond, Vancouver or any other part of the Lower Mainland, and see instantly where each of his trucks is. He can even click another menu to find out how fast the truck is going. "I'm going to have a great time with this," he said in demonstrating the system prior to launch. More importantly, the system enables dispatchers to select the best truck for the job. And Dwarf will now always have an answer when a client asks that annoying question, "Where's my parcel?"

With the hand-held units' two-way communications capability, dispatchers can now assign pickups digitally, with the directions appearing on the drivers' screens. No more garbled radio messages or spelling out of street names. Eventually the system will also put local maps on-screen, enabling drivers to find the best or shortest route to each destination. That's especially important because many new drivers don't know their way around sprawlng, traffic-tied Vancouver. Ramnauth even thinks it will reduce employee turnover, by ending the heated arguments that often occurred between harried dispatchers and frustrated, inexperienced or lost drivers. "The drivers love this," he says. "No dispatchers yelling at them all the time."

Ramnauth expects big changes as a result of the new system. By taking much of the guesswork out of dispatching, it should allow him to cut his dispatch staff from four to two. But that loss was already compensated for. In anticipation of the new system boosting client service and satisfaction, he hired four salespeople to start calling on new accounts. He expected the system to pay for itself in two years, although he was crossing his fingers that it would generate enough new business to pay back in eighteen months.

But automation is a never-ending process, and Ramnauth isn't finished yet. For 1998 and beyond he expected to expand his electronic system to cover Dwarf's operations on Vancouver Island, and to introduce computer guided package-sorting using bar codes and a "smart" conveyor belt. He even hopes to extend his computer intelligence network to his ten bicycle couriers swooping through the congested streets of downtown Vancouver. Eventually, the computer might be able to take over all dispatcher duties, relaying orders to drivers based entirely on known routes and postal codes. But before all that, Ramnauth was looking forward to a local-courier first — a fully functional Web site that would let customers key in a code number and find out exactly where their parcel is at any given time. Improved customer service without any staff interaction, that's Dwarf's idea of a perfect payoff.

PRODUCTION AND INFORMATION SYSTEMS

When most companies adopt technology, they aren't usually out to reinvent the business. More often, they're just trying to keep up with suppliers or customers. But even what looks like good housekeeping can be a key strategic move. In many industries, keeping up with technology is becoming a minimum condition for participation in many markets, especially with the advent of electronic data interchange. When big retailers such as Canadian Tire or The Bay demand their suppliers pay, bill and share documents electronically, it is up to the supplier to evolve fast, or risk losing the contract entirely. But when they make the leap, these companies often find the benefits spreading throughout the company. The same production and information systems that let you serve your customers better also give you increased control over your own operations.

Fantom Technologies Inc. (1997): This producer and marketer of high-tech vacuum cleaners got credit in Chapter 3 for its product savvy and in Chapter 4 for its innovative distribution method — infomercials. For its next act, the Welland, Ontario, manufacturer is overhauling its production technology to keep pace with US consumers' demand for its Fantom vacuum cleaners and their dual-cyclonic cleaning power. In 1996, Fantom tripled its capacity by installing two state-of-the-art, computer-controlled assembly lines. By streamlining its parts-receiving systems and contracting out shipping to specialists in Toronto and nearby Buffalo, NY, Fantom created a just-in-time manufacturing and distribution system that could be the envy of any modern automaker.

But President and CEO Allan Millman didn't just settle for overhauling the company's production technology. Tripling production in response to its astonishing growth from $13 million in sales to $59 million in 1995 and $98.4 million in 1996, Fantom needed an injection of professional management systems. Millman had to learn to control this burgeoning activity fast. In 1996, he agreed to set up Fantom as a "beta site" — basically, a test site — for a new combination of computer hardware and software that would transmit real-time information on revenue, orders and production to everyone in the company who needed it, simultaneously. Using software from SAP Canada Inc. running on a Windows

NT platform, the "Enterprise Resource Planning System" shortens the time consumed by routine business transactions, thus speeding up the entire order-delivery cycle.

With the system in place, orders are logged into the computer as soon as they are received. Orders are then transmitted electronically to every department: manufacturing, purchasing, distribution, finance, sales and senior management. Each department then takes responsibility for managing the progress of the order, instantaneously, so the product can be assembled at the same time as the order is being booked, the invoice created and the shipping arranged. All progress is noted and transmitted instantly, so everyone on the system knows the status of every order, and changes or problems can be noted instantly. In essence, where orders on paper used to flow sequentially around the company, from office to office, they now move constantly and achieve resolution much sooner, Millman boasts, "This gives our company a tremendous advantage over any competitor who is not using a 'real-time' system."

Another plus is that all relevant financial information is updated continuously. With every purchase, sale or expense now being logged, Fantom executives have instant access to the latest financial statements. The income statement, balance sheet and other key reports are continually updated, allowing for faster reading of the company's financial situation and ever faster decision making, which is the only way to run a just-in-time production system in the "zero-notice" nineties.

PROFIT 101 **Leetwo Metal Inc.** (1996): This Pointe-Claire, Quebec, sheet-metal fabricator produces metal housings and other precision parts for high-tech equipment makers. To meet the high standards expected by his customers, founder Mike Lee is continually investing in new equipment. One computer-controlled machine, for instance, is now punching 450 holes a minute in metal, compared to fifteen with the previous machine, which required a full-time human attendant, to boot. "The new software does in fifteen minutes what it would take a person one week to do," says Lee. "The machine cost $50,000 to $60,000 but paid for itself very quickly."

Lee sees continued modernization and automation as the only assurance of his firm's long-term survival and success: "The technology keeps the company competitive."

Aliments Fontaine Santé Inc. (1997): This Montreal-area manufacturer of preservative-free convenience foods began with a single juice counter in a mall food court, but now supplies major grocery accounts such as IGA, Provigo and Price Club. To keep pace with its growth it moved into a new production facility in late 1995, complete with a 22,000-square-foot food preparation area. It's so big that President Michael Mourani isn't sure whether to call it a production facility or kitchen, although he's leaning to the latter for old times' sake. At $6 million in sales, Fontaine Santé has become a big player that needs to meet its customers' needs for electronic data sharing and keep a closer eye on orders and shipments just for its own planning needs. As a result, it recently automated its entire delivery system, equipping every truck with computer notepads so that drivers can record orders and deliveries, and bill customers on site. Daily sales information is downloaded onto the company's computer system each night, providing updated sales figures every morning and keeping all parts of the company informed on a daily basis.

COMMUNICATIONS TECHNOLOGY

No owner/manager ever had it as good as the entrepreneur of the nineties. If the essence of successful entrepreneurship is building an organization that combines professional business competence with the vision, drive and judgement of its founder, today's communications tools are the catalyst. Increasingly, the cellular phone, pager, laptop computer, fax and e-mail are multiplying the knowledge, power and influence of the individual. And that empowers entrepreneurs, who have always rued their inability to be everywhere at once. Even in many sophisticated organizations, the founder, president or CEO still has to be alerted to every new opportunity or consulted on decisions, even though they're probably going a mile a minute in their never-ending quest to identify new clients, suppliers and opportunities. The good news is that with today's communications technology, you still can't be everywhere at once, but you can have your finger in every pie.

Raymond Simmons, president and CEO of **CRS Robotics Corp.** (1990, 1992, 1996-97) of Burlington, Ontario, is still astounded by the new power of e-mail to help him get things done. "It has created very effective ways of keeping in touch with people all over the world," he says. "When I travel to Europe I used to be on the phone every day for more than an hour to coordinate activities. Today I write and receive e-mail, and the cost is not even comparable. I used to spend $1,000 a week on long distance, now it's $10 a month." More to the point, e-mail allows instant transmission of full details and even entire documents, which is not possible with the phone or even voice mail, allowing more complete communication and better, faster decision making. "When I arrive back after a trip I've already delegated all the work, I'm already up to speed," marvels Simmons. "I don't come back to a cluttered desk any more."

Many PROFIT 100 entrepreneurs are fiends for technology. Take Brian Richards, president of Surrey, BC-based **Canned Heat Marketing**, the number two fastest-growing company in 1994. As his business, distributing natural-gas fireplaces, grew, Richards made sure all his sales reps had fax machines and computers at home so they could communicate at all hours of the day or night. Later, he even had fax machines installed in their cars. Before most people had ever heard of the Internet, Richards was sending and receiving e-mail from his laptop computer. He even set up e-mail and a fax machine in his trailer, since he spent most weekends following his first love, the car-racing circuit, from track to track. That way, he says, he can enjoy his hobby and his work — and neither of them is tied into artificial constructs such as 9:00 to 5:00 or the weekend. " I work really strange hours," says Richards. "I do Saturdays and Sundays without even blinking." With instant communication, he says, he can work when he wants and snatch extra time for his family. "Really," he says, "you go when you go."

Steven Stein is president of **Multi-Health Systems Inc.**, a Toronto publisher of psychological tests (1993-95). Everywhere he goes he takes his notebook computer to help him keep up with work at home or on the road. Along with the usual software, it includes a fax modem, scheduler and personal organizer. He uses it to write business letters and contracts, create marketing and advertising pieces, send and receive documents, and even demonstrate his company's computerized testing products. "It saves me from downtime," he says. "You can't afford much downtime; you've got to be active, keeping productive, moving. That's the way business is these days."

It goes without saying that these high-tech instruments, like any tools, can be a curse as much as a blessing. Entrepreneurs have to learn to let go. Even with cellphones and faxes, you can't make every decision; you can't always be "on call." The trick is managing the technology, to get the most from it and still be able to find time for yourself. Managed properly, you should find today's personal communications media empowering, not devouring.

Terry Bergan, president of **International Road Dynamics** (1993), a Saskatchewan firm that sells truck-weighing systems, carries around a cellphone, laptop computer, personal organizer and, occasionally, a portable printer. "Time is of the essence these days," he says. "People want to have a confirmation tomorrow." But doesn't all this heavy-duty communicating create more pressure than it relieves? Not according to Bergan, "I find it more stressful to be out of touch than in touch."

The Internet

Only a few facts are known for sure about the Internet. Here they are:

• The Internet will change the way business is done.

• No one knows how, when, why or how much.

Beyond these facts, no one has a clue as to how the converging of computer and communications technologies via the Internet will affect business over the long run. But Canada's Fastest-Growing Companies are confident that the Internet represents the dawn of a new opportunity. And they are eager to stake a claim in cyberspace and, frankly, see what happens.

They all laughed when Jean J. Robillard of **Avant-Garde Engineering Inc.** (1997) of L'Assomption, Québec, proposed a Web site to promote his company's products. Avant-Garde's hydraulically-powered scaffolding products, lighter and easier to assemble than conventional work platforms, were targeted mainly at masonry companies, which were not generally thought to be avid Web-surfers. But "gut feel" told Robillard that potential customers were looking for new-product information, so he ordered up a twenty-five-page Web site with lots of pictures and product descriptions. The site soon caught the attention of a contractor in Texas who was looking to build a new plant for Texas Instruments. He requested more information and eventually placed an order worth $217,000. The cost of Avant-Garde's Web site was $3,000.

According to the PROFIT 100, now is definitely the time to be on the Net. In March 1996, twenty-eight of the 1996 PROFIT 100 reported they were hosting Web sites on the World Wide Web. A year later, that number had doubled. Fifty-five of the 1997 PROFIT 100 companies had Web sites, with many more companies promising they would have theirs on-line within a few months. But Web sites are not the most popular use of the medium. Even more firms are using the Net for e-mail and basic research. Here's how fast-growth companies used the Internet as of April 1996 and April 1997.

The Internet Takes Off

What do PROFIT 100 companies use the Net for?

	1996	1997
E-mail	44	73
Research	24	66
Marketing/promotion	37	56
Web site	28	55
File transfer	20	46
News groups	10	20
Direct selling	N.A.	5

Clearly, fast-growth companies have taken the measure of the Web and found it appropriate for some activities and not others.

Craig Thomson, president of **Paradon Computer Systems Ltd.** in Victoria, says his computer dealership was quick to embrace the power of the Net. Paradon's Web site allows customers to find out more about Paradon's products, or track the status of special orders or products returned for servicing. The site even includes information on products Paradon is buying, so that suppliers can call Paradon, and not vice versa, to offer better deals. Paradon staff also use the Net regularly to track down more information on new products and software updates, as well as for e-mail and to participate in newsgroups. Paradon went way out in front by including a function on its Web site which allowed long-distance customers to talk directly through the Net to the company's staff. But six months after it was introduced, nobody had used the feature yet.

You'd expect a company named **Online Business Systems** to be a power user on the Web, but the Winnipeg-based computer consultant politely begs off. Online's Web site is primarily used for general company information, advertising job openings in the company, and on-line registration for the company's training courses. President Charles K. Loewen believes the Net's primary benefit is e-mail communication, both with clients and between the company's branches. Staff members also regularly use industry newsgroups when they have questions worth posing or solutions worth posting to a worldwide audience. But Online doesn't expect to become a cyberseller, "Our services are too customized to sell over the Net," says Loewen.

Certainly **Corel Corp.**, the Ottawa-based graphics giant, thinks the consumer model is the right way to sell on the Net. Its "Corel Club" is an on-line supermarket that sells low-priced entertainment and utility software from the Corel Home collection, as well as books and magazines, and downloadable on-line images for professional use. Because fears about credit-card security have hampered the growth of Internet commerce, Corel offers a telemarketing number that lets you call the company and provide your credit-card number over the phone.

Another one of just five brave souls on the 1997 PROFIT 100 selling directly over the net is long-distance reseller **Sprint Canada**, the main operating subsidiary of **Call-Net Enterprises Inc.** of North York, Ontario. Sprint offers product information and ordering on its site, giving consumers a chance to sign up on-line for its "The Most for the Least" long-distance savings program. "It's catching on more than last year," says Call-Net Chairman and President Juri Koor. So far, however, "compared to how we get most of our customers, it's pretty small." Eventually, however, he sees Internet selling picking up. Eight years ago, he notes, nobody looked askance if you didn't have a fax machine; today it's essential. In a few years, he says, a functioning Web site will also be mandatory, and he wants Sprint to be ready.

Some PROFIT 100 companies find they need two Web sites, one for the general public and one for trusted, password-endowed clients to access certain features or confidential documents. "We use our hidden Web site to give us an edge in providing service to clients," said the president of one PROFIT 100 high-tech company, who didn't want his name used. "It's a technical Web site that has software updates. You need a special password to get to it." A regular Web site, he says, "is not important to have at all"; in fact, he has warned some clients against wasting their money on a Web presence. "A Web site isn't necessary in every case," he says. "It's got to address a business issue. Otherwise, it's smoke and mirrors."

But don't expect things to stay slow for long. Internet use is still in its infancy. A late 1996 report by US-based Forrester Research predicted that the overall Internet economy will approach US$200 billion in 2000, up from just US$15 billion in 1996. With the rapid development of more secure encryption programs and protocols to encourage on-line selling, the Net may yet be the place to be, as astute PROFIT 100 companies know. By 1997, twenty-eight companies said the Internet had already had a major impact on their business, and that number will only grow.

WOW
SERVICE

"We're a hand-holding, cradle-to-grave kind of company."

John Gajdecki, Gajdecki Visual Effects.

It's become a favoured cliché of management and marketing consultants that good service isn't enough any more. You have to deliver outstanding, unmatched, superlative service.

This may come as news to all those consumers who have ever taken a day off work to stay home to wait for a furniture delivery that never arrived, wasted a lunch hour searching for a retail clerk to wait on them, or waited in despair for a bank, government agency or travel agent to call them back. In fact, a 1996 PROFIT cover story on customer service ("Retail Report Card," April-May 1996) determined that Canadian store-owners have largely failed to carry out their oft-cited objectives of beefing up their customer service efforts to fend off the new influx of US competitors now swarming all over their territory. PROFIT hired two marketing experts to "mystery shop" nine Canadian retail outlets. By their count, just three offered friendly, well-trained staff who seemed capable of helping to make an informed purchase. The staff at the other six were judged inattentive, uninformed or downright surly. That's not the way Canada's Fastest-Growing Companies do things.

In Antigonish, Nova Scotia, John Dobson built a five-store giftware retail chain across Atlantic Canada that grew 1,263% in five years. At **South of the Border**, "our game plan has been to have the best customer service," he says. That means cash refunds, free gift-wrapping year-round, and employees who are trained to know their products and empowered to make decisions that favour the consumer. The result is loyal customers who return again and again and spend $500 to $700 in the stores every year. Across the country at **Just Kid'n Children's Wear** in Langley, BC, Kelly Cahill stresses personalized service, a 100% satisfaction guarantee and a frequent-buyer club that offers discounts to loyal customers. At Calgary-based **Dino Rossi Footwear**, President Doug Pinder pays his sales staff bonuses not for chalking up more revenues but for bend-over-backwards customer service, "We believe that if we treat you right, you'll find something to buy."

Clearly, better service can make a huge difference in industries where customers have traditionally been neglected. So how much more important must this be when it comes to business-to-business markets, which is where most PROFIT 100 firms derive their growth? Business customers are used to higher standards of service, and indeed their expectations are growing almost daily.

Consider the increased competition in courier services, where overnight international delivery is now standard, and sweat-drenched fleets of bicycle couriers can now promise local deliveries in minutes instead of hours. Look at telephone banking, which provides customers with instant information on balances, interest rates and other bank services without having to wait for a customer-service rep to come back from lunch. In business, the bar is being raised ever higher. Increased efficiency is drawing more and more companies closer together in a web of mutual dependence, forcing service standards to an ever higher level. With just-in-time manufacturing, auto parts companies have learned to produce customized batches of parts and deliver them to the big carmakers' loading docks just minutes before they are needed on the assembly lines. Based on the new technology of electronic data interchange, major retailers are now ordering goods for same-day delivery from many of their suppliers, eliminating the retailers' need for expensive warehouse space and forcing manufacturers or distributors of sporting goods, clothing, mattresses and other goods to meet strict service measures or risk being cut off entirely.

Clearly, the pressure is on for companies that market to business. Entrepreneurs who intend to make their mark must learn to meet and exceed the levels of service in the sector they wish to conquer. One PROFIT 100 entrepreneur calls it "WOW" service.

• IKOR INTEGRATED FACILITIES INC.: "WE ONLY DELIVER WOW!" •

The definition of service, PROFIT 100-style, was set when freelance writer Marlene Cartash interviewed Igor Korenzvit, the astute founder and president of Toronto office-furniture dealership **IKOR Integrated Facilities Inc.** IKOR was thirteenth on the 1993 PROFIT 100, with sales of $9.2 million, and ranked fifty-third on the 1995 list when sales jumped further, to $11.6 million. That's a heady achievement for an office-furniture dealer in any market any time, but especially in a Toronto market that had been dominated by business failures and real-estate retrenchment since the beginning of the decade. In 1993, Korenzvit estimated that the Toronto office-furniture market was worth just $120 million, down from a peak of $300 million three years earlier. But his philosophy could apply to entrepreneurs in any troubled industry, "Even though this business has suffered more than most, life doesn't stop," he said. "Rather than worry about a declining market, we decided to go after the $111 million we didn't have yet."

To do that, "we decided to work hard, be patient, and provide our customers with the best service," says Korenzvit. Especially the service. Throughout its showroom are signs that say, "WOW service by IKOR." It's a concept that Korenzvit constantly drums into his staff. "There are three kinds of service you can give to people," he says: "Less than they expected, which we call 'Yuck;' what they expected, which we call 'Blah;' and more than they expected, which is 'Wow.' We only deliver WOW."

His service strategy isn't especially innovative, but in its old-fashioned simplicity backed by day-to-day commitment, it works wonders. "If somebody asks me to call them tomorrow, I call them today. If they want a price on a chair, I'll get them the price, and then tell them there are two other chairs that are just as good but cost less. If we're supposed to install 100 workstations in a week, we'll do it in four days. And then, we'll ask what else we can do, like moving their old furniture into the basement. You'd be surprised how many dealers wouldn't think to do that."

WHAT'S WOW?

Where does WOW customer service come from? It's not a narrow concept limited to sales staff or a desk of order-takers. It's a company-wide imperative that depends on a multiple of business disciplines, all converging ultimately at the "front," whether it be the sales floor, the cash register, the telemarketing centre, the delivery truck, the field worker or the customer-support operators — anywhere where your organization and its customers interact. WOW service is an attitude that must permeate the entire organization, since it's not just about sales or even marketing but product design and production, distribution, information systems, recruiting, training and compensation, and executive leadership. Without support from the top and continuing pressure to make service a priority, WOW service becomes now-and-then service.

TOP-DOWN SERVICE

Not everyone on the PROFIT 100 puts a label on the quality of service they try to provide. But Korenzvit isn't alone in putting the stress on service. While PROFIT 100 companies outdo the competition in many areas, superior customer service is almost always cited as their key competitive edge. And this finding is in line with the results of a 1994 Statistics Canada study of 1,480 growth firms called *Strategies for Success*. Respondents were asked to evaluate their organization's strengths relative to those of their main competitors in ten key areas: employee skills, flexibility toward customers, labour climate, customer service, new-product frequency, price, product range, production costs, quality of products and R&D spending.

Surprisingly, in only three of those areas did the entrepreneurs grade themselves significantly higher than their competitors: customer service, flexibility, and product quality — in that order. They all recognize the importance that outstanding customer-centred behaviour can play in prying open tight markets and distinguishing winning organizations from their competitors.

FirstService Corp. in Toronto has made the PROFIT 100 five times, from 1993 to 1997. The word "service" in the title comes from the types of business the company engages in — consumer services such as lawn care and house painting, and business services such as order processing and security. But founder and CEO Jay Hennick is determined that service also be a state of mind. If its people can't give consumers a healthy, weed-free lawn or respond politely, quickly and efficiently to customer calls and questions, they're not going to get another contract next summer from any neighbour on that block. To maintain the service he requires, Hennick told PROFIT that he would call the customer service desk at some of his companies two or three times a week, disguising his voice, to ask questions and poke and prod and try to determine what kinds of service customers and potential customers were actually getting. When he encountered problems, he would mention them to the president of the subsidiary in question, hinting very strongly that there was a problem here needing to be fixed.

As a result, everyone in the organization understood that customer service was a priority, and it helped management focus on a related goal of finding ways to link compensation to customer-satisfaction levels. But the benefits from his sustained extra effort went even further, says Hennick. "Because I do these sorts of things, they're now doing it and their people are doing it, too. So the whole organization over time is very concerned about what their customers think of them and what we can be doing better to generate more customer interest."

SEVEN SERVICE SECRETS

SEVEN SERVICE SECRETS

1. Set a new standard for your industry.
2. Don't make clients pay for your mistakes.

3. Measure the service you provide.
4. Speed.
5. Relieve your customers' stress.
6. Use feedback to stay in touch with customer needs.
7. Surround your product with customer benefits.

Set a New Standard for Your Industry

From aerospace component manufacturing to cable-TV installers, every industry has its service standards. To break in and seize market share, you have to reinvent those standards to match your organization's expertise and catch competitors flat-footed.

That's how it worked in Winnipeg when Glen Behl and Michael Gorum, who ran a produce store, decided to begin wholesaling to restaurants in 1987. They saw the market dominated by just a handful of distributors whom they considered "lazy." These firms offered limited service hours and no price lists, and rarely made sales calls. **Garden Grove** entered the market like a new broom, promising lower prices (a result of buying direct from California brokers, which also resulted in fresher products) and better service. Among the innovations Garden Grove brought to the local market were weekend deliveries and no minimum order levels. Some rivals used to refuse orders worth less than $200, no matter how much the same restaurant bought from them a day earlier or the week before. Within five years Garden Grove's sales had bloomed from $300,000 to more than $3 million, landing the company on the PROFIT 100 twice, in 1992 and 1993. It also prompted Behl and Gorum to close their retail outlet and concentrate on the restaurant trade, where the appetite for better service spawned success.

Raising the bar is tough work. You have to build a service credo into your organization and nourish it continuously. That's what happened at **Unity Business Machines Ltd.** (1997), an office-equipment dealer in Victoria. President Frank Buruma says Unity's service edge comes from its people. Their hard work and enthusiasm have helped the company respond to service calls in just two and a half hours, compared to a four-hour average in the industry. And, he notes, "we fix it right the first time."

Service is an ethic, too, says Buruma. In his industry, he says it's not unusual for salespeople to lie about the attributes of a fax machine or photocopier in order to make the sale. "We never lie when it comes to sales, even if it'll lose us a sale," says Buruma. After all, if you're in business for the long run, disappointed customers will come back to haunt you. How do you get staff to take the long view of quality and customer service? Unity puts everyone on the same team, by offering profit-sharing and wide-open employee training. "They can have as much training as they want when they want," says Buruma. And not just in customer relations or bookkeeping. "Russian, linguistics, whatever they want to take," he says. "It makes for more rounded, happier people."

In the trucking business, Mississauga, Ontario-based **Transpro Freight Systems** (1996-97) has raised the ante by meeting ISO 9002 quality standards, ensuring its clients a consistent level of service quality. "We're mighty proud of that," says President Frank Prosia. "We've experienced tremendous growth because we've positioned ourselves to be industry leaders." By emphasizing systems and spending 2% of sales on employee training, he says Transpro offers "a professional edge in a non-professional industry."

Don't Make Clients Pay for Your Mistakes

Professionals set their own standards and blame only themselves when they fall short.

"We're very aggressive and we try hard to keep our customers happy and give them as much service as possible," says Kevin Fitzgerald of **Aurora Microsystems Distribution Inc.** (1996-97) in Copper Cliff, Ontario. Once in a while that aggressiveness means making a mistake, usually in computer installation, but Fitzgerald has it all worked out. "If we make a mistake we typically eat the cost and don't pass it on. Other competitors tend to pass mistakes on to their customers."

It's a similar story at **Logical Design Inc.** (1996-97), a Richmond Hill, Ontario, computer consultant. "We do good work, and we guarantee what we do," says President Mario Costabile. "My philosophy is that if you're going to do a job, take responsibility for that job. We take full and absolute responsibility if it's not done right; we'll do it again and not charge for it." He says Logical Design goes the extra mile for its customer, often putting a lot of research time or project-management effort into a contract that never gets included in the bill. Some customers appreciate the gesture, others aren't aware of it, but Costabile doesn't care. "That's just how we do business. We don't do it for recognition or thanks. It just takes longer to get a new customer than to keep an existing customer."

Measure the Service You Provide

To improve your customer service, you have to find some way to measure it in order to quantify the results. That's not usually easy.

Brian Luborsky, chairman and CEO of **Premier Salons International** of Markham, Ontario, Canada's Fastest-Growing Company in 1996, is probably typical in that he offers many different products at different prices, so quantifying quality is hard. "Because of the different markets we are in, we can charge $300 for a haircut or $8 for a haircut. We've got so many different service levels, our challenge is to figure out what constitutes appropriate service." Unlike many organizations, Premier can't make very good use of mystery shoppers, hired snoops who visit stores disguised as customers. After all, you can only use so many haircuts.

Still, Premier creates an opportunity for feedback and measurement in its Magicuts stores by supplying clients with a comment card, and offering them an incentive, such as a discount on their next haircut, for filling it out. The cards use fairly broad benchmarks, asking clients to judge the quality of their service as poor, fair, good, very good etc. But Luborsky says even these broad brushstrokes can be useful. "It's pretty subjective, but we're just looking for the broad swings. For example, if there's one store where nobody sends the cards back, you know you have a customer-service problem."

In the US, Premier takes advantage of customer-service evaluations conducted by Sears Roebuck, where 300 of Premier's hair salons are located. Sears uses telephone surveys of customers and a small army of mystery shoppers (it can afford more than Premier could alone) who visit various stores and score the experience. Typical categories are environment, friendliness, and how long it took to be approached. In late 1996 Premier's score was 87.5, which Luborsky said was the highest of all Sears licensees.

Speed

No, it's not a movie. It's a key service advantage in the nineties.

MSM Transportation Inc. (1996-97) of Bolton, Ontario, has carved out a niche in freight traffic from the US to Southern Ontario by offering specialized expertise (its drivers know the route and they understand Customs) and faster service. "We deliver to Canada from Los Angeles in five days and most US competitors take ten days," says managing partner Mike McCarron. "We match their rates and provide better service." If the shippers don't think that extra timing edge is important, MSM will call the customers itself and ask if they would like to receive their goods 30% faster. The answer is always yes, and MSM is only too happy to make the arrangements.

How does MSM move so much faster? It has identified a number of efficiencies, such as using a highway truck for all pick ups, so the cargo does not have to be shunted from one truck to another. Further, since all of MSM's runs are direct, there are no central hub delays where shipments are consolidated. Most US truckers are concerned with the domestic market only, and can't offer MSM's brand of service, says McCarron. "It's a niche. It's not a big enough piece of business for them to do right."

But MSM has also worked hard to build a service culture, by fostering positive employee attitudes and offering customer-service training and incentives. MSM stresses instant decision making, fast pick ups, and getting back to customers on a timely basis. It offers an aggressive bonus plan, based on such core values as on-time service and customer satisfaction, all of which MSM measures. And it looks after the soft stuff, supplying driver uniforms, publishing a newsletter for drivers, offering pizza luncheons once a month, and fun activities such as boat cruises, Christmas parties and paintball games. "We treat drivers like kings," says McCarron. "Everyone has trucks and terminals and rates. MSM's competitive advantage is people, so we put time and money into them."

Another speedster is **Entreprises Métallex** of Aylmer, Québec (1996-97), a steel fabricator. Métallex produced parking railings, steel staircases and handrails inside and outside the building for the new casino in Hull, Québec. It took eight months, but Métallex finished forty-five days ahead of schedule. Vice-president Pierre Malouin says Métallex stands out in its industry because it makes a point of always finishing ahead of schedule, "which is very unusual in construction." He credits the company's edge to using experienced professional crews, "not kids," and paying the best salaries and benefits to make sure it retains its best people. Métallex also employs its own draftsmen and estimators, which speeds things up by keeping everything in-house.

When asked how Métallex marketed its services, Malouin was caught somewhat by surprise. "Business cards," he said. "And word of mouth." Nonetheless, from 1991 to 1996 Métallex grew to $1.6 million in sales from just $143,000. "We don't have time for marketing," says Malouin, but clearly speedy service talks louder than words.

Relieve Your Customers' Stress

You want a hot tub. What if you don't like it? What if the neighbours end up snickering at you (or even worse, they want to come over every day)? **Beachcomber Spas** of Surrey, BC, sells its hot tubs as stress relievers, but it also knows how to take the worry out of buying one.

Beachcomber Spas, a PROFIT 100 qualifier in 1991 and 1992, knows it is selling a product with which most consumers are still unfamiliar. To reduce customer anxiety, it offers several unusual services. You can ask for a free "wetting invitation," a chance to have an informal pool party at the local dealership with a number of your friends to help determine whether you would enjoy your own hot tub. If you're keen, a Beachcomber sales rep will come to your home to help you decide where in your yard to place your new tub.

And should you worry about getting cold feet over your new $5,000 hot tub, Beachcomber offers ultimate peace of mind: a thirty-day in-home trial. If its hot tub falls short of a customer's expectations within thirty days of purchase, Beachcomber will either repair the unit to the buyer's satisfaction or take it back for a full refund (the purchaser must pay shipping and insurance charges). That commitment to customer service and reassurance helped Beachcomber soak up sales of $25 million in 1996, up from just $1 million in 1985.

Use Feedback to Stay in Touch with Customer Needs

How do you know, really, what your clients want? Are you keeping pace with their changing needs? In a book called *Customer-Centered Growth,** US consultants Richard Whiteley and Diane Hessan studied 200 companies to find out what makes winning businesses. One of the top success factors they identified was "hard-wiring the voice of the customer." Top companies, they said, develop well-defined listening strategies for obtaining customer feedback and then hard-wire what they learn into the organization so employees actually deliver what customers want. Canada's Fastest-Growing Companies may not be hard-wire experts, but they do seek out customer feedback and try to act on the information they obtain.

Eagle's Flight Creative Training Excellence Inc. of Guelph, Ontario (1995-96), creates interactive, role-playing training programs to help corporate clients build motivational and teamwork skills. To sell its programs, which cost about $3,000 plus $99 per person, Eagle's Flight emphasizes feedback. Every session concludes with a comment form, which participants are encouraged to fill out to let Eagle's Flight know what they thought about its experiential training. And the company employs one staff member whose sole job is to call up clients, "not to sell them anything, just to keep in touch," says President Dave Loney.

Eagle's Flight pays attention. One recently adopted program, "Listening: The Quest for Liquid Gold," flowed directly from clients' many requests for a program to improve employees' listening skills. In response to feedback, Eagle's Flight also changed the way it presents its training. To respond to clients' stated preference for on-going courses — as opposed to the single, four-hour session most commonly used — Eagle's Flight offered "Listening" as a series of short sessions lasting twenty weeks. To Loney, customer feedback provides low-risk ideas for better products and better customer service. "We have the ability to meet customer needs in a wider way," he says. "There's many more needs than we've provided solutions for so far."

---

* Richard Whiteley and Diane Hessan, *Customer-Centered Growth*. Addison Wesley, 1996.

Asked what recent management tactic worked most effectively for him, Toronto printer Dennis Low pointed to his decision to recruit a market-research firm to conduct a survey of his customers. The president of **PointOne Graphics Inc.** (1997) hired the team to scope out what clients thought were his company's strengths and weaknesses, and identify any serious gaps between their expectations and the service PointOne provides. "It's been very informative," says Low, providing the company with ideas about where it needs to pull up its socks and in what directions it should be heading next. "We knew a lot of it," he adds, "but this has made it concrete."

Surround Your Product with Customer Benefits

Sure, your product is superior, but if you can surround it with a bevy of services and benefits that add even more value in customers' eyes, you can move from winner to industry icon.

Calgary-based **Image Club Graphics** (1993, 1996) sells clip art images and graphics software by mail to designers, businesses and educators across North America. Image Club has built its reputation as a design partner by providing high-quality images and then surrounding that with a galaxy of service perks, including flexible purchase options, unlimited technical support and a no-risk thirty-day guarantee. To help clients upgrade their graphics skills, Image Club even offers an educational section, "Tips & Tricks," in all of its monthly catalogues.

In Longueuil, Quebec, **Systèmes Zenon Inc.** (1995-97) offers businesses, schools and institutions computer consulting and systems integration systems. It promises to help them select the best systems for their needs, which means that Zenon's level of expertise had better be well above that of the local computer dealer. "We put together a team of ultra-specialized people," says President Eric Bourbeau. "We know the technology better than most, and we offer more service and flexibility than our competitors."

Zenon uses that knowledge to create a multifaceted, one-stop approach to selling computer systems. It doesn't only sell or just consult. "We're able to offer a complete solution to customers, from pure consulting and architecture design to all phases of implementation of high-end networking solutions," says Bourbeau.

Spotting an additional need to help customers get more from their technology, Zenon added training to its bag of tricks. It opened training centres in Montreal and Quebec City to teach clients everything from installing Windows 95 to programming in Visual Basic. "Each division is run like a separate entity but they all feed off each other and allow one-stop shopping," says Bourbeau. "Our competitors don't typically do that. Even today they still haven't caught on." In fact, he says, many of his competitors come to Zenon for training themselves.

The last piece of a complete solution, says Bourbeau, was adding technical support. Each office now offers a twenty-four-hour customer help desk featuring experienced staff with the hands-on experience to solve clients' problems. "We're always there," says Bourbeau. While they could also get help from their software developers or hardware manufacturers, he notes, "some customers would rather deal with us because they know we won't let them down ever." And that, of course, engenders the loyalty that brings customers back for new software or the inevitable upgrade.

A similar script has been written by **Gajdecki Visual Effects**, a Toronto-based special-effects producer for movies and television. President John Gajdecki credits the firm's 1,359% growth from 1991 to 1996 to the fact that "we're good at what we do, plus we have a commitment to customer service." Again, that means top-notch effects (Gajdecki made the legendary Avro Arrow fly again for a 1997 CBC movie, and produced a giant cockroach terrorizing a miniature subway train for a recent Hollywood thriller) and one-stop shopping for harried film producers. "We are the only fully-integrated FX company in the business," he says. "We have our own model shop, FX production supervisors [who work on film sets] and computer composite department."

Where Gajdecki doesn't have the resources, it subcontracts from others in the industry. But its people continue to supervise each project to ensure the quality is maintained and that even outside jobs are completed on time and on budget. Says Gajdecki, "We're a hand-holding, cradle-to-grave kind of company."

THE EIGHTH SERVICE SECRET

Up above, we promised you seven service secrets. But there's one more concept left to explore. And that, fittingly, could only be called:

Exceed Your Customers' Expectations

Always give your clients more than they expect. It's when you keep offering more that they keep thinking and talking about you, creating openings for untold opportunities to emerge.

The day after Craig Thomson left the navy in 1990, he opened a small computer store in Victoria. He wanted to use his computer engineering degree, and figured retail offered the fewest barriers to entry. Today his company, **Paradon Computer Systems Ltd.**, is Victoria's largest systems integrator, helping retail and corporate clients get the most from their computer systems. That strategic switch from consumer to business market was no accident. Businesses buy higher-margin products and generally have fewer support needs.

To Thomson, WOW service means constantly expanding into new areas that serve his customers' needs. As a result, Paradon has moved into financing its sales to lower-income consumers, as well as computer service and support. And now it's even gone past those frontiers into cyberspace, as the first Victoria reseller on the Internet. If you've got a product in the shop getting fixed at Paradon, or you're waiting for a systems product to be finished, you can use the Net to track its status. To help customers, Paradon also seeds on-line discussion groups about service issues and common problems.

For the future, Thomson is gearing up to meet the biggest need he sees developing in the computer business — service. "We will provide service in-house or on-site with eight hours' turnaround," he says. "We'll *fix* any problem in eight hours, not just look at it." He compares that with the current industry standard of forty-eight hours, which he says "is pretty good for Victoria." To provide that service, Thomson is overseeing a major investment in inventory, staff and training. It's not easy, he says, finding staff with both the technical and people skills needed to put them in front of clients. But he's determined to make the client's experience as painless and positive as it can be. "You can only sell so much in a city this size," he says. "We're growing through service. Customers develop loyalty to an integrator and staff and personalities, and it's very hard for competitors to duplicate them."

But the ultimate payoff from service that exceeds customers' expectations accrued to Terry Maxwell of Lachine, Quebec, a mechanic and fanatical stock-car racer. He followed the circuit in the 1970s, setting a few racing records along the way and building a reputation as a painstaking mechanic who could make any car run faster. In time, he started his own repair shop in Lachine, **Zeke's Performance Automotive Inc.**, to serve racers, sports-car buffs and anyone willing to pay a little extra for top-quality service.

Meanwhile, General Motors had decided to move production of its Camaro/Firebird line to Quebec from an assembly plant in California. This affected the plans of a man named Ed Hamburger, founder of SLP Engineering Inc. in Troy, Michigan, who had just signed a deal with GM to upgrade a number of Camaros and Firebirds every year into a special-edition, higher-performance model. Hamburger had just overseen the conversion of twenty cars in 1992. But now, since these were factory-new cars that would be both built and shipped out of GM's Ste-Thérèse plant, just north of Montreal, Hamburger needed a local contractor to do the finishing work. Who did he know in Montreal? He first thought of an old rival from his stock-car racing days. He remembered Terry Maxwell's competitive instinct, his dedication to excellence in his mechanical work, and the fact that he was the only guy at the track who could be found reading the *Harvard Business Review.* Hamburger asked Maxwell if he would be interested in undertaking the work.

Maxwell accepted the challenge. In 1993, he and his hastily trained team installed new hoods, suspensions, tires and exhaust systems on 200 Camaros and Firebirds to transform them into *real* sports cars, the Camaro SS and Pontiac Firehawk. The cars raced off the lot, and GM asked for 500 the next year. By 1996, Maxwell's company, now renamed **SLP Automotive Canada**, had built 5,400 cars. It now had outgrown three plants, and had just opened a new factory to make its own souped-up hoods. SLP Canada boasted sales of $5.4 million in 1996, up from just $425,117 in 1991, on the strength of Terry Maxwell's commitment to service.

Maxwell's obsession with high-quality service continues. In early 1996 he and his team of 200 employees, most of whom had been with the company less than a year, qualified for ISO 9002 quality certification on their first try. "Only 5% of companies qualify on the first try," boasts Maxwell. And in mid-1997 he was scheduled to open a new plant in North Carolina to install custom parts for new vehicles, to help more aggressive US car dealers add some pizzazz to their car lots. It's a long way from car repairs, but Maxwell sees it as a natural progression for someone who always believed in his work and refused to accept second-best in anything he did. "I got the contract because of my reputation for integrity and my hard-working discipline. Everyone knows that we know automotive performance and we're honest. I planned to have my hobby be my business. I wanted to do both and learn as much as I could and it pisses me off when people say I'm lucky." By exceeding his every client's expectations, Maxwell has proved the sky is indeed the limit. Say Wow.

FINANCING
It's Not Just About the Money

"I probably spent six months out of every year begging for money. I was once described as the man with Gucci kneepads!"

Jeffrey Speak, CBCI Telecom Inc.

"I don't like to characterize it as the banks that don't support the company. I think it's the people working for the banks that don't support the company. If you don't get their confidence, then they can't go to bat for you."

Raymond Simmons, CRS Robotics Corp.

When you look at a successful company that has offices around the globe, a public stock listing and bankers falling at its feet, it's hard to imagine that once upon a time it had all the problems of the typical start-up company: uncertainty about its ability to make next week's payroll and cash-flow hiccups that could be alleviated only by judicious use of credit cards.

But that exactly describes the case of one of Canada's proudest but little-known success stories, **Rand A Technology Corp.**, of Mississauga, Ontario. Started by brothers Brian and Dennis Semkiw and Frank Baldesarra in 1986, Rand began as a pioneer in a very new niche, a reseller of hardware and software for computer-aided design and manufacturing. Their thinking was that CAD/CAM systems, which could help companies design and manufacture new products faster and more efficiently, were still very new and very confusing. There were lots of salespeople selling their company's equipment, but very few middlemen, independent distributors without allegiances to any producer, who could advise manufacturers on the best system to suit their needs. The computer industry term for such distributors-slash-consultants is "resellers." These are companies that don't just sell products, but provide customized solutions to clients' information-age problems.

"We saw that this would be a major opportunity, and it's still continuing," says Brian Semkiw, Rand's CEO. By 1996, CAD/CAM had become a $10-billion-a-year industry, and resellers had raised their share of industry sales from zero in 1986 to 50% in that decade. For Semkiw that means that there's lots more room for growth. In that period, Rand itself grew to a $175-million-a-year company. With sixty offices across Canada, the United States, Europe and Asia, it now claims to be the world's largest CAD/CAM value-added reseller.

Having gone public to raise capital in 1993, and being consistently profitable, Rand is now in the enviable position of having the bankers knocking at its door, asking what they can do for Rand. "They call me every week asking if we want more money. People want to send us cheques for $15 million every week," says Semkiw. Fortunately for Rand, it doesn't need the cash.

But it wasn't always this way. When Rand started, it had all the usual cash-flow problems, says Semkiw. "Our first form of financing was credit-card debt." In early days, the Semkiw brothers' goal was just to just sure that their six employees were paid, even if the founders were not. "My brother, who runs the finances of our company, would hand us cheques and then tell us when we could cash them. That lasted for many years." Management's job, says Brian, "was to keep our priorities in the right order. We made sure our employees were paid and the morale was high, because the sacrifice was made by the original partners." When times got tough, he admits, Rand used Visa to pay the MasterCard, or vice versa.

Commercial bankers were little help, because they had no idea how to evaluate the company. Rand was one of those newfangled knowledge-based businesses, which didn't fit into the banks' traditional business models. Rand had few hard assets for collateral, and two-thirds of its sales were to foreign clients, making it tough to lend against accounts receivable. "That made them nervous," says Semkiw. "At the beginning the banks wanted a lot of security. The owners had to guarantee a lot of their personal assets, such as our houses."

As a service company without high fixed costs, Rand eventually overcame its cash-flow crises. But then it encountered another level of financial problems that made the start-up squeeze look easy. "If you could keep enough self-discipline in terms of your own personal cash requirements down to a limit, and kind of bootstrap it on the way up, I found that getting our business to around $5 million was pretty easy," says Semkiw. But it was at the $5-million level, when Semkiw and his partners at last knew they had a viable business that was going to survive and probably grow quite substantially, that they found the real gap in the financing market place.

At that size, Rand needed money to grow. But it was still too small to have developed the professional-quality systems or cost controls that lenders and investors were looking for. "We weren't really in touch with all our finances," says Semkiw. "You sell and sell without building the financial infrastructure; you don't really know what you're making money on. Cash flow is squeezed. You don't have the financial people or structure in place to really know how you are doing."

Eventually, Rand hired a chief financial officer to bring order to the chaos, and found some financial relief through venture-capital investors. But their demands for equity made their funds more costly than any bank lending. "That was hard," Semkiw recalls. "I think that's the point where a lot of businesses fail, right in that zone." The bottom line, however, is that Rand's solutions strategy paid off. Its clients, who make everything from kitchen blenders to sophisticated electronic equipment, obtained quick payback from Rand's technology consulting, and word spread. By 1992, its sales had passed $20 million, and profit exceeded $950,000. In 1993 Rand ended its cash-flow problems by launching its own stock issue. At the age of seven, it was the first publicly traded company in its industry.

THE FUNDAMENTAL RULES OF FINANCING

The moral of the story is that everyone has cash-flow problems. Even the best growth companies (in fact, sometimes particularly growth companies) have trouble finding financing. A lucky few, mainly in the software business, grow out of their financing problems. Their high profit margins provide all the cash flow they need to fund operations, plant and equipment and R&D. Most growth companies, however, have been forced to become much more creative financiers. They may be at different levels, but they are all learning the same skills. Some are juggling credit cards, while others are playing off one banker against another. Some are scanning actively for "angel" investors, while others are preening for the formal venture-capital community. And the lucky ones, are auditioning brokers from Bay Street in preparation for taking their companies public.

Overall, however, there is one principle of financing that every entrepreneur must remember: *It doesn't get any easier as you grow.* The bigger your company gets, the more financially exposed it is likely to be, the more nervous your banker will get, and the more you will need to diversify your funding sources. (For a more detailed discussion of alternative sources of financing, see *Beyond the Banks: Creative Financing for Canadian Entrepreneurs,* by Allan Riding and Barbara Orser, also in the PROFIT series of books published by John Wiley & Sons Canada, Ltd., 1997.)

As they've expanded, Canada's Fastest-Growing Companies have had to contend with this almost universal truth. Growth satisfies their instincts and vindicates their theories of business, but it only alarms their banker. The bank defines success in just one way — your ability to produce collateral to support your growing financial needs. The solution is to build up your capital, whether through retained earnings or some form of equity investment. The search for capital represents a major focus for most PROFIT 100 entrepreneurs; for many, it's the ultimate test of their business abilities. Fortunately, the smartest ones have learned some very fundamental rules:

- **Financing is about more than money.** It's about the structure of your business, how it will grow and how much it can grow. The decisions you make now to raise funds will affect the very future of your company. And the connections you make in your search for capital can make or break your business in its times of trial.

- **Raising funds is not a financial problem, it's a people problem.** If one banker or investor turns you down, you must keep going till you find someone who understands what you're trying to do, someone who can get excited by your plans and wants to help. Once you find these people, you treat them as well as you treat your biggest customer, because they're just as important, and probably more so.

- **You must take the time to learn about individual sources of capital, from your brother-in-law to your bank to Bay Street.** Each funding source is different, with specific needs, requirements, policies and hot buttons. Your financing requirements may be tailor-made for a private placement but not for a venture-capital injection, or your loan application might appeal more to a local credit union than to a chartered bank. It's up to you to research all these areas (usually with the help of a knowledgeable accountant or financial advisor) to determine which funding sources would be most helpful to you, and how you can go about meeting their criteria.

- **For any viable business idea, there is a financial solution out there.** It may not be the one you want. It may take longer than you dream, or cost more than you ever imagined, but forget the media scare stories about the "credit crunch." No matter how tough it looks, there is a financial solution for you out there. The catch, of course, is that your proposition has to be saleable, and you have to be creative, persistent, flexible and very, very patient.

PROFIT 100 "I'm always looking for money," says Jeff Speak, president and CEO of **CBCI Telecom Inc.**, a Montreal producer of videoconferencing systems. For the first seven years of his company's existence, he says, "I probably spent six months out of every year begging for money. I was once described as the man with Gucci kneepads!" After being rejected, he says, "by every bank in the world," he finally found the right niche for his company by tapping private equity investors, including Montreal's fabled Bronfman family. And as Speak found, success breeds success. "Once you pour capital into the business, everyone [at the banks] wants to take you to lunch." The capper was in 1996 when Speak led a $15-million public offering that put his company on the Montreal and Toronto stock exchanges. Speak could have given up anywhere along the line and decided to be a victim, complaining to the newspapers about the lack of capital for entrepreneurs in Canada. Instead he pressed on and became a poster guy for the opposite, and more important, concept: If your story truly has merit, there is a backer for your business somewhere.

A "No" Doesn't Mean a Dead-End

It's in the positive, can-do spirit of these rules that PROFIT 100 entrepreneurs view their financing challenge. Scratch almost any PROFIT 100 entrepreneur and you will find he or she still holds a grudge against a bank or other lender/investor because of some failure on their part in the past to recognize the brilliance or sheer common sense of the entrepreneur's business plan. And yet, when entrepreneurship researcher Eugene Luczkiw, director of the Institute for Enterprise Education in Thorold, Ontario, interviewed a number of entrepreneurs from the 1995 PROFIT 100 list, he made an interesting discovery. When he asked them to name an on-going problem they have faced, financing issues didn't even make the top ten. Banking, lending and capital issues were lumped in among "other issues," as being barely worthy of complaint in their own right.

The reason is that, although PROFIT 100 entrepreneurs may never forgive the lender that gave them the cold shoulder, they don't spend time moping about it either. They set off to talk to the next lender, using the same unflagging energy and confidence that helped their businesses overcome similar indifference and apathy among potential customers. A "no" from the bank doesn't mean a dead end, just a detour.

SOURCES OF FINANCING

Where do PROFIT 100 companies find their funds? Everywhere. Here's a snapshot of the financing histories of the 1997 PROFIT 100 companies:

Sources of Financing

Sources of Financing	No. of Companies
Owner(s)	93
Chartered banks	86
Public stock issues	33
Friends and relatives	27
Government	18
Other financial institutions	17
Venture capital	12
Informal investors	11
Suppliers	8
Customers	3
Employees	3
Overseas lenders/investors	3
Barter	2
Commercial paper	1

A few interesting conclusions can be drawn from this table. Aside from the personal capital injected in their businesses by the owners themselves, banks are by far the most important source of capital to Canada's Fastest-Growing Companies. That comes as no surprise, although it's interesting to note how few of these high-growth firms — only twelve in 1997 — managed to attract interest from venture capitalists, who are always on the outlook for the next big growth company. The creative talents of entrepreneurs are well displayed in other categories on the list. For instance, 27% have managed to raise "love money" from family and friends, a risky proposition that requires trust and faith on all sides.

Eleven firms have succeeded in locating that rare bird, the "informal investor." Often called "angels," informal investors are relatively affluent individuals who like to invest in private businesses for their own portfolio. Research indicates that these people, usually experienced or former entrepreneurs, invest as much for fun as for the anticipated profit. In return for they funds, they expect to have a say in the running of the business, and they usually expect a generous return (30% to 40% a year). These are very choosy investors. They usually stay out of the limelight to avoid attracting unwanted attention, and still they reject thirty-nine out of forty opportunities that come their way. The PROFIT 100's ability to tap at least eleven of these individuals speaks highly of their creative networking abilities and their selling skills.

From stock markets to government grants, from suppliers to customers, the PROFIT 100 seek out all the opportunities they can to balance their cash flow and fund their new ideas and growth plans.

Image Processing Systems Inc. of Scarborough, Ontario, which develops and sells machine-vision manufacturing-inspection systems to international markets, is a past master at balancing funding sources. In nine years it has tapped owners' equity, some bank funds, friends and relatives, export financing, angels, grants from the National Research Council and other government sources and, finally, a public stock issue in 1994. President Terry Graham doesn't think his path has been particularly tough. "Any start-up company in Canada finds it difficult to get money," he says. "The bank was only supportive in the last year, when we didn't desperately need them anymore." In fact, the only resentment he seems to feel is towards the labour-sponsored venture-capital funds, which were specifically set up in recent years by the federal government, and armed with generous federal and provincial tax incentives, to invest in promising small businesses. "The labour funds are incredibly conservative," he says. "They are set up as venture-capital funds, but they don't act like it."

GETTING ALONG WITH THE BANK

By far the most important financing relationship for PROFIT 100 companies, as for most businesses across Canada, is with their bank. And Canada's Fastest-Growing Companies seem to enjoy the same love-hate relationship with their banks as do most other Canadian businesses. When asked if they found their bank supportive of their endeavours in general, 61% of the 1997 PROFIT 100 answered yes. But that figure masks the frustrations that many of them have had with their banks over the years, and the fact that many of them have switched banks in the past to find a more sympathetic lender.

Here, in fact, are some typical responses from recent PROFIT 100 entrepreneurs who said that yes, their banks were supportive of their early endeavours. It's not quite a ringing endorsement.

- "Yes, they were [supportive] before, but not now. Too many changes at the bank manager level is what caused the problem."

- "Yes, in a Canadian sort of way," said one computer consultant with what our PROFIT 100 interviewer described as "an evil laugh." "Everything I have is with Bank of Montreal; my previous banker told me that my type of company goes out of business all of the time. The Bank of Montreal has been helpful, but want lots of guarantees. I'm glad I haven't had to go to the bank for too much assistance."

- "Yes, very supportive. Originally they weren't, but because of the background of the three partners in business and the community, we had a good rapport and history with the bank."

- "Yes, they have been very supportive since the day we started doing business with them. My bank manager believes in me. [My previous bank] wasn't very good. I couldn't get what I needed at the time, so I left. I was trying to buy another company, and needed $200,000 to do that. I had money of my own and had been with the bank for a number of years, but I'd never had much reason to borrow. I got a flat no when I asked, but a friend said to go to a particular CIBC branch. I went there, brought my financial statements, and within one hour had an account with $200,000 on which I could write a cheque. I have no idea why the attitude was so different."

For comparison, here are the responses of a few PROFIT 100 presidents who said no, their banks weren't very supportive.

- "They don't like retail."
- "They don't like the computer business."
- "They don't like funding exports."
- "They didn't understand our business, and we were growing too fast."
- "We had no bank lines [of credit] at all. At the beginning the banks wouldn't return our calls. [Ironically, this company found much more support from the public stock markets than from its

local bank.] And now, the bank calls us. What's the problem between banks and entrepreneurs?"

Consider the experience of Mark Albertine, president of **OpenAire Inc.** (1996-97), a Mississauga, Ontario, manufacturer of swimming-pool enclosures with retractable roofs. It's a fast-growth company of the sort that makes governments proud and bankers very, very nervous. OpenAire grew from sales of $344,000 in 1991 to $2.9 million in 1996, a jump of 731%. In that time, exports, primarily to the US, where pools are more common because of the longer season, grew from 20% to 80% of sales. All that, of course, drives the bank crazy. "They don't like the fact that so much of our business is in the US," says Albertine. "They don't give us credit on our receivables for the exchange rate, and they don't even like having US receivables; they're afraid we won't get paid." But the reality is, according to Albertine, "that all of our slowest-paying customers are Canadian."

Like the first three complainants above, Albertine is convinced the banks don't like his industry at all. "They're trying to say that we're in construction, and they don't like construction," he claims. "I say we're manufacturers. They don't understand our business."

With a profit of just $41,000 in 1996, OpenAire depends on its bank line of credit to fund production. Albertine has tried to look beyond the banks for help, but has so far run into the big roadblock of time. For a while he was wooing one private investor, but that fell through. He's currently working sixty-five hours a week on sales and administration, he says. There's no way he has time to look for other investors, or even pursue a public stock issue. "Something would have to give," he says. "If I'm spending my energy on going public, I don't make sales and can't keep the doors open. It would be an advantage to have more capital, but a better line of credit would really help, too."

But at least one PROFIT 100 entrepreneur is ready to admit that the problem wasn't all the bank's fault. "We started our business with $147 and lived on credit cards for one year," says Kevin Fitzgerald, president of **Aurora Microsystems Distribution Inc.** of Copper Cliff, Ontario (1996-97). "Now we have a line of credit; after five years the bank finally recognizes us as a viable business venture." In the beginning,

Fitzgerald admits, "we weren't a proven business. At first we didn't have statements together properly, so I can't blame the banks for turning me down. I wasn't properly prepared. They have a risk element they have to look after, and businesses have to be aware of that."

Of course, this love-hate relationship is a natural state of affairs. There's an inevitable tension in the banker-entrepreneur association that is found in few other business relationships. Bankers and entrepreneurs tend to approach the world from opposite ends of the spectrum. To generalize only slightly, one tends to be visionary, outgoing, optimistic and oriented to risk, while the other is trained and paid to be cautious and conservative, to shun risk above all else. Neither side is necessarily "right." It's just that the combination doesn't always work out.

Growing companies in particular tend to frustrate their bankers no end. Lenders are uncomfortable with high-growth companies. They are always coming back looking for more money or a higher line of credit, or to present a new opportunity for which they need just a little more help. In fact, one Western Canadian banker, in learning about the PROFIT 100 survey (with its implicit assumption that growing companies should be identified and supported) held up her hand in a motion to stop. "I'm not sure," she said, "that this is something our bank wants to encourage." The fact that her bank had been supporting the PROFIT 100 program as a ballot distributor for five years seemed not to have penetrated yet.

But this story does underscore the differing views that individual bankers, even within the same institution, may hold regarding small business success. And it suggests that problems can result when an entrepreneur has the wrong banker.

The Bank Shuffle

Despite all the money that banks spend to advertise themselves as banks that can make things happen or that understand small business, the fact is that the name on the front door of the bank you deal with is less important than the relationship that you have with the people inside.

Norbert Bolger of **Nor-Built Construction** (1997), a homebuilder in Amherstburg, Ontario, recalls being initially quite impressed with his bank. But in five years he watched four bank managers breeze through his local branch, to the point where he no longer even knew his account manager's name. When Bolger finally went to meet manager number three a year or so ago, he expressed some dissatisfaction with the high interest rate the bank was charging. "It doesn't sound like you want my business," said Bolger, looking for reassurance. Instead, the banker's reply was, "Not really." "Well," said Bolger, "maybe I should go look somewhere else." "Go ahead," said the banker. Bolger recently completed his switch. (To the bank's credit, sort of, Bolger says the manager was later fired. "He wasn't a people person.")

Switching banks is nothing new to savvy entrepreneurs. It's all part of the importance of dealing with people who are on the same wavelength as you are, whether they are suppliers, customers, employees or bankers. What's most interesting, however, is the lack of pattern in the switches that are taking place. If you ever really wondered whether one bank was better than another, you'll find no evidence for that among the PROFIT 100. In the 1997 PROFIT 100 survey, twelve companies reported switching banks recently. They were asked where they were, and where they went. See if you can spot any pattern.

Switching Banks

	From	To	Then To
1.	Bank of Montreal	Royal Bank	
2.	Royal Bank	TD	
3.	CIBC	TD	
4.	TD	Royal Bank	
5.	Royal Bank	Bank of Montreal	
6.	Royal Bank	Bank of Montreal	
7.	CIBC	Royal Bank	
8.	Royal Bank	CIBC	
9.	Royal Bank and Bank of Montreal	TD	
10.	TD	Credit Union	
11.	Credit union	Royal Bank	
12.	Bank of Montreal	Royal Bank	Canada Trust

Brian Munholland had a background in finance with a number of large corporations before joining **McGill Multimedia** of Windsor, Ontario (1996-97), as vice-president, finance. He takes a fairly sympathetic view of the problems that banks have in keeping good people on small business accounts. "You know, banks, like accountants and lawyers, are only as good as the individuals you encounter within the firm. But accountants and lawyers, because of the value that the firm recognizes, are fairly compensated for it. If I had a really good banker, the odds are he's going to be promoted out very quickly and not stay at that level anyway."

For those who think bankers are all bad, it should be noted that in at least one case, a PROFIT 100 entrepreneur shifted his account to a new bank to follow his bank manager. "She was excellent," says the entrepreneur. "When she left [to move to a different bank], we decided to go with her."

While the banks staunchly maintain that their high standards provide equal levels of service across the country, small-business bankers on the firing line know that the quality of a banking relationship depends as much on the chemistry as it does on the math. And they know that if a relationship isn't working out, it's up to the entrepreneur to find another one that will. "You've got to look for a banker who's enthusiastic," advises Neil Hollingsworth of the CIBC. "Don't be scared to ask the individual what makes them tick. The right fit is important."

Managing Your Bank Manager

PROFIT 100 entrepreneurs didn't get where they are by passively accepting every situation that confronts them. They know that success stems from altering circumstances in their favour as much as they can, and that applies to dealing with the bank.

When Robert Murray, president of **MSM Transportation Inc.**, a Bolton, Ontario, trucking firm, tells his banking stories, it's a classic saga of adapting, reacting, and then turning the tables.

MSM, which mostly carries freight from Southern Ontario into the US, was started in 1989 by three partners who put up $45,000 in capital. "We lived on tight budgets for the first two years until we built up enough cash flow to make things a little easier," says Murray. "We certainly didn't have any help from the banks in the beginning. We had to lease different types of office equipment. Even getting corporate Visa cards out of the banks was quite humourous. We had to actually sign over our receivables and personal guarantees. Any assets that the company had at that time were on the books for the bank to take, and this was for a total credit facility of about $6,000, about $2,000 apiece on each of the Visas."

With a background in credit and collections, Murray has been able to maintain a tight leash on creditors and keep MSM rolling to this day without a line of credit. That's given him the credibility, and the time, to seek out bankers he can work with on his terms. But, as he explains, then that age-old problem crept up. The manager was transferred. "It took me two years to develop a good relationship with our bank manager," he laments. "As I got to like him, and was working up a very good rapport, he was very quickly promoted into heading up a business branch." But Murray didn't take that lying down. When the new manager started on the account, Murray and his partner Michael McCarron called the old manager and made sure he stayed involved in the transition. "We just did not have the time to educate a new account manager on the trucking business, what we are doing and why are we doing it," says McCarron. "We really did have to call in some markers by picking up the phone and saying, 'we need you back until we finish this exercise,' but he did come back and he did do a good job."

Still, if MSM was going to have to start all over again with a new banker, its owners decided they should have the say in who it would be. Murray and McCarron actually interviewed different banks to see which one they should deal with, the opposite of the usual state of affairs, where entrepreneurs feel they are the ones on trial. Among Murray's more important questions were, "Why would I want to deal with this particular institution?" and "What type of people are here?" "I prefer to work with MBAs or commerce-type people," says Murray. "The typical traditional bank managers I've dealt with in the past didn't even know how to read a financial statement." Murray admits that the banks seemed a little uncomfortable about being interviewed. "I don't think they're ever asked things like, 'Why should I buy from you?'"

And when the opportunity came, MSM wasn't afraid to play one bank off against another. "The banks seem to be most competitive when they really believe that you will switch," notes Murray. For some time he and McCarron had been trying to get CIBC interested in their business. Finally, they let it slip that the Royal Bank was starting to show an interest and the CIBC banker perked up his ears, says McCarron. "If I hadn't said that the Royal was interested, his answer would have been, 'Oh, you're in the trucking business, we're not interested.' Instead, it was, 'Can we have lunch next week?'"

The benefit can be substantial. With their plans to build a new truck terminal requiring some outside financing, McCarron and Murray used a strategy of playing good cop/bad cop with the two banks. Each partner appeared to favour a different bank, which McCarron says got both banks moving. "It played into our hands because the Royal came back three times with better offers, based on perceived involvement by the Bank of Commerce."

Another PROFIT entrepreneur, who asked not to be named, said she followed a similar course of action to spark the banks' interest in helping get her service company off the ground. "Knowing their competitiveness, we would change banks a lot," she said. "Canada doesn't have enough banks, as far as I'm concerned."

But while there is no denying the short-term gains that can be made from switching banks or playing them off against each other, the best payoff for the long run is to find a sympathetic banker and work with them constructively.

Kyu Lee, thirty-three-year-old managing director and CEO of **Queue Systems Inc.** (1997), a Markham, Ontario, computer-consulting firm, offers this instructive story. "Our bank has been supportive, but in 1996 we went to them because we were scared. We didn't need any money, but we wanted to establish a banking history to help promote our growth. We thought it might be easy to get financing when we were only $1 million in sales, but it would get harder when we get to $3, $4 or $5 million in sales. We wanted to be ready, so we established a lending history early on."

The bank proved very receptive, he says, "because we had done our homework. We didn't just go in and say please lend us money. We worked with accountants and lawyers and put together financing proposals; everything was laid out. I had little to do with it. We're not business people, we're technology nobs, but we hired business people to help us out."

For a "technology nob," Lee and his co-managing director, his brother Alex, did things right. They approached the bank for money well before they needed it, giving them time to get their application in order and put the best face on their situation. And they hired experts to do the job, knowing that their own time was better spent looking after their clients and their company.

Raymond Simmons, president and CEO of **CRS Robotics Corp.** (1990, 1992, 1996-97) of Burlington, Ontario, believes that partnership is the key to successful banking relationships, and that long-term relations work best for everybody:

"We went looking for a bank back in 1985 and ended up with the Royal Bank, and with this account manager who was just outstanding. The banks were relatively all the same, but he was very enthusiastic. Twelve years later, we still have the same bank manager, even though he's been promoted a number of times. I think when the account manager likes your business and understands your business, he'll take you with him. And because of the strength of that relationship, I've met everyone at the Royal Bank right up to some board members. I mean, he likes to show off this company that he's created. He's as proud of what we've accomplished as we are, because he's a member of the team that built this company."

Can a Bank Change?

There's no doubt that entrepreneurs have always complained about their banks, and probably always will so as long as banks put depositors' security above risk-taking (which is to say, as long as the banks stay banks). But given that so many entrepreneurs feel hard-done-by, are the banks getting better?

The banks themselves certainly think so. Under pressure since 1993 from an activist federal government that has seen banks and their billion-dollar profits as an easy target, the banks have been forced to find new ways of serving the new entrepreneurs of the nineties. They have worked hard, through training and education and targeted recruiting, to help their people come to grips with the new economy, the special needs of internationally oriented entrepreneurs, and the fact that equipment, bricks and mortar may no longer be a company's most valuable assets. "I think the bank is learning a lot," says Claude Lestage of Bank of Montreal, who like CIBC's Neil Hollingsworth was named one of "Canada's Best Bankers" by PROFIT in 1995. He told PROFIT writer David Hatter that attitudes at the banks are changing, although not always fast enough to suit every client. The old attitude, he says, was that, "If it's good for the bank, it must be good for the customer." Now, he says, the bank is more likely to say, "What are you looking for?" and "How can we help you?" Says Lestage, "I think the bank realizes that entrepreneurs are partners in our evolution."

Even some PROFIT 100 entrepreneurs agree the banks are evolving in the right direction. **MSM**'s Robert Murray says he notices his bank has taken, "a much different approach to hiring more people with a commerce background for their account managers. They're setting them up to literally go out and sell. They tend to be getting a lot more aggressive towards 'buying' business accounts."

"When we first started, the banks didn't really have a way to handle technology companies," adds the CEO of one Quebec high-tech company. "They didn't understand our assets, which were software and people." Now, he says, "the banks have changed quite a bit. They're much more able to lend money on intangible assets — like software and people." But still, he says, one thing never changes, "The better you're doing, the more supportive they are."

INVESTORS: THE PAYOFF
FROM RELATIONSHIP-BUILDING

If relationships are the key to better banking, does that also apply to other forms of financing as well? The PROFIT 100 say yes. Whether you're looking for a line of credit or an investment of $500,000, you're still dealing with people. You have to be honest, upfront and well-prepared. You have to give them your best sales pitch, and if you strike out, move on. (Although not before asking for any referrals, suggestions or other feedback that will help you hit the ball out of the park next time.)

Many entrepreneurs, feel reluctant to go looking for capital infusions from formal or informal equity investors. Some are intimidated by the process, while others dread the idea of giving up any of their ownership of the company to an outsider. However, most of those who have done so are glad they did. Getting more equity into a company relieves it of some of its credit burden, opens new financial horizons, and often involves other synergies created by the new investor(s) taking interest in the company and its activities.

"The smartest thing I ever did was take my company public," says Jock Chong, echoing the words of a number of PROFIT 100 entrepreneurs. Chong is chairman and CEO of Vancouver-based **Canadian Medical Legacy Corp.** (1995-97), a $3-million-a-year distributor of medical products. "As a newly landed immigrant [from Malaysia] seven years ago, without having a lot of business and community roots, I recognized that one of the best routes for growing my company was to go public." He arranged an initial public offering in 1993, and while he admits there were "lots of growing pains and aggravations in the public market," the company has survived and is in a position to grow further. "Going public opens up avenues for obtaining public financing and the use of equities for acquisitions," says Chong.

Indeed, in April 1997 he announced that Legacy would raise $4 million through a special warrant financing, doubling the capitalization of the company. Along with that news, Chong announced the recruiting of two new executives, Dave Pearce and Rob Thornton, who had worked together previously in founding the Vancouver-based Mega Movies chain, a former PROFIT 100 company, which they later sold to Rogers Communications. With the additional cash and executive brainpower made possible by his stock listing, Chong hopes to boost revenues from $3-million to $10-million a year through a series of acquisitions of medical-equipment distributors in the US and Canada.

Chong's experience demonstrates, once again, the connection between people and money. Going public puts him in a different league than the average $3-million company, making it possible for him, not only to raise money more easily, but also attract interest from experienced executives who have the chance to increase their incomes by buying shares or stock options. While the owners of many private companies detest the idea of "living in a fishbowl" with a public company, where all financial reports and major executive decisions must faithfully be made public, Chong's experience shows just how productive that fishbowl can be.

Raymond Simmons has spent a lot of time thinking about business relationships. His company, **CRS Robotics**, which makes human-scale robots (automatically run machines that duplicate some of the movements of the human body, such as turning a screw or the bending a joint), works to build lasting relationships with all of its suppliers and customers, including its financial contacts. Indeed, he tries not to think of these suppliers in terms of the institutions they work for, but simply as human beings. "It has really been people that have assisted us," he says, "not 'banks', not 'venture capitalists.' All through the development of the company, it's been relationships we have established with our banks, with our vendors, with our customers, that have all led to our success in financing the business."

It's not just talk. CRS, founded by Simmons and three robotics-research scientists from Hamilton's McMaster University in 1981, has always had a healthy appetite for cash, from the cost of funding inventories and manufacturing equipment to meeting the payroll of a highly professional staff that now numbers 175, half of them engineers. That means it has had to tap a wide range of lenders and investors, not even counting its helpful banker. "We've probably gone through every financial phase that exists in the development of a company," says Simmons. "It started with the founders putting a small amount of capital in [$20,000], then employees putting capital in, then family, then private angel investors and venture capitalists, and then we went public." From the very beginning, Simmons used a single strategy to woo investors and lenders, the same strategy he used to win the goodwill of suppliers, which was building a relationship rooted in trust, confidence and even excitement.

"I characterize the success of our financing strategy as getting the people with the money to buy into our vision and dream, and keeping them informed and communicating with them.

When I started CRS, the very first thing I did was go out to our banking people, and I got them to understand what our dream was, what our product was, what our target markets were, where were we going. Today we're a successful company and the banks are chasing me, so it's been quite a role reversal. But I realized that I was the vendor to the bank. I was trying to convince them to put their money into my business, so I behaved like a vendor, trying to sell them on what my business was all about, even our components, and going in there and meeting their credit managers and mapping out our business plan. At the time, we had $20,000 on our balance sheet and we were trying to take on a global market in manufacturing robots. So, we had to do a lot of selling in the early days on the finance side."

The same tactic worked for negotiating favourable terms from suppliers. Simmons spent time with them, showed them his business plans, and talked about his dream of building a globally competitive robotics manufacturer. The payoff was, "Once I got them to buy into our vision, getting 90- or 120- or 180-day terms was actually relatively easy. Once I got those people on my side, I no longer characterized them as my vendor, I characterized them as my partner in my business. And I treated them as a partner by keeping them informed and showing them financial statements and really treating them like a strategic element in my business."

CRS treated its banker the same way. It's not "the bank" that decides to support or not support a business, Simmons insists, but a person working for the bank. "If you don't get their confidence, then they can't go to bat for you with their next-level management, so we have always considered the account manager as another member of our team, and shared our dream, or business plan, or financial statements." It started from the beginning, when Simmons walked in and handed his banker a detailed balance sheet and full financial statements. "When we first established the bank relationship, you couldn't walk into the plant and see robots being built and operating. It was only a dream at that time," says Simmons. But his full-court press impressed the banker immediately. "I've heard him say a few times that, for the size of our business, he was impressed with our business plan, he was impressed with our financials. We gave him full balance sheets, forecasts and cash flows, and he said it was pretty rare for a company that had a couple of hundred thousand dollars worth of sales to have such an in-depth analysis of where they were going." Simmons continued to meet with the banker regularly to update him on the company's progress, ensuring he was onside and would go to bat for them if CRS needed a favour or a bigger line of credit. Simmons' focused strategy has been an unqualified success over the years. "He understands our business and our vision. He's been very supportive as we've grown and our needs have changed."

Mind you, Simmons has worked hard to keep that relationship going. He has made himself active in community affairs with the Chamber of Commerce, for instance, knowing that he could meet valuable contacts there, especially since the banks usually expect their people to get involved in local activities. If the Royal Bank is holding some sort of local reception, he'll make sure to go, as a way of getting to know the rest of his bank manager's colleagues, and of demonstrating that he's prepared to give a little of himself to keep the relationship going. Most entrepreneurs would say they don't have the time to make that kind of extra effort, but it was important to Simmons. "Sure, I was working twenty-two hours a day, sleeping one hour, and drinking coffee for the other hour that was left just to keep going, but I made sure I had time for the events that I felt helped my business." Now that CRS Robotics is publicly traded and has a little more breathing room on the finance side, Simmons admits he doesn't maintain this networking pace with his bank any more. Instead, however, he has decided that the output side of the business can use his attention now, so he is devoting the same energies to meeting with customers and industry associations.

How Do You Attract Investors?

How do you attract investors to your company? The same way you woo lenders, suppliers, employees and customers — by having a good story to tell, by persuading others to share your dream.

Most companies follow a traditional path when it comes to equity investing, not unlike CRS's process outlined above by Raymond Simmons. After putting in their own savings, entrepreneurs in need of more cash usually tap the wallets and goodwill of friends and family, followed by local investors they know, then angel investors, and finally, if they're very ambitious, successful or lucky, the public markets. Although the numbers and players are very different, in many cases the process of tapping these sources will be very similar.

Wooing Start-up Investors

Jeff Hunt first hit the finance wall in 1984. He was trying to start his own carpet-cleaning business, but he had no money and no prospect of getting any from the bank. It probably didn't help that he was nineteen years old. By 1996 Hunt's company, **Canway Ltd.** of Ottawa, had sales of $39.5 million and 200 full-time employees in the US and Canada (plus another 500 part-timers). Canway's growth qualified it for the PROFIT 100 for the sixth time in seven years, a record bettered only by its Ottawa neighbour, software giant Corel, which made the PROFIT 100 six years in a row.

How did Hunt break through his financing wall? He sold equity early on, to friends and partners. He persuaded two friends from affluent backgrounds to invest a total of $6,500 in residential carpet-cleaning equipment. To get the business off the ground, another five of Hunt's friends started working for the company, contributing their muscle and time in return for "sweat equity." Hunt had no business plan, no assurance of success, just his previous experience working summers in the business, and his gut feel that the industry needed another player that would put professional cleaning and quality service first. But he also had a secret weapon, his maturity, his confidence and his contagious enthusiasm that what he was doing was going to work.

Hunt bought out his original shareholder-friends many years ago, but he continued to use that same strategy with other key contacts. When Canway owed money to certain employees, lawyers, accountants or suppliers, Hunt would offer selected individuals a chance to buy shares in the company instead. By sticking with people he liked and who obviously had a feel for the company, he was able to turn a liability, an account payable, into a long-term asset. The more shares an individual had, the more determined they were to see the company succeed. Hunt made the offer only to a select few, but, he told PROFIT writer Deborah Read, "I've never been turned down." In early 1997 he still owned 60% of the company but was considering taking it public within a few years, a move that would benefit his fellow shareholders as much as himself.

THE GAPS IN THE MARKET

One group Jeff Hunt couldn't sweet-talk, at least at first, was the banks. He says bankers were less than supportive of Canway for two reasons. First, they didn't understand his business, selling carpet-cleaning franchises across North America and distributing their services under the Sears brand name. And second, Canway was just growing too fast for their comfort.

Hunt's problem points up a common element in the financing problems facing Canada's Fastest-Growing Companies, Their worst financing problems don't necessarily occur at start-up. The biggest gap between the funds they have and the capital they *need* may occur at any stage in the companies' development. Sometimes the problem can be foreseen and prepared for; other times, it strikes out of the blue. Either way, it is the companies that have followed the conservative financial path, trying to stay a step ahead of their bankers and investors, that have the best chance of coming through the crisis and continuing their steady growth record.

Where does the finance gap most often manifest itself? At a 1996 round table on entrepreneurial financing, three PROFIT 100 leaders shared their moments of crisis, and their solutions.

• MCGILL MULTIMEDIA INC.: PENNIES FROM HEAVEN •

Brian Munholland, vice-president, finance, says, "The toughest part for us has probably been after the start-up stage. We could find the seed capital to get going. Where it became a real problem was once we felt we had a viable business, but we didn't have enough history yet to convince the banks of that. We actually got to the point where I was holding a purchase order from Chrysler Canada and had trouble financing it."

Munholland, a former senior financial executive with Pepsi-Cola Canada, was brought into McGill specifically to deal with problems such as these. Fortunately, with his extensive background in finance, he knew a number of angel investors, people who might be interested in investing in the company to cover the upfront cost of developing some of its state-of-the-art multimedia training and promotional products.

Brian brought McGill's founder, Robert Whent, and other top people to meet one target angel, an older man who had already made significant money by building and then selling his own business. "We sat around his kitchen table for a few meetings and he finally concluded, 'I like you guys. I'll do this.' But it was in that order: I like you, so I'll do this." In other words, like most private investors, McGill's angel was judging people first, opportunity second.

The investor put in enough cash to get the company past its big cash-flow hump. At the same time, the deal was structured so that McGill could buy him out early, as soon as it had the funds and the required economic stability. Based on the revenue from its big Chrysler contract and other projects, that happened in less than a year. "He takes the dividend while he's there and then he takes a great buyout when he leaves," notes Munholland. "It was a great return for him."

In the meantime, the investor also joined McGill's board. That's a common condition for angel investors, who like to keep an eye on where their money is going and how it is used. In this case, it worked well for both sides, says Munholland, because the investor was able to contribute some important strategic insights. "He gave us some great advice, and that was important."

But Munholland warns that not every angel investment works out so agreeably. Since it is as much about a relationship as it is about an investment, the chemistry is important. In most cases, says Munholland, entrepreneurs are right to be wary about offering significant equity to an outsider. If the relationship goes sour, or the promised returns don't emerge on time, you can find yourself with one very angry angel making things very difficult for you at the board level. "If you can find the right people for your business concept it may be worth gambling on," says Munholland, "but it is a bit of a gamble." In McGill's case, there wasn't much choice. At the time, it needed the money.

By 1995, however, McGill was earning $694,000 on sales of $6.1 million, so it had pretty much overcome its funding gap. "We have a significant positive cash flow right now and we don't seem to have any serious financing requirements," says Munholland. "So, needless to say, we have a lot of people now wanting to buy into the company. We have the banks coming after us wanting to finance it and everybody offering to help because we really don't think we need it any more." Nonetheless,

McGill recently arranged a line of credit anyway. "With the bank, the best time to set up your credit facility is when you don't need it."

• MSM TRANSPORTATION INC.:
EXPLORE THE ALTERNATIVES •

Bob Murray, MSM president says, "Probably the biggest cash crunch next to start-up capital came in purchasing capital equipment — the guarantees that were required by some of the financial institutions. Every piece of equipment we buy is a long-term investment. Tractors for example are $100,000 per unit, and trailers are up around the $30,000 range. It can become pretty costly. We ended up actually going outside of the traditional banking institutions to the parent companies of truck manufacturers, their credit corporations, and they've been great to deal with. I basically kept searching until we were able to find financing where there were no personal guarantees involved — which is really what our mandate was at the time."

• EXCELL STORE FIXTURES INC.:
INVESTORS, FACTORS AND ALLIES •

Fritz Winkels, Excell's vice-president of finance says, "We're an eight-year-old company manufacturing check-out counters, display cabinets and wall systems for specialty retail chains like Blockbuster Video. We found our difficult times were at the end of our second year when we went from jobbing out our production to other manufacturers to producing it ourselves. That's where we needed to get some equity capital — which was when I came into the company.

"I was involved in another business which we had sold out, so I had some money to invest. I'm a chartered accountant by profession, and Excell didn't have anybody in administration and finance, so there was a pretty good fit at the time: a place to park my money and myself, and contribute something to the business.

"The second cash crunch we had was when we did accelerate our sales tremendously in the fourth year, but we could get no serious bank support for our inventory. Our inventory's highly customized; no other customer would possibly take these funny designs, so that's where we had a real serious cash crunch. To overcome that, what we ended up doing is factoring our receivables whereby the minute the product went out the door at least we got our cash right there. We paid our bills and that got us to the next level of sales. And then after that, things eased up because we got a track record and the banks started knocking on our doors."

In between those two cash crunches, Excell faced another problem common to growing businesses, a continual cash-flow squeeze. Although Winkel's investment helped Excell fund its move into manufacturing, there continued to be long lead times in which the company was buying supplies and paying people to build its products, but couldn't hope to be paid for weeks or months yet. Excell had no choice but to put off paying its creditors, begging them for more time and in some cases even borrowing from them to pay other bills. "We'd work things out with those that trusted us," says Winkels. "They could see the product at least was in our warehouse just waiting for delivery; we could show them our orders from very reputable customers. So as long as they saw that their product was still on our floor and we had orders to ship at some point in the near future, they went the extra mile."

Excell did more than forge strong relationships with its suppliers. Winkels calls them "strategic alliances," and makes it clear that he hasn't forgotten the suppliers that helped them bridge the gap. "There's one that we probably buy 30% of our material from because they helped us in the early days," he says. "We won't forget them for helping us out."

GOING PUBLIC: NOT THE LAST STEP, JUST ANOTHER

For many entrepreneurs, issuing shares to the public represents the final phase of financing, the giant step that turns your company into a big player. It doesn't work that way. Many companies that go public find they need more money again and again in future, because the pressures of growth never let up. Going public doesn't mean the end of your financial needs, although it does makes them easier to solve.

Raymond Simmons figures that one of his biggest mistakes at **CRS Robotics** was not going public early enough. While CRS was growing as a private company (it made the PROFIT 100 in 1990 and 1992), it really hit growth stride again after going public in 1995. The proof is that CRS qualified for the PROFIT 100 again in 1996 and 1997, becoming the only company to appear on the PROFIT 100 across a seven-year time span.

In the early years, says Simmons, "we took a more conservative approach to developing the company. That delayed our market entry dates and product launch dates. Going public was our first shift away from a conservative investment strategy to a more aggressive strategy." Indeed, since going public CRS has acquired two companies that produce machine-vision systems (one in Germany and one in Burlington, Ontario), and appointed a new vice-president of sales and marketing and a new chief operating officer. It also managed to lose $4 million in 1996 on sales of $21 million, but Simmons considers that part of his investment strategy. "We're investing in technology and market share for the future. We feel there's enormous opportunity in automation of health care with pressures on the health-care systems in Europe and North America, and we want to be first there."

Simmons says robotics is still an industry in its infancy, ripe for consolidation by companies with vision and financial wherewithal. "In every city of every state or province there's somebody involved in robotics or machine vision — there is no standard, no multinational that dominates our industry. We feel that we have the opportunity to do some of that by consolidation, buying up some of these smaller local competitors." To do that, he says, being public proved critical. "When we go to talk to these people about acquiring them or doing a joint venture with them, they see our balance sheet being very strong compared to theirs, and that we legitimately have capital to fund the acquisition, so they take us far more seriously."

Besides the financial freedom, Simmons says going public on the Toronto Stock Exchange has helped solve other problems as well. It has exposed the company to institutional shareholders that are providing useful advice. It's also helped attract higher-quality staff, and given some reassurance to potential customers, "in terms of giving them confidence that the business is well financed and has a long-term vision." As well, he says staff morale is on the rise. "Our financial numbers are now reported every quarter, and the story gets picked up in the local newspaper. Our staff are very proud to work for the company because there's a much more public awareness of the company in our community."

Finally, says Simmons, being public has forced him to talk about the company more, especially to analysts working for Bay Street investment houses, and that experience too has been a good thing. "I feel, if anything, my 300 meetings with analysts over the last five weeks or five months has been very helpful. I now understand the strategy of the company today better than I've ever understood it, because I've had to explain it in ways that I never had to explain it before."

With his company trying to compete globally in a capital-intensive industry, Simmons knows CRS will be back looking for funds again. "We viewed our initial public offering as only the start of our public strategy for raising money. It was opening the door, giving us access to capital as we need it as we grow." He says the current financing plan is to borrow money for strategic investments, and then pay for it through future equity issues. "Our strategy would be to use as much debt as possible, completely saturate our debt capacity, then go back to the market to clear the debt. We'll just keep trading debt, equity; debt, equity." In other words, he says, CRS is treating its public stock issue like a fuel rod: "when we need it, we know we can issue more stock."

The issues and concerns around raising capital may vary among Canada's Fastest-Growing Companies, but one thing is clear. Financing issues must take second place to a company's strategic vision. Put the needs of your company and your people first, and the money, if you work at it hard enough, will follow.

CHAPTER TEN

VALUE-ADDED COST-CUTTING

"I call them up and say, 'Here's my yearly volume. Give me your best price.'"

Pierre Malouin, Entreprises Métallex.

As mostly young companies that are still hiring rather than downsizing, the **PROFIT 100** haven't had much experience with the ruthless and dispiriting brand of cost-cutting that overtook business during the recessions of the 1980s and '90s, with cutbacks, rollbacks and layoffs. Most of these companies, in fact, are still locked psychologically in start-up mode when it comes to expenses, eschewing the fancy offices and company cars normally associated with business success. They prefer to concentrate their efforts on their clients' needs, thereby keeping overhead growth to a minimum while continuing to expand sales and profits.

It would be easy for growth leaders such as these to zero in on top-line growth and obsess on keeping those revenue figures expanding, but few **PROFIT 100** entrepreneurs fall into that trap. They know that what counts is not how much you make, but how much you keep. To sustain growth means being able to control the bottom line, by minimizing costs and enhancing cash flow and profits so that you have the funds to deal with the increasing obligations and overhead of running a larger business. Profits, after all, aren't just what's left over when you subtract costs from revenues. They're the foundation of your organization, and the only guarantee that its mission will be able to continue.

While "cost-cutting" is a word that drives fear into many corporations, mainly because it's an occasional activity they associate with bad times, it is a way of life for the canniest growth companies. In fact, their focus on value for money and creative alternatives to spending cash results in cost-cutting initiatives that are more productive than restrictive, and more often than not motivate their staff rather than depress them.

TEN METHODS OF VALUE-ADDED COST-CUTTING

Here are ten ways PROFIT 100 companies have proven adept at value-added cost control.

TEN WAYS TO CUT COSTS

1. Avoid the King Midas disease; keep overhead down.
2. Pounce on accounts that are owed you.
3. Invest in technology to save production costs.
4. Don't pay for experience you don't need.
5. Look for cash-free ways to acquire services or supplies.
6. Vet your suppliers; make sure you are getting the best deal.
7. Keep your money in the company.
8. Boost profits by sharing them.
9. Make growth a team effort.
10. Plan your financial needs in advance.

Avoid the King Midas Disease

They keep overhead down throughout the organization. Bankers and venture capitalists will tell you that many promising firms sow the seeds of their own demise when they start getting more hung up in expensive sideshows such as office design, executive perks and corporate cars than with the details of running the business. For some companies, moving up to Class A office space in some gleaming bank tower or putting their name on a building may be a strategic marketing move, but for most firms they are costly frills.

Jim Estill, founder of **EMJ Data Systems Ltd.** (1991), today runs a $140-million public company. But when the Guelph, Ontario-based computer distributor opened in 1979, Estill was just twenty-three, and determined to do it all himself. He paid himself no salary for the first few years, lived in a "student-type" apartment and made do with a car he had to "jump-start every morning." If the office needed painting, he did it himself. "I had a significantly lower standard of living than my classmates for the first four or five years," he told PROFIT writer Deborah Read. Today he controls two public companies with operations in Canada, the US and Hungary and manages or advises several other growth firms, including **Puresource Inc.**, a 1997 PROFIT 100 company.

When **Oasis Technology Ltd.**, the number one company on the 1997 PROFIT 100, moved into new space in North York, Ontario, it inherited one luxury, oak-panelled office left over from the previous tenant, a financial services giant. It sits empty. President Ashraf Dimitri refused to move into that office, and everyone else on staff turned it down, too. "It just isn't us," says Dimitri.

Pounce on Accounts That Are Owed You

Fast-growth companies become adept at collecting their receivables as quickly as possible. Because they don't usually have the credit resources that would let them fund their customers for two or three months, they learn to deal with companies that pay faster, or find new ways to encourage them to pay up.

PROFIT 100 At **Trump Systems Inc.**, (1997), a computer consultant and reseller, President Kevin Leach says managing receivables is the key to sustaining his company's growth. The standard in his industry, is to be paid in sixty or ninety days, "but we expect clients to pay in thirty or forty-five days," he says. "It's important to discuss receivables at the beginning. We tell them we'll be a true partner and in return we expect them to pay promptly." Leach says they don't mind the friendly warning if it means they can continue to receive Trump's promise of top-quality systems at the best prices. "The price for admission is paying on time," concludes Leach.

PROFIT 100 At **Kee Transport Group Inc.** (1996-97), a supplier of drivers to companies with truck fleets, payroll represents 80% of costs, says President Kieran O'Briain. Staff won't wait to be paid, so he can't wait long either. He says his customers have all been told they must pay their accounts within twenty days, and he is now trying to get that figure down to ten. Since he's in the fortunate position of having more demand for his services than he can fill, he's been able to drop clients who have insisted on industry standard thirty to forty-five-day payment periods.

PROFIT 100 How do you collect your accounts faster? Just keep the pressure on, says Bob Murray of **MSM Transportation Inc.** (1996-97). "We're not afraid to ask for what's needed. I've got a credit manager who does a super job; basically, we collect what's owing and don't make any bones about it." MSM doesn't offer any terms for early payment. "We're not a bank." he adds. Sheer persistence has worked his company's debts down to an average of forty-two days outstanding, versus about sixty for his competitors. "I'd like to get to thirty," he says, "but I certainly won't cry about forty-two days. It has certainly kept us away from the banks."

Invest in Technology to Save Production Costs

Smart companies keep reinvesting in technology, to cut costs and provide the increased quality or production quantities needed to keep pace with their growth.

PROFIT 100 In Pointe-Claire, Quebec, sheet-metal fabricator **Leetwo Metal Inc.** (1996) uses the latest technology to provide precision metal parts for high-tech equipment makers. One $50,000 computer-controlled machine worked thirty times faster than the human it supplanted, paying for itself very quickly. Founder Mike Lee says the company also designs more of its parts electronically, using software programs that can complete a project in half an hour, rather than the week or more for a human designer using conventional tools. The key to successful technology adoption is being able to convince employees that investing in more productive equipment doesn't eliminate jobs, it creates them. By enhancing the company's efficiency and turning out more products faster, Leetwo's technology investment has helped the company boost sales and profits, and grow from five employees in 1990 to eight-five by 1996.

Many other PROFIT 100 companies offer similar testimonials for technology's ability to reduce costs and boost output or service. Richmond Hill, Ontario-based **Phonettix Intelecom Ltd.** (1996) has invested $3 million in developing its own software to allow its 1,500 call-centre employees to become more productive and perform more services for callers and clients. In 1996 Phonettix invested 8% of sales in R&D to give it an edge in electronic commerce and voice-response capabilities. "We have to keep enhancing our software," says chairman and CEO Michael Jarman. With technology advancing so fast and clients' expectations rising, he says, "as soon as you stop, you're eighteen months away from being dead."

Don't Pay for Experience You Don't Need

Many companies complain that they can't find motivated workers, or people with the precise skills they need. By establishing employee training as a priority, Canada's Fastest-Growing Companies can avoid hiring expensive experienced workers and instead recruit people with the appropriate attitudes or other skills they are looking for. Through judicious use of training and performance feedback, they can bring these employees up to speed quickly, to the point where they are usually out-producing more experienced workers.

Take a look at **SLP Automotive Canada** (1997), which has created more jobs faster from a standing start than virtually any other company in Canada. SLP, which customizes a growing number of high-performance

Firehawk and Camaro SS sports cars every year for General Motors, grew from seven employees in 1991 to 220 by mid-1997. In 1996 alone it created 157 new jobs. Founder and President Terry Maxwell needed workers who could learn fast and perform with a high degree of skill. But he turned down people with industry experience, because he didn't want other employers' bad habits infecting his organization. He targets people in their twenties with little experience but loads of heart. Maxwell says SLP can teach employees all they need to know, "We've trained 95% of our employees in-house. Most are multiskilled — they can do five or ten different jobs."

If they have the skill and desire, he says, the pay increases will come. Twenty-one of SLP's twenty-four executives have come from the ranks of its six-dollars-an hour wage earners. Even when Maxwell has recruited employees from the unemployment and welfare rolls, SLP's screening system and in-house training have more than made up for the lack of experience. In February 1997, the company qualified for ISO 9000 quality certification in its very first try, an amazing feat considering most of its employees had been there less than a year.

Indeed, employee training is an increasing priority for most growth companies. In 1997 the PROFIT 100 invested 1.8% of revenues in training, up from 1.2% in 1996 and 1.1% in 1995.

Look for Cash-Free Ways to Acquire Services or Supplies

To conserve cash, savvy growth companies look for alternative ways to acquire needed supplies without paying upfront cash. Leasing is one popular strategy. Jeff Hunt of **Canway Ltd.** (1991-95, 1997) remembers when his company, with less than $3 million in sales, leased trucks and equipment worth more than half a million through fifteen different leasing companies. In the early days at **Excell Store Fixtures Inc.** (1995-96), says vice-president of finance Fritz Winkels, "We didn't lay out the cash to buy a thing. We leased everything from a hand tool to a fork-lift."

Another growing source of non-cash investment is barter, a fast-growing system in which companies share "credits" that allow them to tap each other's products and services at virtually no direct cost.

One 1996 PROFIT 100 company, **Akran Systems Ltd.**, an Ottawa systems integrator, first discovered barter when it closed its retail showroom and needed to liquidate $500,000 worth of inventory in a quiet, orderly fashion, so no one would panic and think the company was going out of business. President Raman Agarwal faxed his list of inventory to four different barter organizations and managed to dispose of $200,000 worth of stock that way, building up credits that let him access everything from airline tickets, car rentals and hotel rooms to film developing, microwave ovens and accounting services. He says bartering offers more than a chance to move products (at full retail value, he notes: no discounts). It also provides good networking opportunities with other members of the barter network, which he says has also resulted in cash sales as well.

L.E. Cherry & Associates is a 1997 PROFIT 100 company in Markham, Ontario, that operates a mail-order retail service called **Computer Buyers' Warehouse Direct**. To launch the company, which sells Apple Macintosh computers and compatible clones, founder Lorne Cherry bartered for advertising space through Toronto's Barter Business Exchange. It's not exactly free — he has to pay for the equipment or supplies he barters away, as well as a percentage fee on each transaction — but it helps expose his wares to a new audience even as it reduces the high cost of entering new markets.

Vet Your Suppliers

Keep the pressure on to make sure you are getting the best deal.

Pierre Malouin, vice-president and co-founder of **Entreprises Métallex** in Aylmer, Quebec, says his smartest management move has been to begin comparison-shopping for key supplies. As the metal-fabricator builds a new $450,000 workshop to handle growing demand, Malouin says he's saving big money by sourcing quotes from other suppliers or consulting with other customers to find the best deal. "Once you're well established with a supplier, they don't tend to give you the benefit of price breaks," he says, even if volumes are increasing. Recently, a reliable Métallex supplier was selling bottled gases at $130 each; Malouin called around and found someone who charged only $69. Another supplier who had been charging Métallex the same price for years lost the business when Malouin found someone else who would offer a 15% volume discount. The original supplier only won the business back by pledging 25% off.

Malouin doesn't dicker. "I don't want to negotiate," he says. "I call them up and say, 'Here's my yearly volume. Give me your best price.'" He figures that vigilance will cut Métallex's costs this year by up to 6%, and says it has already made suppliers more proactive about offering deals. "Now they know I'm checking."

Keep Your Money in the Company

When PROFIT 100 entrepreneurs were asked about their salaries (on a strictly confidential basis, of course), just over half revealed their greatest secret. But many did so almost reluctantly, not for fear that people might find out how much money they're taking out of their company, but because people might find out how *little* they're drawing. As the CEOs of companies that are still enjoying their prime growth years, most PROFIT 100 presidents are choosing to leave as much money as possible in the company. There's nothing altruistic about it. The funds will be taxed less onerously in the company treasury than in the owner's hands, and they will help build future growth which will provide the owners with an even greater payoff down the road.

"We draw what we need to survive and live," says one co-owner of a growing multinational company on the PROFIT 100. He says he drew $100,000 in 1996, which he considers peanuts compared to what he would be earning anywhere else. "Normally people at this level in a company this size would be getting $300,000 to $400,000," he says. "My payday will come as the stock grows."

Another PROFIT 100 owner pointed out that his bank had always been supportive of his endeavours, demanding personal guarantees for its loans but never actual mortgages, for instance. He credits that cooperation to the fact that he has always reinvested profits in the company, demonstrating his faith in his firm's future and thereby reassuring the bank that its money is safe too. "It's a two-way street," he says.

Another growth leader reported he earned just over $400,000 in 1996, but says he poured "the bulk of it" back into the company in the form a shareholder's loan, "I thought we should use it to get more office space." Sure, he says, he could have bought a new house with the money, "but none of it would give me as much satisfaction as watching the business grow."

Boost Profits by Sharing Them

To most PROFIT 100 companies, overhead is anathema, but they don't mind paying for performance. In 1996, 17% of PROFIT 100 companies reported they had some sort of profit-sharing plan in place to ensure that employees shared in their employers' good fortune. And 26% offered their employees stock options, to let them cash in on the company's success over the longer term.

As one 1996 PROFIT 100 company in a very competitive industry noted, "we only pay about average for our industry. But we have a profit-sharing system that proves quite generous at year end." Profit-sharing allows a company to give its employees above-average returns in good years, while keeping its costs in line should the roof fall in.

The increased productivity shows up in other ways, too, reports Grant Reynolds of Mississauga, Ontario-based **Auto Control Medical Inc.** "With some individuals there has been an obvious change in attitude since we introduced profit-sharing" three years ago, he says. "It's not as if before profit-sharing they were bad and now they're good; the differences are subtle, but they're there. There is a willingness to do things that they would have dragged their feet on before."

Make Growth a Team Effort

One of the hottest concepts in US business circles these days is open-book management, sharing your company's financial details with all your employees. While letting staff in on management's secrets has so far proven less popular in Canada, some PROFIT 100 companies have embraced the idea as a way to focus staff attention on all factors affecting the company, including costs.

At **IntelaTech Inc.** (1995-97), a Mississauga, Ontario, supplier of electronic components to the computer industry, "all information on the company is shared," says President Michael Ruscigno. "We reveal all key company performance statistics [including sales and profits] to each employee on a weekly, monthly, quarterly and annual basis." That helps focus employees on the bottom line, but it also does much more. With a better understanding of all that's going on at the firm, says Ruscigno, "Each person in the company is aware of all major opportunities as well as major threats."

Plan Your Financial Needs in Advance

Other than a few lucky software firms or service companies that can finance their own growth internally, most PROFIT 100 companies know their financial needs will only increase with growth. That's why the best of them start planning where and how they will meet their future funding needs well in advance.

"Never ask for money when you need it," affirms Muneeb Khalid, president of **Gage Applied Sciences Inc.** (1995-97), a Montreal computer-component manufacturer. He says entrepreneurs should plan their affairs so that they are lining up funds "at least twelve months before you need it."

It's not easy to do. Entrepreneurs hard-pressed by immediate operating issues often overlook long-term financing strategies. But adopting a more proactive approach can help you build relationships with bank managers, investors or other financial partners, saving you time and money in the long run. If your company is caught short with a cash-flow problem, rescuers will be hard to find, and they'll be able to name their own price.

CHAPTER ELEVEN

HIRING, FIRING AND INSPIRING

"Treat employees as people of immense worth. Give them a vision of their potential."

Dave Loney, Eagle's Flight Creative
Training Excellence Inc.

PEOPLE: GREATEST ASSET, BIGGEST CHALLENGE

The dean of modern management gurus has a bone to pick with today's businesses. "All organizations say routinely, 'People are our greatest asset,'" Peter Drucker wrote in his 1995 book, *Managing in a Time of Great Change.** Yet, he noted, "very few practice what they preach, let alone truly believe it. Most still believe, though perhaps not consciously, what nineteenth-century employers believed. People need us more than we need them."

Every employee knows the profound truth of that statement, and yet there are exceptions, and none more prominent than the

---

* Peter Drucker, *Managing in a Time of Great Change*. (New York: Truman Talley Books/Dutton, 1995).

PROFIT 100. Canada's Fastest-Growing Companies subscribe wholeheartedly to the idea that their employees are the source of their success. In big businesses today, the usual object of study for management maestros such as Peter Drucker, value and competitive advantage have been built up over decades. Today their most important business assets are measurable ones, whether they be long-time monopoly status (think Bell Canada, TransCanada PipeLines, Rogers Cable); brand equity (think Molson, Nabisco or Procter & Gamble); a national charter to make money (consider the chartered banks); or millions of dollars tied up in factories, real estate, equipment or distribution systems. Smaller, fast-growth businesses don't have those assets to provide a long-term return and a cushion against incompetence or misfortune.

Canada's Fastest-Growing Companies owe their success to a good idea, well executed. But in today's competitive markets, good ideas don't last long by themselves. Companies that want to keep growing have no choice but to put their efforts into creating an organization that can spin off more good ideas, and can execute the best of them quickly, efficiently and with flair. Innovation and market savvy are the most important challenges these companies face, and these jobs can't exactly be done by traditional balance sheet assets such as buildings, equipment and goodwill. It's a task for creative, motivated, energetic people, and the companies that hire, motivate and develop these people most effectively are the growth leaders of tomorrow.

Raymond Simmons, CEO of **CRS Robotics Corp.** of Burlington, Ontario, sums up the challenge facing fast-growth companies today. "We want to grow this business to over $100 million in the next five years [from $21 million in 1996], and that means we need very qualified people," he says. "The market is there and capital is there, but we need to attract high-level, high-quality people. That will be our biggest challenge: getting the people and developing a culture and environment that motivates them and attracts them to the business."

A lot of his PROFIT 100 colleagues agree. When they were asked by entrepreneurship researcher Gene Luczkiw, for a 1995 study of growth entrepreneurs, to name the key issue facing their organizations, the majority of PROFIT 100 respondents picked "people issues." Finding the right people, and training and motivating them, constituted a more serious problem than (in declining order of importance) increasing global competitiveness, productivity, taxation, environmental regulations and government red tape.

TACKLING THE PEOPLE CHALLENGE

How do Canada's Fastest-Growing Companies tackle their greatest problem?

• They make human resources an important part of their operations strategy. Management at Toronto-based **KL Group**, for instance, holds regular meetings where they discuss the performance and career path for every one of their employees.

• They incorporate employee input and feedback in everything they do. BC-based **A.G. Professional Haircare Products Ltd.**, number five in 1996, hired a consultant to analyse the satisfaction of its fifty employees. It immediately acted on staff suggestions for an employee newsletter to provide more information on the company and where it was headed, for more employee-recognition programs, and for more opportunities for employees to try new or more varied tasks.

• They try to encourage and empower employees to greater performance through stimulating independent thinking, problem solving and decision making. "Whenever anyone asks me anything that shouldn't have come to me, the first thing I ask them is, 'What do you think?'" says Dean Whitford, president of **A1 Computers Ltd.** in Edmonton (1997). More often than not, he says, they already know what should be done. He likes to tell his twenty-one employees, "You knew the answer. Next time, you don't have to ask me; just trust your instincts."

• They constantly review compensation and motivational systems to ensure they attract and keep the best people. Computer integrator **Trump Systems Inc.**, of Bolton, Ontario, recently offered bonuses based on performance. "Our people are disciplined and work hard," says President Kevin Leach. "I wanted to reward their efforts with something on the table now. I want everyone who is here to retire here." To keep your best employees you must always keep changing and improving your incentive packages, says Leach. "If they feel taken for granted they might start looking, but if not they stay put."

• And they never forget their roots. Almost all the companies on the PROFIT 100 began as just one or two people with a good idea. They owe their success to individual achievement, not to inheritance or inertia. As a result, these entrepreneurs remain devout believers in the potential of the right individual to make a difference, to create value, and to transform a product, an organization or an entire industry.

THE FOUR BIG CHALLENGES

Entrepreneurs' solutions to their human resources problems tend to fall into four areas: recruiting; developing, training and motivating; compensation; and rooting out the occasional bad apple to keep the barrel from rotting. While many entrepreneurs admit they're not very good at the last step, most are quite proud of the time they have invested and the skills they have developed in hiring, inspiring and rewarding.

HIRING

Because they are growing so fast, PROFIT 100 entrepreneurs are in almost perpetual hire-mode. They seem to be always on the lookout for new talent and skills. In 1996 alone, the companies on the PROFIT 100 created 4,089 new jobs. In other words, they each hired, on average, forty new staff members — or nearly one new employee a week.

What are they looking for? There's no question. In his 1995 growth company study, researcher Gene Luczkiw of the Institute for Enterprise Education in Thorold, Ontario, asked forty PROFIT 100 entrepreneurs what characteristics they considered most important in filling their human-resource needs: attitude, knowledge or skills. The hands-down winner was attitude, with 80% of the vote. Far behind were knowledge, at 5%, and skills, at 3%.

HOW DO YOU GET A JOB WITH A PROFIT 100 COMPANY?

According to the 1995 study by Gene Luczkiw, these are the attributes PROFIT 100 entrepreneurs look for most in new employees:

ATTITUDE:
- motivation
- initiative
- sense of responsibility
- determination/perseverance

(Less important are empathy and understanding for others, confidence and receptivity to change.)

KNOWLEDGE:
- knowledge of subject
- ability to find and use information
- ability to manage projects

(Less important are business or economic knowledge.)

SKILLS:
- communications and interpersonal skills
- problem-solving ability
- creativity
- ability to work as part of a team

(Less important are literacy, ability to plan, ability to negotiate.)

The Importance of Attitude

These survey findings might come as a bit of surprise, given the supposed growth of today's information economy and the importance of knowledge workers. But PROFIT 100 leaders remained adamant that they could teach their employees most of what they need to know. More important was their attitude—their ability to work hard, to understand the company's mission and to accept the entrepreneur's work motivation as their own. Not quite sharing those sentiments are several high-tech companies on the PROFIT 100 who need qualified software developers who can get to work the same day they start. Having pretty much scoured the country for qualified programmers, ambitious

PROFIT 100 companies such as **Oasis Technology** are now looking to India or the Philippines to supply their software needs.

The champion of attitude-based hiring is Terry Maxwell, president of **SLP Automotive Canada** in Lachine, Quebec (1997). When his car-repair business won a contract to upgrade hot-off-the-assembly-line General Motors Camaros and Firebirds into higher-performance sports cars, he needed help fast. His solution was to hire young, inexperienced people who made up for their lack of experience with a sense of responsibility and a work ethic equal to his own.

"I like to get young apprentices who say 'I want to work,' and don't ask about the pay," says Maxwell. When he had to hire more than 100 people to keep pace with production increases in 1996, he called government employment offices and said, "Send us bodies. We can train them." Replacing the hood, wheels, exhaust systems and other components on each car is skilled work, but, "you don't have to be skilled to learn it," he says. "You need your heart and your head in the right place."

Maxwell's results have been impressive. Of SLP's twenty-four managers, all but three have been promoted from within. And in the process of qualifying for ISO 9000 quality certification in early 1996, he says, two ISO consultants told him how impressed they were with the "unreal" amount of employee loyalty, to both Maxwell and the company. "Employees really believe I'm doing what's best for them and the company."

Like most PROFIT 100 companies, including SLP, **New Systems Solutions Inc.**, an Ottawa computer consultant, believes in hiring based on word of mouth, referrals and recommendations. It's a "virtuous" circle, says President Mark Quigg. If you hire the best people and make your shop a good place to work, he says, word will get around and more good people will want to join you. "Quality people attract quality people," he says.

FOUR QUESTIONS TO ASK *YOURSELF* WHEN YOU'RE INTERVIEWING

Attitude is a key consideration when hiring for any job, but it's especially important when the candidate will be representing your company to the outside world. You want character and integrity, but neither is usually evident from a résumé. To help you separate the doers from the talkers, you can learn from construction-equipment dealer William Trainer, president of **Trainer Brothers Equipment Services Inc.** in Langley, BC. He offers four examples of the type of questions you should ask yourself when interviewing candidates for sales or management positions:

- "Would I trust this person with my money?"
- "Does he or she show real enthusiasm?"
- "Is he or she for real, or is this a fake persona?"
- "Is this the kind of person I'd ask over for dinner?"

Senior Hires

While many PROFIT 100 entrepreneurs are happy hiring young and inexperienced people for production or entry-level positions, they take a different approach to filling their management needs. As their companies grow they know they need higher and higher levels of skills in operations, finance, marketing and sales. Particularly tested is a young company's commitment to promoting from within. But the smartest and most far-sighted of PROFIT 100 entrepreneurs understand that the future of the company cannot be entrusted to amateurs, so they do their best to recruit high quality, professional help.

At **KL Group**, President Greg Kiessling filled out his management team with experienced professionals in sales, finance and planning. The key is to fill in the gaps — the things you and your current management team either don't know how to do or don't want to do — with experienced people who have been trained for just such an opportunity. Indeed, one of the mantras of the PROFIT 100 entrepreneurs is the boast that, "I like to hire people who are better than I am."

It's hard for some people to admit that they don't know everything there is to know about running their company, and to hire people with different skill sets who will forge their own power base in the company. But it's all a part of making the leap from upstart start-up to corporate maturity.

"The only way to grow this company is to bring in people who are smarter than me to help run it," says Lorne Cherry, president of **L.E. Cherry & Associates** (1997), a mail-order computer dealer in

Markham, Ontario. He knows his role as his company passes the $2-million mark in sales. "I can be the driver and motivator, but one person can't do it all." His first order of business was to hire a controller to help keep costs in line.

TRAINING, DEVELOPING AND MOTIVATING

Once you've assembled a staff, the old techniques of mushroom management — leave them in the dark and buried in fertilizer — no longer apply. Your company depends on a spirited, motivated workforce that will put their best into everything they do. You don't own them, you owe them, warns Peter Drucker in his book, *Managing in a Time of Great Change*. "Organizations have to market membership as much as they market products and services — and perhaps more. They have to attract people, hold people, recognize and reward people, motivate people, and serve and satisfy people." Because your best workers have so many other options, he says, management's job today, "is not to command. It is to inspire."

PROFIT 100 leaders agree that the future of their organizations hinges on their ability to provide a stimulating and rewarding environment for their staff. "You have to take care of your employees," says Mark Diamond, co-founder of **Gage Applied Sciences Inc.** (1995-97), a Montreal producer of high-performance PC accessories. "You have to create a sense of fun, challenge and participation." Turn that off, he warns, "and your product will disintegrate over time."

Indeed, most PROFIT 100 entrepreneurs try to address all three of those concerns in the workplace: fun, challenge and participation. **KL Group** offers a foosball table for building teamwork and relieving stress; similarly, the offices of **L.E. Cherry & Associates** boast a pinball machine; while **Vantage Securities** installed a pool table as the centrepiece of its new office in Vancouver.

As for challenge, Allan Millman, president of **Fantom Technologies Inc.** in Welland, Ontario, sees that as an implicit component of the new type of job contract that information-age companies have with their employees. "We have a productive and motivated group of people who are challenged to grow personally," he says. "I say to them that I can't guarantee employment, but I can guarantee employability. So that when they leave here, they've improved their skill sets and knowledge; I believe in that and I think they appreciate that." As a result, Fantom employees are encouraged to pursue their interests and learn new skills, and to speak out and push back if they disagree with management decisions. "We encourage conflict and opinion as a positive business tool," says Millman. "We hold people accountable for expressing concrete viewpoints. If you disagree with your boss you have a responsibility to say why."

"Corporate culture" plays a major role in PROFIT 100 companies' attempts to retain and motivate employees. Flat hierarchies, fast decision making, improved communications and employee empowerment are all part of the mix. The point is to *prove* that employees are the important asset that management likes to claim they are. Calgary software developer **Merak Projects Ltd.** (1994-96) had an innovative way of demonstrating just that. When it won a Canada Award for Excellence, it sent two rank and file staff members, not its head honchos, onto the stage in Ottawa to accept the award. The message was, we're a team.

In a similar vein, **Transpro Freight Systems** in Mississauga, Ontario, planned its new office with people in mind, furnishing it with more employee-friendly equipment such as chairs with lumbar supports and $160 headsets that make telephone work less straining. President Frank Prosia says the company tries to ignore hierarchy and rank. Its business cards don't carry employees' titles. "We give everyone the opportunity to be whatever they want," he says. Doesn't that just confuse things? Prosia says no: "No one is pigeonholed, there are no power-play struggles, everyone gets to earn respect."

Besides its foosball table, **KL Group** offers a combination of monetary and "cultural" perks to create a satisfying and fulfilling workplace. "In a small high-tech company people can get job offers tomorrow, so it has to be a place where they're happy and having fun," says President Greg Kiessling. KL fosters a laid-back atmosphere, no dress code, and a funky downtown address in a renovated warehouse. The company finds any reason it can to celebrate, with a summer party on a sailboat, a Christmas party, and more parties whenever a major new product ships. In addition, the firm's engineering staff, probably the company's most valuable group, get one all-expense-paid seminar per year anywhere in North America. "They try to pick one in Hawaii," says Kiessling.

In Winnipeg, surprise seems the order of the day at **Online Business Systems** (1995-97). In addition to offering staff three personal days a year to do whatever they want, it also offers surprise bonuses and dinners. And recently it pulled a fast one when three staff wanted to take their wives along to a conference in Florida, but didn't have the ready cash. They asked if the company could cover the extra airfare and hotel costs, which they would repay over time. "We said sure," says President Charles Loewen. But as they boarded the plane the staff members were given vouchers telling them they wouldn't have to pay the extra costs. Such generosity isn't altruistic, of course. Like other PROFIT 100 companies, Online needs its workforce motivated and ready to work everyday. "Our next big challenge is to keep the enthusiasm and drive of the whole team going as we continue to evolve and grow in an ever changing world," says Loewen. "We'll do it with lots of planning, lots of teamwork and lots of hard work — and some surprises."

Getting To Know All About You

To cement better relations with their employees, a number of PROFIT 100 companies do surveys and studies to find out what staff needs are not being met. The results can surprise you. Employees want more than just more money or time off.

When **CRS Robotics** conducted an employee survey, it found that staff wanted a better program for setting employee objectives and measuring their performance against those goals. Now, says President Raymond Simmons, CRS has a performance evaluation and development program in which all employees establish personal and career goals for themselves at the beginning of each year, and then receive bonuses for meeting their performance targets. Even Simmons participates, negotiating his goals and objectives with the board of directors. The system has worked out much better than Simmons ever expected. "We thought it would be enormously bureaucratic, but the benefits have been overwhelming," he says. "It's been a terrific communications tool, and it got people focused."

PROFIT 100 In Toronto, **Endpoint Research Ltd.** (1997) hired a human resources consultant for a full year to conduct psychological profiles of all forty employees. The point, says President Wendy Porter, was to break down communications barriers and get people working better together by helping them analyse the way they think and behave. The results were released to each employee, who could decide whether or not to share them with his or her co-workers. "It increases self-awareness and from that a confidence to deal with other people," says Porter. And where results were released, they have aided employees in putting together more effective teams. If a project requires someone who is good at follow-through, for instance, the test results help identify appropriate team members.

Getting the most out of its people is essential to Endpoint, which manages clinical trials for pharmaceutical and biotech companies. "The only asset I have is the people and their skill sets," says Porter. She tries to create a strong learning environment, to keep her well-educated employees learning and eager to stay. "I don't want to be a training ground for a competitor." Porter also works hard to keep employees in the loop so they feel at home and in touch with the company, even the twenty out-of-towners who work out of their homes in cities across Canada. She keeps in touch via e-mail and flies the whole group to Toronto three times a year. "We have to keep the humanness," she says. "Our employees are people-oriented, they can't feel isolated. I lose them when they feel isolated." Porter says the consultant has helped a lot with her human-resource development, and since he is semi-retired, his services haven't broken the bank. "There's a real science to human resources," she says, "but it doesn't have to cost a fortune."

Training Tools

Another non-monetary motivational tool is employee training. Enlightened entrepreneurs have found that the proper training program can not only boost employee skills, but act as a prized benefit or incentive. For some employees training is the route to new skills, a better job and more money. But to many others, especially where training funds are used not so much for on-the-job skills training but a variety of educational purposes, it's a sign that the company cares, and is willing to invest money in their future.

A 1994 StatsCan study of 1,480 growth firms found that 53% offered their employees training. The PROFIT 100 survey, which represents the veritable tip of the iceberg when it comes to growth companies, found an even greater commitment: Eighty-one of Canada's 100 Fastest-Growing Companies invest in employee training. In fact, the amount they spend on training has grown consistently over the six years that PROFIT has researched that statistic, to the point where PROFIT 100 companies now spend a full 1.8% of revenues upgrading the skills of their employees.

Investing in the Future

Percentage of revenues spent on training by PROFIT 100 companies

Year	%
1992	0.8
1993	0.7
1994	1.0
1995	1.1
1996	1.2
1997	1.8

One of the PROFIT 100's most industrious trainers is **Unique Systems Corp.** (1997), a Calgary-based systems integrator specializing in oil and gas, manufacturing and telecommunications. Unique devotes 15% of revenues to employee training as part of a package of perks designed to appeal to young, enthusiastic technical employees. Says President Gary Nevison, "We don't pay the most, but they get lots of training, and it's fun to work here. We have leading-edge technology, and to a techie, that's a turn-on."

Unique has prided itself on its ability to recommend, supply, install and maintain the most effective and sophisticated information systems for its corporate clients. Training teaches staff more about selling and being client-focused, and familiarizes them with the latest equipment and software. "You need to be very cognizant of technology changes," says Nevison. "One year in technology is almost like a dog year, it's constantly changing and adapting." He says ongoing training is especially important since business itself is changing so fast. His work obviously paid off. Not only did Unique Systems grow 1,284% from 1991 to 1996, but in early 1997 the company was bought out by GE Capital. Nevison attributes the company's success to its well trained staff and customer-service orientation. "We had a five-year business plan, but we got through it in a year and a half."

REWARDS

All sharp business people know that employees are motivated more by non-monetary factors such as respect and encouragement than by cash. But man does not live by empowerment alone, so PROFIT 100 entrepreneurs work hard to create total compensation and reward systems that motivate employees without breaking the bank.

At **Tescor Energy Services** in North York, Ontario (1996-97), management offers a combination of money and "soft" benefits to create an open and supportive climate for its seventy-five employees. It pays above-average wages for its industry, offers a generous benefits program featuring medical and dental coverage, pensions and flexible hours. Tescor reserves a portion of its profits for a performance incentive plan, which pays employees a bonus for meeting team and individual goals, and it also offers an employee share-ownership plan.

Yet it is the softer benefits that are stressed by chief administrative officer Gary Johnson. He planned Tescor's move into a new office in 1997 to reflect the company's values, from environmental stewardship to "affirmation of people's value," through more ergonomic furnishings and layouts that stress informal gathering areas and "community-building." "We work well as a business and a community," says Johnson. "Life is short and we have the ability to make a positive impact through what we do." Tescor stresses open communications, whether that means disclosing financial statements to all staff quarterly, or the fact that the company's three most senior executives have dividers instead of offices. "It's very open," says Johnson. "Everyone can see each other, and we have the same kind of furniture as everyone else." He admits there are risks to such open-book leadership, but says there is more to gain than to lose. "Our hierarchy is as flat and open as you can squish it."

Alnoor Sheriff believes that one of his most important moves as president of **Shikatronics Inc.** of La Prairie, Quebec, was to reward his fifty employees with a blockbuster company gathering once or twice a year. At Christmas 1996, Shikatronics, a computer-memory producer that ranked second on the 1997 PROFIT 100, booked all its employees into a ski resort at Mont Tremblant for food, drinks and fun. "We were supposed to go to the Bahamas," says Sheriff, "but 60% of employees voted no. It was Christmas and they wanted to stay with family." Next time, he says, the firm will go south. "We do it as a thank-you to staff and to build morale." That bonus comes on top of Shikatronics' established profit-sharing plan, which is paid every month. "Immediate reward is very important," says Sheriff. "It came by request from our managers, and it's really working."

Shikatronics and Tescor are not alone in putting cash on the line as a way to thank and continue to motivate their best people. Some 17% of the companies on the PROFIT 100 offered some sort of profit-sharing program, while 26% offered employees stock options or share-purchase plans. Beyond that, PROFIT 100 companies engage in a riot of creative perks, benefits and off-the-wall incentives to reward, reassure and retain their employees. Kevin Fitzgerald, president of **Aurora Microsystems** (1996-97) in Copper Cliff, Ontario, puts the challenge plainly. All seven staff members have both salaries and incentive plans customized to their jobs, he says. "We offer an incentive to perform better, because these days just getting to keep your job isn't incentive enough."

PIZZA, PERKS, PROFIT-SHARING

How do PROFIT 100 companies reward their people? In a nutshell, here are some of the miscellaneous and sundry perks PROFIT 100 entrepreneurs have offered. How many of them would work in your office?

- Pizza parties or a free lunch in the office to celebrate a new order or contract, a day off on your birthday, bonuses to non-sales employees for referrals that result in sales, "lunch and learn seminars" for informal on-the-job training, a new-baby bonus, best monthly performance awards in different departments of the company, "best employee suggestion" awards, full access to company library with over 100 magazine subscriptions, employee purchase plans for computers or accessories: **Akran Systems Ltd.**, Ottawa (1996).

- Profit-sharing, share ownership for key personnel (private company), higher than average pay scale, flex-hours, cash bonuses amounting to 20% of net profits: **Datalog Technology Inc.**, Calgary (1996-97).

- Stock-ownership plans (public company), stock-option plans, flex-time, above-average vacation time, extended out-of-country health coverage, employer contributions to group RRSP, casual atmosphere: **Andyne Computing Ltd.**, Kingston, Ontario (1994-97).

- Group insurance, life-medical-dental-disability coverage, pension plan, above-average pay levels, group activities such as hiking days and ski trips, off-site weekend retreat every six months: **Systèmes Zenon Inc.**, Longueuil, Quebec (1995-97).

- Pay 10% to 20% above industry average, flex-hours and flexible regarding time off, occasional big event such as twenty-person fishing trip: **Logical Design Inc.**, Richmond Hill, Ontario (1996-97).

- Share-purchase plan (before and after going public), incentive plan for new employees to buy in, profit-sharing, above-average pay, casual days, subsidized training even if not job-related, "lots of social events": **CRS Robotics Corp.**, Burlington, Ontario (1990, 1992, 1996-97).

- Employee stock options (public company), performance bonus, above-average salaries and vacation time, medical/dental coverage, flex-hours, subsidized health-club memberships (up to $400 a year), paid training courses, showers in office (for employees who jog or ride bikes), days off for work with local charities: **Fulcrum Technologies Inc.**, Ottawa (1994-97).

FIRING

There's another element to any human-resource policy that can't be ignored: weeding the garden once in a while. When asked to name their biggest management weakness, a surprising number of PROFIT 100 leaders have said they are too soft on people. Many say their biggest mistake was not pulling the plug on bad performers or bad attitudes soon enough. Even Terry Maxwell, the stock-car racer who now builds sports cars for GM and refuses to hire people who ask about the pay, admits that he's no good at firing people. "I'm too soft-hearted," he says. "It's great that my managers do it now, so I don't have to do it any more."

Putting off the inevitable can be a deadly mistake in small, growing companies built on teamwork and attitude. Failure to eliminate one bad apple will not only permit the rot to continue, it actively encourages further decay; morale among other team members declines as they perceive management's inability to deal with the problem. In admitting their errors, some PROFIT 100 entrepreneurs confess they have often handed off the dirty work to others. Whether you do it yourself or through others, the important thing is that it must be done. Proactive firing is at least as important as creative hiring and inspiring.

At **PointOne Graphics Inc.** (1997) in Toronto, President Dennis Low says some of his best management talents relate to people skills. "I'm good at getting everyone to pull together as a team, and I break the ice when it's really busy and people are going crazy." But he says the dark side is that, "sometimes I'm a little lenient. I give people too many chances. I've been burned by former employees that I placed a lot of trust in." He says he's just going to have to work on that aspect of his character. "I don't want to change my personality, but sometimes you have to."

"One bad weed can ruin your garden or negatively influence your office," notes Allan R. Ward, executive vice-president of **Norris Transport Ltd.**, a four-time PROFIT 100 company (1993-96). Continuing his gardening metaphor, he says, "a bad attitude can spread like a weed, choking off the healthy growth of the people who want to succeed." His advice is to get your hands dirty if you must, but root out the weeds as early as possible — before they crowd out and demotivate the rest of your carefully tended garden.

SYSTEMS AND STRATEGIES

Putting It All Together

"Business is about mastering a comprehensive skill set and the disciplines needed to succeed."

Jeff Hunt, Canway Ltd.

YA GOTTA HAVE A SYSTEM

Experiencing growth, or even surviving it, is not the same as mastering it. For the most part the companies on the PROFIT 100, having grown at least 600% in five years, have achieved greater success than they ever imagined. But now the hard part begins.

In the early years of a growth company, a good product, solid marketing plan and competent execution will go a long way. For a company that wants to hold on to its gains, however, or even continue growing, tactical excellence is no longer enough. Growth transforms an organization as inexorably as it changes the job of the founding entrepreneur. The organization itself must make the leap from product-driven entrepreneurial organization to strategy-driven professional corporation. And the entrepreneur who started the company on a whim and a credit card must become a visionary executive who operates through mentoring and leadership rather than hands-on operation and periodic dictates. Mastering this evolution — "Barbarians to Bureaucrats," in the memorable phrasing of a classic book on business life cycles by Lawrence M. Miller* — determines whether an entrepreneurial company will continue to succeed, and whether the founder is indeed the right person to carry it forward into its new, mature era.

At the time PROFIT published its 1997 PROFIT 100 in June 1997, 89% of the companies on that list were still being run by a founder or co-founder. Eleven companies had made the transition to "professional management" — almost invariably, executives with senior-level experience at other companies. In most cases, they were recruited to take over the corporate reins. In a few cases, they were brought in to beef up the management ranks and ended up being asked to take charge. In other words, some outsiders rose to the top because the founder or founders realized they lacked the right stuff to run the larger, more corporate entity. Others were put in charge by minority shareholders or directors after they determined it was time for the founder to move along or be kicked upstairs.

Whether the transition is voluntary or not, it is essential that entrepreneurs realize there is no shame in reaching the limit of their expertise and abilities. Everyone has limits. As Stanley Samole said regarding his selling of **Fidelity Electronics Ltd.** of Mississauga, Ontario (1992-95), one of only five companies ever to make the PROFIT 100 five years in a row, "I'd be lying if I said I knew everything there was to know about running a $50-million company."

Indeed, that 89 founders on the 1997 PROFIT 100 have survived so long is remarkable in itself. In 1991, the companies on the 1997 PROFIT 100 averaged sales of less than $2.7 million, and a payroll of only twenty-eight people each. As that's an average, many companies were much smaller than that, some of them just two- or three-person shops grossing under $200,000 a

---

* Lawrence M. Miller, *Barbarians to Bureaucrats: Corporate Life Cycle Strategies.* (Atlanta: Miller Howard Consulting Group Inc., 1989).

year. By 1997, these companies averaged sales of $41.7 million and 260 employees. The task of managing organizations of such different sizes demands two quite different sets of skills.

A Tale of Two Companies

Here are the jobs you need to do to run a:

$2-million company	$25-million company
Day-to-day operations	Long-term planning
Hands-on sales	Strategist
Develop market positioning	Create a vision of where the organization is going and what it can be
Seek financing	Scout acquisitions and strategic partners
Quality control	Guardian of company's values
Recruitment	Morale officer
Production supervisor	Question or review all company's products and processes
Liaise with accountant, banker	Set financing strategy
Conduct employee reviews	Assume responsibility for systems and training that help employees avoid mistakes and encourage creative problem solving
Clean the toilet, order supplies and answer phones when necessary	Media, investor relations
Take the heat when things go wrong	Take the heat if things go wrong

Clearly, running a bigger organization requires not just a revamped job description but a whole new set of skills, and a different attitude towards the concept of what actually constitutes work. Making the jump from barbarian with a mission to bureaucrat with a vision is a difficult transition for anyone to make. But it's pretty much impossible without a carefully planned set of structures and systems that help your business evolve from a one-person show to a successful, sustainable organization that is capable of continuing, and indeed possibly thriving, without its founder at the helm day-to-day. It's not uncommon for entrepreneurs to feel left out and perhaps a bit at a loss as they see their companies learn to adapt and grow without them, just as parents feel a twinge of sadness when their child goes off to school for the first time.

"At first it's hard to let go," says Wendy Porter, president of Toronto-based **Endpoint Research Ltd.** "I used to do it all myself." As her clinical-trial-management company surpassed $2 million and then $3 million in sales, Porter learned to delegate. She created a five-person management team to encourage better decision making, and now brings all personnel and business-related issues to the group. She has even learned to hand off sales, although as she confesses, "the first time it was hard to send someone on a sales call by themselves."

"Everyone who starts their own business is a control freak at the beginning," says Alex Habrich of **Lemire & Habrich Consultants Inc.**, a $20-million computer-aided-manufacturing consultancy in Montreal. "My biggest mistake was not delegating enough authority at the beginning. You want to know everything, but you just can't do that any more as the company grows." But there's a trade-off, Habrich notes. While hands-on operators lay awake nights, second-guessing whether or not a particular job got done, delegators sleep more soundly, "because they can feel comfortable that the job got executed."

In the long run, moving on and letting go helps the entrepreneur grow as well as the organization. As a leader, your job is to learn and to communicate, which can be much more fulfilling than slaving on the loading dock to get the last delivery out on Christmas Eve.

THEORIES OF EVOLUTION

In moving out of their one-man-band phase, growing companies need to adopt policies and systems that let them access and develop ongoing expertise in all the disciplines of business: operations, finance, purchasing, sales, marketing, customer service, technology, recruitment, training, compensation, promotion, intellectual property, security, communications, and more. How do you get started, and then master all these areas? Examples from 1997 PROFIT 100 companies illustrate a five-step program:

> ### A FIVE-STEP PROGRAM FOR PULLING IT ALL TOGETHER
>
> 1. Recognize the problem.
> 2. Hire experts to impose order on chaos.
> 3. Adopt systems.
> 4. Restructure for better results.
> 5. Increase exposure to professional expertise.

Recognize the Problem

Don't bury your head in the sand. Acknowledge what bankers and investors and management consultants take for granted, that most entrepreneurs — as professional renegades who are happier kicking in doors than adjusting doorknobs — are unfit to run big, professional organizations. Only when you admit this to yourself do you stand a chance of becoming an exception to the rule.

Once you have acknowledged the problem, you can work on improving your own abilities as a manager and executive (get used to that word). Shoring up their own management weaknesses and upgrading their executive and leadership skills constitute the most important job for any entrepreneurs who would like to think they've got a job for life.

PROFIT 100 **KL Group**'s Greg Kiessling, a software developer and marketer whose unheralded start-up business boasted international sales of $9 million and a staff of sixty by the end of 1996, is one entrepreneur who would like to stay on top as his company grows. His chances for success look good. He has been quick to surround himself with good people and delegate his tasks one by one. "I haven't managed a company this size in my life," he admits. "I don't have the management skills to run a medium-sized company." But by keeping his eyes open to the problem, he's probably halfway there. "I pick up skills through thinking, talking, watching and getting mentors," says Kiessling. "Everything is common sense, but I have to be focusing on it all the time."

At **Image Club Graphics**, a two-time PROFIT 100 company in Calgary, President Brad Zumwalt is under extra pressure. Not only is the company a growth leader, but in the mid-1990s it was acquired by US software powerhouse Adobe Systems Inc. While Adobe has tried to preserve Image Club's unique culture and environment, Zumwalt left nothing to chance, "I left school to join this company, and now I'm back in school taking MBA courses."

Hire Experts to Impose Order on Chaos

It's always hard to share the wealth, but most PROFIT 100 entrepreneurs recognize that the best tactic is to increase the size of the pie by bringing in top people with complementary skills and a record of achieving results. As president of **Canned Heat Marketing Inc.**, the number two company in 1994, gas fireplace distributor Brian Richards put it best: "I want to surround myself with people who are used to more zeroes on the end than I am."

Where do you find the good people you need? Most PROFIT 100 companies count on friends, former acquaintances and personal recommendations. At **KL Group**, Kiessling hired Deric Moilliet, a former colleague at Sun Microsystems, as vice-president of sales. Paul Davis, president of **Accu-Rate Foreign Exchange**, PROFIT's number one company in 1994, hired his bank manager to guard the company's finances after they both had been commiserating about the problems of finding skilled help.

Adopt Systems

The most important thing entrepreneurial companies can do to act more like big corporations is to adopt policies and reporting systems that turn seat-of-the-pants organizations into smooth-running information factories. The very phrase "monthly reports" strikes fear into many entrepreneurs' hearts, but there's no escape. As leaders phase out of day-to-day decision making, they need to develop standards, measures and reporting mechanisms that reflect exactly what is going on in the company at any given moment.

PROFIT 100 With his advanced computer manufacturing company jumping from sales of $2.5 million in 1991 to $33 million in 1996, Michel Gareau of **Teknor Industrial Computers Inc.** of Boisbriand, Quebec, had no problem naming his most effective management decision. It was isolating five specific management reports and having them e-mailed to him every day, no matter where in the world he might be.

PROFIT 100 Similarly, **Fantom Technologies Inc.** in Welland, Ontario, installed a state-of-the-art computerized ordering and planning system that allows instant monitoring of all key aspects of the company, from sales and orders to payments and cash flow.

But it's not just financial systems that are important. Written policies, procedures and strategy statements are equally vital to growing organizations, to guide them as they continually move into new markets and indoctrinate new employees. While only forty-four of the companies on the 1997 PROFIT 100 said they had a business plan when they started out, by 1997 a full seventy-nine of them had a written business plan. And most of them said they were revisiting and revising their plans regularly, as market shifts required.

PROFIT 100 Faical Farhat of **Aliments Fontaine Santé Inc.** of Montreal says his company, although founded in 1985, only recently adopted a business plan. With sales reaching $6 million in 1996, he said, "to control our growth and to be more focused, we felt we needed a more focused plan."

PROFIT 100 At **Andyne Computing Ltd.** in Kingston, Ontario, President Cameron Thompson says the company's once-unwritten business plan has been supplanted by an annual strategic planning review and an operating plan that is updated regularly once a month.

Operational systems are also in need of overhaul as companies grow. At **Just Kid'n Children's Wear** in Langley, BC, President Kelly Cahill identified setting up new cash controls and tighter production systems as his next priorities.

And while **Yogen Früz World-Wide Inc.** of Markham, Ontario, run by three bothers the oldest of whom is just thirty-two, would appear to be a business built on fun and pleasure, Executive Vice-President Aaron Serruya attributes much of the company's success to uncompromising management systems. "In taste we're comparable with our competitors, but the most important thing is control of theft," says Serruya. Through strict measurement and portion control, he says, "we have zero waste. We never throw anything away."

In business today, the ultimate in systems control are the ISO 9000 programs geared to meeting international quality standards. Companies operating under ISO 9000 must meet rigid production and performance standards. The standards don't actually relate to qualitative elements, but to a company's ability to regulate its inputs and produce consistent output, time after time. In 1996, 31 PROFIT 100 companies reported they had instituted ISO 9000, while many more were considering getting involved.

"It's the trend of the future," says Mike Lee of **Leetwo Metal Inc.** in Pointe-Claire, Quebec. "ISO doesn't mean you're making a better product, just that the process is consistent: the lines of process are clearly defined and delineated." He says his eighty-five employees have become more attentive to what they're doing since Leetwo started the ISO process. "It has created tons of paperwork, but employees understand the process and what is expected of them better than ever before," he says. "Customers demand ISO now, and Leetwo would be perceived very differently without it."

Restructure for Better Results

As companies grow, they often find they need new management structures to enable them to meet the new demands of their size and their markets. Sometimes sole proprietorships become partnerships, and sometimes cooperative partnerships need to turn into more authoritative hierarchies.

Iris Power Engineering Inc. of Toronto bit the bullet in 1996, when the four founding partners, three of them engineers, decided to abandon the idea of a management committee that arrived at every decision consultatively. "We managed well that way for a while, but as we get bigger that structure doesn't work," says President Resi Zarb. To obtain more focused strategic thinking and faster decisions, the four partners decided to defer to a president — and appointed Zarb, the sole non-engineer, to the position. "It's weird," she admits, going from collegial joint decision making — which often meant that the most persuasive argument won out, whether or not the decision was right — to the more traditional executive model. Among other things, she's now her husband's boss, although so far, she says, "it seems fine."

Increase Exposure to Professional Expertise

While hiring more professional managers and executives is a key way to acquire additional expertise in systems and standards, you don't always have to buy that resource. You can also rent it, or even borrow it.

Similarly, special effects whiz John Gajdecki of Toronto-based **Gajdec-ki Visual Effects** says his $2.8-million company is now at "that critical stage where we have to make the transition from a mom and pop operation, which is me, to a larger organization that has to function more smoothly." Until now, he says, "we've operated according to the whims and desires of the people who work here." Now he intends to appoint a board of directors that will bring order and controlled growth to operations and strategy.

DIRECTION AND DISTANCE

Of course, when it comes to imposing standards and order on your company, not everyone gets it right the first time. Andrew Campbell, a management consultant in Oakville, Ontario, spent some time interviewing companies on the 1993 PROFIT 100 list to try to figure out what made them successful. He found that even Canada's growth leaders were at varying stages of maturity as far as systems and strategies were concerned. "My tour was exciting and eye-opening," Campbell wrote for the June 1994 issue of PROFIT:

ANDREW CAMPBELL ON SYSTEMS
AND STRATEGIES OF PROFIT 100 COMPANIES

I saw companies where employees shared a single vision and a commitment to succeed, and others where no one on the shop floor would meet the president's gaze. There were companies confidently riding the crest of the Age Wave and the Quality Wave, and others visibly rudderless or sinking. Clearly, fast growth brings its own set of problems. So the focus of my study became not just how these firms got where they are, but whether they have the smarts and the structures to stay the course.

At one high-tech company I found a raft of problems. Stymied by high overheads as they mushroomed to 100 employees, they were experiencing serious cash-flow problems. There was tension among the shareholders. Their growth was exciting, but it was testing the full breadth of their skills. Yet the problems they faced were typical of those that confront every growth company:

- **Poor communication.** The company faced growing employee discontent, high staff turnover and new employees who received poor orientation to the company.

- **Unclear structure.** There was duplication of management, confusion over who reported to whom, and questions about what constituted a job well done. Employee performance suffered.

- **Inadequate policies, procedures and systems.** Personnel policies and computer systems that worked fine when the company was small had started to fail. It was time to upgrade.

- **Weak controls.** There was no formalized capital budget, operating budget or business plan. Management did not know what was going on. And this made the company's bankers reluctant to finance the cash-flow problem.

- **No training.** Skimping on staff training had led to weak middle management, and could derail future development.

How to Cope With Growing Pains

Campbell had seen enough. He refocused his study to find out how successful companies cope with growing pains. Based on his decade of consulting experience with growing companies, he developed questionnaires to probe three key areas: organization, culture, and owner's personality.

Organization

The Growth Index assessed five disciplines generally under stress in any growing company: communications, structure, controls, systems and training. Sample questions: Is there an organization chart which is known to all? Are there departmental meetings that occur at least monthly? Do the statements provide meaningful management information? Is the incentive system appropriate for the structure? Are performance appraisals regularly prepared?

Culture

The Culture Index probed the vision of each organization (which Campbell dubbed "direction") and its ability to convert that vision into reality (dubbed "distance"). It inquired into whether a company has a general philosophy statement that tells employees what is expected of them; offers employees training and testing that lets them fully explore opportunities for learning new skills; emphasizes delegation of authority; pays for performance, not just loyalty; and holds people accountable for results.

Owner's Personality

The Personality Index examined the individual attitudes of company leaders, and how they relate to others. Typical of the twenty questions, participants were asked to agree or disagree with statements such as: "I like to start and finish on time and have a tendency to become angry at those who do not"; "I like to adhere to a fixed agenda"; "I consider myself a very confident and secure person who has no fear of failure"; and "I enjoy a good argument and tend to be aggressive in making a point."

Index Survey Results

For the **Growth Index**, the results of Campbell's study were mixed. Ten percent of entrepreneurs were rated very good and 57% were good to satisfactory. Campbell concluded that PROF-IT 100 entrepreneurs turned out to be "the sort of people you want on your side in tough times: market-savvy, go-for-gold, action-oriented street-fighters." But 33% showed danger signals, signs they were neglecting the fundamentals of systems and procedures and controls. Having gotten where they were on the strength of their personalities and entrepreneurial ideas, they found their personal assets dissipating in their ever-growing organizations. Many felt they were no longer in control, a problem often compounded by their reluctance to delegate.

For the **Culture Index**, Campbell found most organizations scored better for direction than for distance. They had strong leadership vision, but only a moderately healthy support system. PROFIT 100 leaders proved good at defining the direction in which they were going and raising expectations of all employees to generate excellent performance. The best also had systems to help their people go the distance and convert the vision into reality. As a general conclusion, Campbell reported, "the better that staff were informed and trained, and the more plans and systems were in place to help them get the job done, the more likely these companies were to sustain their fast growth."

For the **Personality Index**, Campbell found that PROFIT 100 executives tended to be sales and marketing-driven, and all displayed a high receptivity to change. That's a powerful combination, but he also found that in some cases egos got in the way of success. "There was an inverse correlation between companies that were doing well and entrepreneurs whose impatience and dominant personalities scored well above average on the 'relating' scale. These were the people who still thought they knew it all. Such personalities left a trail of red flags in their wake: administrative chaos, problems in production, no clear policies and procedures, and, often, problems in their home life. Not surprisingly, these individuals were usually the hardest to get in to see — and the least interested in seeking outside help."

> Clearly, the way to growth is to abandon ego, work on your strengths, and seek help in doing what you can't, don't want to, or don't have time to do any more.

MANAGEMENT

Fortunately, more recent classes of PROFIT 100 entrepreneurs seem to recognize their management and structural deficiencies.

When asked to identify their next challenges, they pointed more often to management issues that needed tightening than to any other challenge.

The Next Big Challenge

Expansion into new geographic markets (mostly foreign markets, especially US)	23
New products	13
More sophisticated structures and systems (e.g., grow infrastructure and organization on par with demand; add senior management; refine business systems; raise management team standards)	12
Improve profits, cash flow and capital	9
Marketing	8
Sales targets (e.g., reach $50 million in sales)	7
Personnel issues, such as improved training	5
Production issues	5
Target new markets	4
Maintain standards as company grows (e.g., product quality, customer service or staff motivation)	4
Complete specific projects (e.g., construction of new truck terminal)	3
Achieve leadership role in industry	2
Strategic industry issues (e.g., set up lobbying group)	2

SIX KEYS TO ENTREPRENEURIAL SUCCESS

PROFILE 10 Talk about your winning moves. Stanley Samole founded **Fidelity Electronics Ltd.** of Mississauga, Ontario, in 1983 to market a line of computer chess games. As the computer game market exploded in the 1980s, he teamed up with Nintendo, the biggest name in the business, to distribute video games. By the mid-1990s Fidelity was the largest video-game distributor in Canada, representing sixty game developers and selling to more than 6,000 stores. As sales boomed, Fidelity made the PROFIT 100 five times, from 1991 to 1995.

By 1995, Fidelity's sales were nudging $50 million and Samole was feeling stressed out. With a young family and a part-time career as a professional jazz guitarist, with several CDs to his credit, Samole was ready to bail out. When the opportunity came, he sold his company to Canada's largest video distributor, which could help Fidelity consolidate its gains and benefit from its established practices and systems. As Samole noted, "the computer they use to run their air conditioning is bigger than the one I use to run my entire company."

SIX KEYS TO ENTREPRENEURIAL SUCCESS

In growing Fidelity over ten years, Samole came up with the following six keys to entrepreneurial success.

1. **Take Accounting 101.** "From my experience, the reason businesses fail is that entrepreneurs don't know an asset from a debit."

2. **Earn the trust and partnership of your employees, your trading partners, and your peers.** "Always tell the truth," says Samole. Clearly, he doesn't think this commitment is widely shared. "You can beat up on your competitors because you'll be telling the truth and they won't."

3. **Test the end-use performance of any product or service you intend to come out with.** Don't leave room for any surprises come launch day.

4. **Tightly control your operations.** You've got to turn inventory over as quickly as possible, and always know where your money is going. That's the tough part because it takes work. Samole adds, "You have to be there. You have to make that commitment."

5. **Assume you know nothing.** "Seek expert advice from friends and family," he says. "I surround myself with geniuses in my business. Everyone can run the company better than me."

6. **Learn your market place; it's always changing.** Samole advises seeking out information wherever you can, and he offers a secret formula for picking up vital intelligence from suppliers and customers: "Don't sell. Ask."

CHAPTER THIRTEEN

CHARACTERISTICS OF FAST-GROWTH ENTREPRENEURS

"You could say these people specialized in creating havoc where there was peace and predictability."

Management consultant Andrew Campbell, based on his study of the personal strengths of **PROFIT 100** entrepreneurs.

IT'S ALL IN YOUR MINDSET

To this point, this book has been about management: about how ordinary people can achieve extraordinary results through the intelligent application of certain business skills. But business is all art, not science. Two people could follow the exact same business plan, identical in every detail down to the colour of the shoes they wear, and generate completely different results. (In fact, this happens in franchising all the time.) The difference is the human factor. The skills, background, experience and above all the attitude of the individual remains the biggest single determinant of success in business. In the end, the niche you choose, the marketing techniques you develop and the quality of the product you produce, all play secondary roles to your most important business asset: yourself.

Each year, the PROFIT 100 includes an astonishing range of people: young and old, male and female, Canadian- and foreign-born, PhD and high-school dropout, technologically adept and street-smart. What do they have in common? Attitude. For the most part, they are bright, self-confident and creative. Most importantly, they are curious about the world and as optimistic as a kid on Christmas morning.

Almost invariably, they look forward to getting up and going to work each day, interacting with an enthusiastic and motivated staff and matching wits with the world. They see the world as filled with opportunities, and wish only for the time and resources to explore them all. The most optimistic among them have faith that they can accomplish the impossible in an afternoon. The pessimists figure they'll have to consult their lawyers, accountants and business advisors, but they should be done by Thursday.

Take Terry Maxwell of **SLP Automotive Canada** (1997) in Lachine, Quebec. In 1993 the former stock-car racer turned mechanic took on a whole new challenge when he agreed to customize Camaros and Firebirds for a low-volume line of high-performance muscle cars for a subcontractor to General Motors. Starting with 200 cars in 1993 and 500 in 1994, SLP Canada was scheduled to assemble 7,500 vehicles in 1997. But that's just one accomplishment. Recently Maxwell got into the auto-parts business, opening a new plant to turn out the plastic hood needed for the GM upgrade. Before long, he expects to be manufacturing a whole range of auto parts for GM and, possibly, other carmakers. "When I see a mountain I need to climb," says Maxwell, "I just take it one step at a time until I get there."

AGENTS OF CHANGE

For a clue to perhaps the most important characteristic for success in high-growth business today, take another look at Terry Maxwell's résumé. Stock-car racer. Mechanic. Repair-shop owner. Automotive sub-assembler. Car-parts manufacturer. Clearly, Maxwell has a remarkable ability to grow, learn and change, and that description would fit most of the entrepreneurs on the PROF-IT 100. They adapt well to change, both personally and managerially. They don't pigeon-hole themselves as mechanic or computer programmer, salesperson or company president. They adjust to each opportunity that comes their way, developing within themselves or acquiring (from their team or outside the organization) the skills and resources needed to meet each challenge.

Consider the findings of Andrew Campbell, a management consultant in Oakville, Ontario, who works with growth companies. He conducted an in-depth study of more than thirty companies on the 1992 PROFIT 100 list to identify common strengths, weaknesses, problems and success factors. By subjecting the PROFIT 100 entrepreneurs to a gaggle of questionnaires dealing with the companies' structures and policies, corporate culture, and personal characteristics, Campbell was able to identify specific success factors by plotting individual scores against company success.

His most important finding was that the key determinant of company growth was the owner-managers' personality and the culture they created in their company. "Virtually all the leaders had similar personality profiles, whether they were MBAs or Grade 12 drop-outs," he noted. "They tend to be rebels, not followers. They prize freedom and challenge. They need to be in control, and have trouble delegating. They act quickly and aggressively, thriving on flexibility and uncertainty. They sort out their ideas by dreaming and talking, and they love being recognized for their work. You could say these people specialized in creating havoc where there was peace and predictability."

Campbell summed it all up with one observation. He concluded there was one personality characteristic that best summed up all of the above attributes, and showed the greatest correlation with sales growth — receptivity to change. Successful growth companies don't avoid change, and they don't just endure it, they embrace it.

Think back to the challenges they have overcome already. Most PROFIT 100 entrepreneurs started in small businesses with just a few employees. In most cases, they were responsible not just for making policy but for making coffee. Their ability to change and grow as they try to meet the ever-increasing challenges of running a growing company is a huge part of their success. Change is all about them. Executives running fast-growth companies must keep their firms abreast of changes overtaking their industry, lead change within their own organizations, and grow personally — as people, as leaders, and as business decision makers — to meet the changing requirements of their own job. Even the weekly management meetings at **KL Group** (see Chapter 14) are really all about coping with change.

The equation also works in reverse. Entrepreneurs who find themselves uncomfortable moving from hands-on operations or sales to a more administrative and mentoring role are unlikely to be able to lead their organizations to the sort of success that the PROFIT 100 companies have enjoyed. And indeed, those who are uncomfortable with change or unable to change are probably better off where they are. Some PROFIT 100 entrepreneurs have even identified this characteristic as key to their own success.

When asked to name his key strength in business, Herman Yeh of **Northern Micro Inc.**, a four-time PROFIT 100 company in Nepean, Ontario, said, "I'm good at anticipating change. I accept change and in the trade, I can see what's coming next. In our industry new product comes out every six months, so we have to be good at it." To ensure his systems-integration company retains that ability, Yeh put Northern Micro through ISO 9000 certification in 1993, making it one of the first companies in its industry to adopt formal procedures and standards. Yet Yeh himself continues to change and grow to adapt to the demands of his $35-million company. "I'm now trying to be good at finance," he says. "My training is technical, not financial, but understanding finance is key to a successful business."

THE PARADOXES OF GROWTH

There's another factor pushing adaptability and willingness to change as a determinant of growth. To succeed in business today, you have to be open-minded and resilient, because success requires a combination of skills and attitudes that most people would consider contradictory. Only a chameleon-like personality, able to move quickly from challenge to challenge and switch hats faster than a teenager changes TV channels, could deal with the paradoxical demands of business today.

What's paradoxical about business? Based on the stories reviewed in this book, we can better understand the oft-conflicting nature of the challenges facing today's growth-oriented entrepreneurs:

- a driving determination to succeed and yet the patience to do it right;

- an obsession with detail and an overarching sense of strategy;

- confidence that borders on bullheadedness, and acute sensitivity to customer needs;

- the ability to see around corners, as well as what's under your feet;

- the confidence to hire people who know more than you do, and the gut instinct that tells you when to overrule them;

- the ability to focus doggedly on a plan and yet learn and adapt based on experience;

- the persistence to learn all about a new market, yet the courage to proceed before all the answers are in;

- a penchant for risk and an obsession with avoiding or reducing it;

- an ability to get the best from yourself and those around you, and the tolerance to forgive those who make mistakes;

- a strong ego, and a willingness to share the glory when things go right;

- a healthy distaste for failure, and the largesse to shoulder the blame when things go wrong.

Few entrepreneurs master all these personal paradoxes. Yet somehow, successful entrepreneurs do achieve this most delicate of balancing acts. The contradiction is inherent in business itself. Entrepreneurship attracts the impatient but rewards the patient; it heaps glory on the risk takers but punishes those who gamble too often. As we have seen in our tour of niche markets, business success today demands a specialist's vision, but a generalist's touch. It requires the systematic rigour of the accountant and the creative instincts of the artist. Any entrepreneur who hopes to succeed must be aware of these conflicts, and learn to grow themselves and their organizations in order to master the challenge.

PERSONAL CHARACTERISTICS THAT LEAD TO ENTREPRENEURIAL SUCCESS

So, are the people behind Canada's Fastest-Growing Companies some kind of saints or superheroes? Of course not. What they possess are strong skills in a few key business areas — usually, operations and marketing — supplemented by a rigorous self-knowledge that helps them shore up their weaknesses and fill in the gaps in their knowledge or experience before these short-comings can inflict any lasting damage to their businesses.

Based on entrepreneurs' own comments and the general observation of successful fast-growth businesses and their leaders over a number of years, it's possible to come up with one more top ten list: a listing of personal characteristics and attitudes that seem to correlate best with business growth and success. What's important in perusing this list is noting how few of these charac-teristics are personality-driven. Most of them represent behav-ioural characteristics that can be learned, as opposed to inherited abilities (an affinity for math, say, or an outgoing personality) that infer ongoing advantages on just a lucky few. In other words, suc-cessful growth entrepreneurs are made, not born.

THE 10 CHARACTERISTICS OF SUCCESSFUL ENTREPRENEURS

1. Experience
2. Strategic Vision
3. Impatience
4. Willingness to Share
5. People Orientation
6. Enthusiasm
7. Ability to Deal with Stress
8. Persistence
9. Lifelong Learning
10. Ability to Communicate

Experience

Some entrepreneurs are successful straight out of school, but most growth leaders have put in time in their industry. As a result, they possess an in-depth knowledge of their field and its products, their competitors and their customers, that play a key role in their success.

As Brian Edwards of **MPact Immedia Corp.** in Montreal says, the best way to understand your industry is to use instinct born of long experience, because in today's fast-changing markets you can't grow your business based on market surveys. "If you can accurately size and figure out the players and the opportunities in a market today, then you've probably missed it," he says. "We're in a business that requires that you go into uncharted territory to be successful, because if you're in charted territory so is everyone else."

Strategic Vision

To grow your company, you must be able to articulate a vision for your company, and set a strategic pace that will keep your organization moving forward. To do this, you will seek input from key employees and advisors — but as noted by Brian Luborksy, president of **Premier Salons International Inc.**, the number one company on the 1996 PROFIT 100, the final decision must be yours.

"The one thing you will notice with successful entrepreneurs is that, whatever business they're in, they are pretty good strategists," says Luborsky. "They can see ten steps down the road, they know they should be generally heading in this or that direction. There are lots of times as an entrepreneur when you're in the room with your ten key people, and they're all shaking their heads 'no' and you're nodding your head up and down — and that's the way you proceed. You might get their advice and their input, but if you're not a good strategist, I think you're going to have trouble."

Impatience

A number of PROFIT 100 entrepreneurs cite impatience as a management strength, while others call it a weakness. Either way, impatience can be a positive force when it is channelled into an ability to act quickly, to seize an opportunity or react to changing market forces.

"I'm the fastest guy on my feet that I know," says Kieran O'Briain of **Kee Transport Group Inc.** "I think quickly and I jump on opportunities quickly. I'm not a plodder." Another PROFIT 100 entrepreneur confesses he doesn't move quite so fast, but he's learning. "My strength is sales and general operations; my partner is a forward thinker and he pushes me and the company. Sometimes I can be a little slow in reacting, but I'm learning to move faster — that's something my partner taught me."

Willingness to Share

It sounds old-fashioned, almost childish, but PROFIT 100 entrepreneurs believe in sharing: sharing information, sharing risk, and sharing rewards. They know that organizations are at their best when everyone has the same goals so they can work in the same direction. The best PROFIT 100 companies share operating information with their staffs, develop profit-sharing programs and even employee share-ownership programs, which constitute the ultimate sharing of risk and reward. But there's another aspect to sharing, which is based on the concept that no business can succeed unless its customers do, too.

Eric Goodwin, chairman and CEO of **Fulcrum Technologies Inc.**, believes in "sharing the wealth" with all his business partners. He claims his greatest strength in business is "my ability to deal with partners and customers and be sure that any agreement we strike is a win-win agreement." A lot of business deals and contracts, he says, represent posturing or one-sided gains that might have some short-term impact, but no long-term value. "Only win-win," he says, "has enduring value."

People Orientation

Successful entrepreneurs have to like people. They are betting their savings, their careers and their hopes and dreams on people—customers, suppliers, partners and employees. To get the most from employees, to build customer loyalty and get the most from suppliers, they have to show a genuine interest in working with these people, and take joy in their association. Entrepreneurs are not lone wolves, they are social animals who thrive on their contacts with others. When asked how much his salary was last year, one multiple PROFIT 100 winner admitted he had no idea. More important to him was that he still knew the names of everyone who worked for him. Indeed, for a number of PROFIT 100 entrepreneurs, a typical workday involves spending most of their time just hanging out with their staff, to tap into their enthusiasm and ideas. As one PROFIT 100 CEO says, "My office is always empty, because I'm out there with the troops." Alex Habrich of **Lemire & Habrich Consultants Inc.** says his management philosophy is simple, "Treat others the way you want to be treated, with respect and kindness. Keep your heart, mind and office door open."

Enthusiasm

Growth entrepreneurs didn't get to dominate their markets by complaining that the glass is always half-empty. They are professional optimists, tapping enormous reserves of enthusiasm as they go about their business, urging employees and customers alike to get as excited as they are about their business.

Al Hildebrandt, president of **Total Care Technologies Inc.** in Kelowna, BC, says his biggest strength as a manager is "lots of enthusiasm, never being down, my tremendous personal drive to keep going. I'm always challenging others to do better." It's the sort of attitude that wins sales as well as friends. As another PROFIT 100 entrepreneur says, the reason she can sell to reluctant customers is that "I'm passionate about what I do." Or consider the approach of Kyu Lee of **Queue Systems Inc.** in Markham, Ontario, which he co-founded in his twenties with brother Alex. "Queue Systems is part of what I am," he says. "It's part of us." He says he's not in business to save the world or become a multimillionaire, but to finish what he started and serve his customers. "I don't look at it as work. In hindsight, I would have done it all for free."

Ability to Deal with Stress

Despite their enthusiasm and passion, even fast-growth entrepreneurs have bad days. In fact, they undoubtedly face more setbacks and gut-wrenching decisions than do most businesspeople, whose companies are evolving at a much slower pace.

For the entrepreneurs who make it onto the PROFIT 100, however, success often stems from their ability to channel the stress of their positions into more positive energies, leaving them free to attack problems without sliding into depression or frustration. There is no one way they deal with stress. At **L.E. Cherry & Associates**, founder Lorne Cherry keeps a pinball machine in the office that everyone uses — including Cherry — to work off nervous energy, as well as a doll that everyone can beat up on when they feel rage or frustration building up inside. Still, most of the tonics cited by PROFIT 100 entrepreneurs when they feel stressed are considerably more conventional: reading, spending time with family, travel (usually to the Caribbean), visiting with friends, and playing sports (especially golf and skiing, but also racquetball, hockey, tennis, biking and boating). A few of the less common responses to stress reported by PROFIT 100 entrepreneurs were:

- driving my convertible with the top down;
- helping load the trucks;
- going for a swing on the swingset in a park across the street from the office;
- hiring more good people to relieve the stress;
- pulling out of my desk my list of the 50 things I want to do before I die.

Clearly, however they deal with stress, the important thing is that successful entrepreneurs recognize the importance of family time and play time as well as work, to head off burn-out and maintain balance in their lives.

Persistence

Everyone knows you have to be persistent to be an entrepreneur. You can't give up when things look bleak; you have to persevere.

The PROFIT 100 proves this is still true, and that the results can be extraordinary.

Consider the case of David Lui, a Vancouver retailer who was just twenty-five when his company, **Theme Holdings Ltd.**, first cracked the PROFIT 100 in 1996. At the age of nineteen, Lui saw his first Theme store while travelling in Hong Kong. Drawn by its sense of style, its attractive store design and sensible prices, he asked Theme's Hong Kong management to grant him the licence to open Theme stores in North America. The company turned him down. Undaunted, Lui opened his own women's fashion store, and went back to Theme again and again until they bowed to his superior lobbying skills. By the end of 1996 Theme had twelve stores in Canada and was plotting its first US expansion, into fashion centres New York and Los Angeles, for late 1997. To succeed, you have to know what you want, and work tirelessly to earn it.

Lifelong Learning

"I make twenty decisions a day and only two of them are right," admits Theme's David Lui. Indeed, PROFIT 100 entrepreneurs have confessed to a myriad of mistakes over the years, from buying too much merchandise and trusting the wrong partners to failing to ask for a deposit before starting work on a contract. The key in business is not to stop making mistakes, but to never make the same mistake twice, and to learn from each as you go along. "I've made tons of mistakes; it's all part of the deal," says Doug Pinder, president and CEO of **Dino Rossi Footwear** (1995-96). "But I've learned from all my errors, so I don't consider them mistakes — just learning experiences."

Ability to Communicate

In the end, entrepreneurs are successful to the extent that they are able to verbalize a vision, rally people to their cause, attract the attention of their target markets, and enlist the support of outside agents, from dealers to bankers to venture capitalists, to supply the help needed to overcome specific problems and reach the next level of growth. In other words, entrepreneurs must be deliberate, strategic and eager communicators. Businesses today are massive engines that run on one fuel — information. As owner/manager, chief possessor of company information and architect of the systems and structures through which key information is communicated, entrepreneurs must recognize that they are in the communications business. Morning to night, their job is to communicate their vision of their market, their products and their company to employees, customers, suppliers, media and anyone else with a role to play in the organization's future.

Communication Challenges

Just think of the communication challenges that must be overcome in your business every day. Here are seven crucial ones:

- **Marketing:** You must reach out to customers and potential customers, and listen to them in return. In niche marketing, you must know your market inside out, which means you must establish ongoing communications channels that let you get your message out, and keep on top of market changes you need to know.

- **Human resources:** Your organization's success depends on communicating tasks and strategy to your workforce, as well as continually working to motivate and inspire them. Again, you must establish a two-way feedback loop so that they can reach you in return.

- **Advertising:** You have to know the market you want to influence, how to reach it, and what your message is. Sure, an ad agency or marketing person can work out the details, but you must articulate the vision and the message.

- **Internal systems:** Is your marketing department talking to production? Have you maximized efficiencies between your sales people and the shipping desk? Do your financial people and your customer-support staff understand each other's values and needs? Does everyone in your organization have timely access to the information they need, not just to do their jobs, but to do their jobs better? Leaders must ensure that their people have the tools to succeed, and that means not just information, but continuing, ongoing structures that encourage intramural communication and mutual understanding.

- **Liaison with partners or board of directors:** When partnerships fail or directors lose faith in management, communications have usually been broken off for some time. Ongoing, open and honest two-way communications, which expose and help solve problems rather than sweep them under the rug, strengthen organizational sinews and provide for faster decision making and better, more timely idea generation. Dealing with partners on important strategic issues requires sophisticated communications skills, from the ability to persuade to conflict-resolution. As one successful PROFIT 100 entrepreneur says of his partner, "We argue, but we never fight."

- **Intelligence gathering:** The best entrepreneurs are plugged into their industries. They talk to suppliers, customers and even competitors on a regular basis to identify new opportunities and head off new threats. A commitment to sustained, open communication is the key to staying in touch, and staying on top.

- **Electronic commerce:** As more and more companies move into formal electronic documentation with suppliers, distributors and customers, the essence of business is revealed — timely, accurate communication. Entrepreneurs who understand that their job is to facilitate information flow to produce more responsive and orderly markets will have the easiest time moving into the era of real-time, on-line communications, and a huge advantage over competitors who think business is about things, not people.

For years, IBM's motto was "Think." Canada's most successful growth entrepreneurs take that instruction for granted, and find that the highest value-added component in business has moved on to the next stage, where ideas and innovations meet their markets, "Communicate."

CODE RED

A Day in the Life of KL Group

"Do you like wearing a tie? Do you enjoy office politics? Do you hate change? Do you like the steadiness of working nine-to-five? Is a job something you do so you can afford to do something else?

If you answered yes to any of the above, you should probably give KL Group a pass."

KL Group Inc.'s recruiting manifesto,
as posted on its Web site.

What really goes on inside Canada's Fastest-Growing Companies? From where do they draw their inspiration? How do they deal with the problems engendered by such rapid growth? And are they genuinely committed to creating a new style of business as they seem? To find out, I spent a few days with one of the youngest and most dynamic companies on the PROFIT 100.

"THE FOX IS IN THE LAIR. CODE RED."

The marketing staff at Toronto software developer **KL Group Inc.** have seen a lot in their day, but this announcement over the company's PA system has them gazing at each other in bewilderment.

Bizarre goings-on are nothing new at KL, a young, fast-growing company given to programming management seminars that feature clips from old movies like *Twelve O'clock High*, or staging rousing tournaments at the foosball table in the company's so-called lounge. But on this Monday afternoon in March, no one has any idea what to make of this enigmatic "Code Red" declaration from President Greg Kiessling, KL's thirty-six-year-old co-founder.

The joke's on them. Code Red is just one of Kiessling's little pranks, a line stolen from yet another movie (*A Few Good Men*). The announcement is Kiessling's way of informing his key programmers that an overdue conference call is about to begin in his office. Those who've been awaiting the summons know what this means — and what's at stake. The "fox" is actually a group of programmers from a global technology giant which we'll call GTG (confidentiality agreements are part of the high-tech culture). They're on the line to discuss one of KL's new software products with the hope of determining — within a day or two! — whether it's the right tool for a new project they're planning. This one deal alone could be worth $20,000 to $40,000 (US) to KL, but the real stakes are higher still. In today's technology industries, getting your foot in the door of a big client is almost always a prelude to bigger and better things as more divisions or departments get to know you and your products. And GTG is a $4-billion company. Kiessling and his team are eager, but more confident than nervous. They've been in "shoot-outs" before, and they've won more than their share.

KL Group is a laid-back slice of Silicon Valley just east of downtown Toronto, a place where jeans and running shoes are standard business attire, weekly strategy meetings are held at a nearby pancake house, and new employees get a "rookie bonus" of $1,000 worth of company shares once they pass their six-month probation. To most of the staff, a forty-hour work week is as alien a concept as a pinstriped three-piece suit. This is an archetypal new-economy company — casual and informal on the surface, yet deadly serious about its mission. Its employees, all young, well educated and highly motivated, are driven by a personal sense of commitment and contribution, not by duty. It's a far cry from the traditional business model where employers and employees are presumed to be alienated from each other, and time clocks, rule books, grievance processes and annual reviews replace trust, flexibility and communication. Together, the KL team are creating a successful global business in a market niche almost nobody else knows exists. The odds against them are staggering. Confronting them are all the everyday problems that face a growing business: maintaining production and customer service levels, upgrading products to keep pace with changing client needs, sourcing financing, finding good help, and adopting new systems and more professional management as their organization gets bigger and more complex. Add to that the fact that KL is competing with equally bright high-tech firms all over the world, in an industry — creating graphical software tools for programmers to incorporate into their own software programs — that must rank as one of the fastest-changing in history.

KL Group is not only leading its field technically, but setting a new pace for business in Canada. For the fiscal year ended March 31, 1997, KL posted a profit margin of better than 30%. As the nation's seventh fastest-growing company in 1996 (and twenty-ninth in 1997), winner of a Canada Export Award in 1995 and recently named one of Canada's fifty Best-Managed Private Companies, KL Group is turning heads, winning friends and influencing markets at home and abroad — and always on its own terms. For these reasons, I decided to spend some time with Greg Kiessling and his colleagues at KL Group.

Even among the successful high-growth companies on the PROFIT 100, KL stands out for its profitability, its international orientation, and its unique window into the brave new world of twenty-first century cyberbusiness. It struck me as a worthy item of study — even for a visitor who wouldn't know Java from a cup of joe.

GOLDEN GOOEY

When you phone the offices of KL Group, you get a recorded announcement: "Thank you for calling KL Group, the leader in gooey components."

At least, that's what it sounds like. But professional computer users and programmers — the only callers KL is much interested in — know that she is really saying "GUI components." To know the difference between GUI and gooey is to begin to understand the rarefied programming world that KL Group and other cutting-edge tech companies inhabit today.

GUI stands for "graphical user interface," a visually based computer operating system such as Microsoft's Windows or the Macintosh operating system. Such systems are widely considered more fun and easier to learn and use than old-fashioned non-graphic interfaces such as MS-DOS, the text-based operating system that IBM selected to kick off the personal computer revolution in the early 1980s.

So much for GUI. But what are the "components" she was talking about? In KL's context, components refer to self-contained little pieces of software code that programmers can use to build their own programs. It's just like building a house. You can construct it entirely from scratch if you want, but if you're not interested in a customized showpiece or you're really in a hurry, you can use prefabricated materials such as roof trusses, doors, and window frames to speed the job along. When software developers are writing new programs for graphical operating systems, they invariably need to include charts, tables, and boxes for organizing information effectively. Sure, they can build them from scratch. Or they can buy these components ready made, pre-packaged and pre-tested, from companies such as KL. That saves them valuable time (and probably money) writing and debugging their software, and lets them employ their programming energies on the trickier or truly original aspects of their applications. As one KL customer at Bell Northern research says, buying components is consistent "with one of our key development principles: reusability. We stick to creating elements specific to the problems that our products are created to solve, while purchasing reusable general-purpose components from KL Group. Our thinking is 'why build when you can buy at a fraction of the cost?'"

It's not the most high-profile market around; virtually no one but the international programming community (and a lot of Bay Street brokers, as we'll see shortly) know that KL even exists. But as is often the case with Canada's Fastest-Growing Companies, the obscure market niche may be the most desirable. Undetectable to most, shared by an elite group of software developers who take their work seriously and want only the best, the GUI component market is "probably the largest opportunity of this decade," according to industry analyst Portia Isaacson of Boulder, Colorado.

For a producer that understands the technology, can anticipate the needs of the programming community, and knows how to move fast to create and update their products, the GUI components market is a niche made in heaven.

FROM HUMBLE BEGINNINGS TO MARKET DOMINANCE

Greg Kiessling and Ed Lycklama, the two founders of KL Group (the K and the L, in fact), know their market. They are both programmers who met while studying mathematics and computer science at Ontario's University of Waterloo. They went in different directions after university but stayed in touch as they moved on to programming jobs with various employers. At the time, the component market was largely undeveloped; programmers had to reinvent the wheel with each new page, document and chart they produced. In July 1989 Kiessling and Lycklama formed KL Group to see if they could fill that gap.

"We both had done a lot of user-interface programming and we saw opportunities for pre-packaging user-interface components that would make developers' jobs like ours much more productive," says Kiessling. It was a new model, he admits. Previously, software companies had targeted end-users, not other programmers. But with typical entrepreneurial moxie, he adds, "It never crossed our minds that if no one had done it yet, there was no market need."

KL conducted software consulting to pay the bills until 1990 when it produced its first product: XRT/graph. Although they co-designed the product, Ed led the development effort while Greg looked after sales and marketing. XRT/graph quickly became the industry standard for two-dimensional graphing in its market: X Windows for the powerful UNIX operating system. In 1993 KL released XRT/3d for developers wanting to employ three-dimensional surfaces. Later products (sometimes known as "widgets") allowed users to create tables to display tabular information and build data-entry forms. KL's XRT family of products, which sell for around $2,000, proved instant hits. Developers working for software companies and the creators of internal computer systems for *Fortune 500* corporations and other big institutions all seized on the opportunity to automate some of the drudge work and finish their systems faster. With KL's products they can add push buttons and tabbed-folder interfaces with text and images, add colourful icons to on-screen toolbars to display all the functions their applications offer, align columns to create more user-friendly forms, or add pop-up help screens to bail out end-users when they run into trouble. Minor fixes here and there not only help developers by speeding up programming time, but provide a familiar interface and a consistent level of functionality for software users.

Of course KL had the market to itself for only about six months. As competitors arose, KL had to learn to defend its turf by developing new products, constantly improving its old ones, and by signing up the best and most aggressive computer resellers around the world to carry their products. In 1990, its first full fiscal year, KL managed to scare up revenues of $195,000 (and a $9,000 profit). The following year sales jumped to $510,000 and profits to $195,563, which offered proof that the company's strategy was bang-on.

KL's revenues and customer base doubled every year for the next five years, culminating in its first appearance on the PROFIT 100 in 1995, in seventh place with sales of $4 million. For 1996, sales exceeded $9 million with profits remaining uncannily healthy at $3 million. Still, KL continues to pour almost 20% of its revenues back into R&D to preserve its product edge in a fast-changing market.

"There was no single reason for our success," reflects Kiessling. "It was a combination of a certain amount of luck combined with solid, technically awesome products, good marketing and an aggressive growth attitude." Pressed a little further, he offers a more detailed answer. "It's technical features and quality. We've tested better for bugs than anyone else and we provide more detailed documentation and more features. We pay high-quality attention to what the market needs. We do lots of trade shows and talk to people on our support lines."

One other thing, adds Kiessling. "Because we were first we were able to sign up the best resellers in each country, and that kind of locked out the competitors." Today KL has a dominating market share of 70% in its UNIX markets. The US accounts for about 70% of KL's revenues; Canada generates just 2%.

Its head start and its willingness to invest in R&D has helped KL dominate its traditional markets. But time marches on. With the advent of network computing, more powerful 32-bit PCs and the rise of the Internet, UNIX is on its way out. While it still accounts for the lion's share of KL's business, Kiessling and Lycklama knew they had to expand into new markets before their golden goose was cooked.

In 1996 KL took its biggest gamble by introducing products for two new operating systems: a charting tool for Microsoft's powerful network computing system (Windows NT) and a tables product and collection of tools for Java (Sun Microsystems' multi-platform system geared to Internet applications). Both lines required KL to learn a new way of doing business. While KL set the pace in the UNIX markets, it is now just one of many players in the Windows sector. That means prices and margins have to be much lower, which requires moving away from direct selling towards retail, catalogue or on-line sales on the Internet. "Our goal is to be number one in all our markets," says Kiessling. But by mid-1997 it was unclear how KL would reach that goal in its two new competitive arenas.

MONDAY MORNING

To get a feel for KL Group's success, I arranged to spend some time in mid-March 1997, visiting its offices and shadowing some of its managers. It's an intimidating place for a non-techie, with terms such as Olectra, JClass, C++, Motif, VBITS, Java Beans and many more being thrown around. But, the people at KL Group were genuinely helpful towards a rookie who didn't always understand half of what they were talking about, even though they clearly couldn't understand how any functional human being could grow to adulthood without knowing all this stuff.

The work week at KL Group begins the way it does at many companies: with an 8:00 a.m. management meeting. Before most people have arrived at work, it's a good time for Kiessling,

Lycklama, and the five top managers to share ideas, update each other on the progress of various projects, and set out priorities for the next few weeks.

On this sunny Monday morning in late winter, the downtown Toronto bank towers look close enough to touch — but they're a mile away. Culturally, however, it's more like a thousand.

KL takes up 15,000 square feet of a converted warehouse on King Street East, right across the street from the *Toronto Sun/Financial Post* building. It's an appropriately funky venue for a hip software company, with high ceilings, shiny wood floors and exposed brick. KL has grown to take up two floors in its building, and is hoping to be able to negotiate for more space soon.

I arrive a few minutes before eight for a short briefing with Greg Kiessling about the issues currently dogging KL. We meet in his office, which boasts all the trendy accessories: a Sharp stereo CD player, a paper shredder, and a fourteen inch Dilbert doll (the nerdy cartoon character who's become the patron saint of software engineers). On Greg's desk sits a computer and a banana.

The big issue at KL this morning is the switch from UNIX to Java. Greg explains that he has been assuming that KL's UNIX market, while mature, would continue to grow for a while longer, mainly on the strength of satisfied customers who now use one KL product buying a few of the others. But for the first six weeks of the quarter, sales have actually been flat — a nasty shock for a company used to 100% annual growth. As a result, KL must lean more than ever towards its Windows and Java products as the engines that will keep the company growing.

On a more upbeat note, Greg is still glowing about KL's most recent coup: being named by the accounting firm of Arthur Andersen as one of Canada's Best-Managed Private Companies. But he sees it as a victory for *everyone* in this young, aggressive company. So management decided on an appropriate thank you: every employee received a gift of 2,000 KL shares.

In the conversation, Greg also casually mentions that he just got married ten days before. He took a day off. "No honeymoon?" I ask. It turns out that he and his bride took their honeymoon trip before they got married. And just to complete the backward theme, Greg confides that he thinks there's a stag being organized for him this coming Friday. I congratulate him and we head out of his office and around the corner to the boardroom.

KL's seven-member brains trust meet in a nondescript conference room. There's coffee and bagels on the table and marketing materials scattered about. One by one, the managers shuffle in. Greg Kiessling is tall and lean, easygoing in a reserved sort of way. Co-founder Ed Lycklama, now vice-president of technology, is pulling away from day-to-day operations to concentrate on strategic issues. Ed will speak the least at this meeting.

The hired guns arrive. John Selles is a bright youthful-looking MBA who has been the jack-of-all-trades operations director since the company had just twenty employees. Now that things are considerably more complex, Chief Financial Officer Larry Goldberg runs finance and administration — as well as the meeting that's about to start. Later, I asked Larry why he runs the meetings; I had just assumed Greg or Ed would take the lead. "I've done a lot of it," said Larry, a chartered accountant who worked briefly for a large accounting firm before getting into the technology field. "I think I'm pretty good at it. I keep things focused." Next to arrive is Steve Rosenberg, KL's tough-talking vice-president of research and development. Two people are missing this morning. Tom Wilkinson, the director of customer service who was hired just three months ago, is on vacation, while vice-president of sales Deric Moilliet is in Denver.

It's not exactly a zany, off-the-wall Silicon Valley team of netheads and cybersurfers. These are serious professionals. Still, none of them wears a tie; they're all in open-necked sport shirts and casual trousers or jeans. Clearly, KL represents a transition in business style. These men are building a business culture that accepts the need for strategy, accountability and regular reports but dispenses with the solemnity and formality that formerly accompanied all that.

Even the agenda for today's meeting has a solid professional feel. Every anticipated item is recorded on the document, followed by the name of the person introducing it, and the amount of time the discussion is expected to take. It's Larry's idea. Before he arrived at KL, Greg affirms, management meetings tended to be, well, directionless. People just got together and talked about whatever they felt like. The intent of Larry's reform is not to choke off conversation but to keep things in line. The time line provides a constant reminder that there is a real world outside this room where each manager's real work will begin once this meeting ends.

Despite the well-structured memo and the managers' gung-ho approach, however, there are some universal constants that seem to afflict all organizations, big or small, institutional or fast-growing. With all the managers' fussing over coffee and buttering their bagels, the 8:00 meeting gets underway at 8:15 sharp.

Larry kicks things off with some positive news. Sales picked up in the last two weeks of February and things are back to normal. Everyone in the room relaxes visibly. "It's about time," says John to nobody in particular. The next person to report is Steve from R&D. KL is just about to ship a new version of Olectra Chart, its Windows product. But late last week, just when they thought they were done, KL's software wizards discovered a small flaw in the new version: an application that worked in one development platform turned out, upon testing, not to work in another.

There was immediate discussion about what to do. Time was short, and Ed thought the bug was so minor they could let it go. But April Dunford, product marketing manager for the Windows line who has been with KL just a few months, had disagreed. (As Ed explained later, "you will never reach the point where there are no bugs. You want to be at the point where the bugs that remain are marginal enough that they will affect very few people, and we can afford to give them updates. It's a judgement call.") By working round the clock, KL's Windows team fixed the bug, and at this very moment they are testing it to make sure the patch holds. By the end of today, says Steve, they should be finished and the product will be ready to go.

A few minutes are then devoted to discussing the logistics of actually producing a product. For an international exporter, KL's production process is remarkably simple and straightforward. When the master CD-ROM disk containing the new program is ready, it will simply be sent to Cinram Ltd., a manufacturer and duplicator of CDs. "We need three days for CD manufacturing," says Steve, "and then two days for packaging and pulling things together." Greg does the math. "So if we can get it to Cinram tomorrow morning, it will be out next Tuesday?" Steve nods. Easy as pi.

Greg's next concern is the direct-mail campaign for the new product. He is concerned about how clean the company's database is. He's assured that it contains 3,500 contact names, all of them users, evaluators and licensees of KL products. "So we can mail to licensees by Friday?" he asks. No problem.

The group then turns its attention to marketing. With Deric in Colorado, Greg takes charge, observing that "the big push this week is to finalize the XRT brochure," promoting yet another new upgrade. The brochure is already in draft form, he notes, but with all the new products KL is shipping, he says, "We've overloaded our ability to produce boxes and brochures." Still, he notes, the Web pages devoted to XRT will be upgraded today, and the finished brochure should be ready for the printer next week. "We'll have it by the 17th."

"It takes a whole week to get printed?" asks Larry, obviously more comfortable with the incredible new logistics of software production, which can see thousands of CD-ROMs churned out in a day, than with the traditional time lags of four-colour printing. "Well, yes," says Greg. "It's a sixteen-page brochure. But the cool thing is that once it's done, it's stable for a year."

The group agrees the brochure will go out with a letter for the sales reps working for KL's distributors. For a few minutes, John, Larry and Steve discuss updating their database so letters can be customized according to the salesperson's territory. "It should be easy to do," says Steve. "But it will change over time, so it should be coded with the date, too," says Larry. In the end, they resolve to buy a few mailing lists as well, from other high-tech marketers such as Hewlett-Packard, to get the word out fast about their latest update.

I begin to sense one of the advantages inherent in smart young software companies. Database marketing — combining information technology and marketing smarts to keep tabs on a very precise target market and communicate with it at appropriate intervals — has become a key marketing tool in the nineties. In how many older, more established companies could the entire management team engage in a constructive discussion regarding the strategy and tactics of database marketing — especially when the marketing manager isn't even there?

The next item is somewhat more interesting. It's all about GTG, the US-based technology giant that wants to hold a conference call this afternoon. Greg reports that GTG called out of the blue on Friday, asking if KL could demo a product for them. It's exciting news. GTG is about to start work creating some new Java applications for internal use and had approached Sun Microsystems (the inventor of Java) for the names of one or two of the best product developers. Sun recommended Rogue Wave Software Inc. of Corvallis, Oregon — and KL.

Rogue Wave is a components developer founded, like KL, in 1989 and active in the Java, Windows and UNIX markets. Judged by sales or numbers of employees, it's twice KL's size, but it hasn't shared KL's eye-popping profitability.

It's a shoot-out, and there's not much time. "They wanted us both to present today," says Greg. "Tomorrow they decide." GTG has brought ten of its software developers to Denver where they will meet at 3:00 p.m. (Toronto time) to discuss the project. The conference call with KL will begin at 3:30. But it's more than a phone call: GTG also wants KL to demonstrate its software over the Internet, using the demo software on its Web site. It could be a wonderful example of the new information economy at work — how organizations use on-line interactive communication with zero notice to move faster than ever and create virtual alliances. Or it could be a complete boondoggle. You never know with the Net, and GTG sounds more than a little disorganized.

Meanwhile, KL has a problem. Both of its Java product managers are away at the same time. It shouldn't happen, but there it is. Greg wouldn't have hesitated to send either of them to Denver to meet with the potential client and show them KL's software. Instead, however, he asked Deric Moilliet to do the job. Armed with a laptop and the barest knowledge of Java, Deric is even now flying to Denver to meet with GTG. "So," says Steve, "He'll have a roomful of carnivorous developers tearing the flesh off him." "Or, maybe they know nothing about it either," says Greg. He adds that he doesn't think Rogue Wave is sending anyone to Denver for this deal. "We're hoping to win points by showing up in person."

Larry shuts down the unscheduled discussion to move onto finance and administration. "We've entered audit season," he notes warily. Fortunately, the auditor has already been in for half a day and seems satisfied with KL's financial statements. "Everything we do on a monthly basis is enough for them," he says. In a way, he's patting himself on the back. Larry was hired last fall to do exactly this: bring some discipline and controls to a company that had always been more concerned with software systems than with financial ones. There are still a few wrinkles to iron out, such as how to declare some new research and development tax credits, but according to Larry, "the audit should go quickly and well...and hopefully inexpensively." With a successful audit behind them, he says, the company will be ready for a share offering, if that's what it decides to do.

Going public is a matter still to be determined. Selling stock on the public markets has good and bad points. Certainly, it's a way for a company to raise money, or for a firm's founders and chief shareholders to divest some of their shares — usually at a premium — and get some cash into their personal bank accounts. It's also an opportunity for a company's employees to cash in on any shares that they have.

But of course there are problems associated with going public. Many entrepreneurs call it the fishbowl effect. Everyone knows what you're doing. You have to file quarterly reports, you have to make time to talk to securities analysts whose job is to determine whether you're a buy or a sell, and you have to suffer increased scrutiny from the often cynical and suspicious media. Greg is also concerned about the pressure from investors to perform every quarter, and wonders whether that might not seriously harm KL's hard-working but on-our-own-terms culture.

In the fall of 1996 Larry orchestrated the first movement of a campaign to go public. KL invited in a group of investment bankers from the golden towers of Bay Street in a series of get-to-know-you sessions. Lured by KL's fantastic growth rate and even more impressive profit margins, six brokerage firms and a few private investment houses willingly came to see *them*. "We had a lot of people get excited about us, and we learned a lot," says Larry.

In the end, however, KL decided it wasn't quite ready to go public. "When we release a product, we want to be ready. We want it to be right the first time," says Larry. He thought the same standard should apply to any public issue, and he felt KL Group just wasn't ready. "We executed real well, but very short term. We need a real formal business-planning process," he says. As a result, "we made it our goal to act and think like a public company, even if we don't go public in the next year."

With Larry's input, KL launched bold new management initiatives to upgrade its planning processes. That's when the monthly financial meetings turned into Monday-morning management meetings. "Monthly meetings don't work," says Larry. "There's too much happening in this company. We might as well never meet at all." A more long-term initiative involved setting up quarterly off-site conferences to accommodate more formal strategic planning. The weekend getaways — held in regional resorts and conference centres — deal with financial and product issues, but also the softer stuff, such as leadership and management issues.

WHO ARE WE? WHAT DO WE DO?

By now it's after 9:00, and time to move to the more tactical items on the morning's agenda. Intriguingly, they turn out be some of the most important discussions of all and as strategic in their own way as anything to be discussed at the quarterly offsites.

Steve notes that a new software developer, who has worked for the company before on contract, starts work on Wednesday. That will bring the company to sixty-one employees, but according to the help-wanted section on KL's Internet site, there are still more jobs available than there are qualified applicants.

Hiring aces is tough. Competition for programmers has driven salaries up to $80,000 for top people in the hottest technologies, and these people can still write their own ticket in Silicon Valley as well as Toronto or Ottawa. It's the main reason, in fact, that KL enjoys the spotlight when they win a Canada Export Award or make the PROFIT 100. It helps reinforce the company's image as a place where something is happening, and helps separate it from the crowd of software companies competing for the best talent. For that reason, KL guards its reputation as a freewheeling, noncorporate kind of workplace. And the very next agenda item provides a sterling example of what happens should anyone — even the company's founder — lose sight of that goal even for a moment.

It turns out that Greg has received a phone call from a saleswoman for a publisher of corporate vanity books. It publishes glitzy coffee-table books on major North American cities, featuring lots of attractive colour pictures and boosterish stories about the city, as well as glowing profiles of prominent companies or institutions in each city. The profiles, of course, are ads, paid for by the companies themselves. Greg hands out a copy of a glossy new book about Boston as he explains that the publishers are just now finishing off a Toronto version of their book. Blue-chip firms such as the Royal Bank or The Bay participate in programs like this one, explains Greg. "We could get a nice buzz from associating with these big companies." The cost of this ad/profile is $7,200.

Reaction is mixed. "Well," says John, "it could be an interesting thing to pass around to resellers." Others are less eager. Larry, who's been with the company six months, says, "It's really out of character for KL Group. Sort of like having an office at BCE Place." Steve warns, "It looks like corporate ego."

John acknowledges that the listing wouldn't do anything for KL within Toronto or Canada, "but it could be good for our profile outside the city." Greg adds that he thinks it might be useful as a recruiting tool, but again Steve disagrees. "Will it win points for us in Waterloo?" he asks. "I think hosting a pub night and buying three beers for everyone would do more."

Larry drops the c-bomb on the idea. "I think it's very counter to the real culture around here." Waving a hand at the **PROFIT** and Arthur Andersen awards on the wall, he notes, "they're not self-referential. I think doing this would run counter to how this company has always acted." Ed, the co-founder who has been silent so far, finally weighs in. "I don't think it will enhance our image with developers; it might even be counter. It would look like we're associating with a larger corporate culture." There's a slight pause, and Greg accepts this rebuff gracefully. "I'm glad I asked you. I was sold." Steve observes, "She must be a good salesperson. Maybe she needs a job."

This conversation strikes me as blazingly significant for two reasons. One, you rarely get to see a company's managers define the culture that drives them. It's easy to define yourself day to day by the things that make you different, such as gifts of stock to employees or even a foosball table. But how does that culture actually work when it comes to corporate marketing? At what point do you stop defining yourself in terms of what you're not, and start doing the corporate things that work for the banks or The Bay? After a useful discussion, the management of KL Group have drawn a line.

Two, you couldn't help but be impressed by Greg Kiessling after this exchange, and not just because he acceded to the wishes of his subordinates so willingly. Kiessling has succeeded in surrounding himself with the best managers possible — people who not only understand the distinctive culture of the organization, but who will work tirelessly to communicate it and advance it — and who won't even hesitate to take him on in their zeal to preserve his vision.

The next subject is a follow-up item to solicit feedback on a leadership course that most members of KL's management and sales teams just attended. It was a brainchild of Deric Moilliet, VP of sales, who had taken the course a few years earlier. Again, the ensuing discussion presents an inside glimpse of a young, growing company still trying to find itself.

The course, Situational Leadership, came in two parts. A few weeks ago, everyone spent a day learning about different personality types and how to adapt their own management style to the person on the other side of the desk. Then, a week ago, they all went back for part two, which was basically a refresher and reinforcement day. The group discussed the issues and refined their understanding of leadership by watching clips from such movies as the 1950 war classic *Twelve O'clock High*. Larry reports that he got a lot of "fightback" from some of the technical managers who didn't want to go back for the second session. They had a lot of work to do, and thought that the first day was enough. There were also reports that some of the women felt the material was too gender-biased. All the examples and all the positioning were male, he reports, and the film *Twelve O'clock High* had just two prominent women: a nurse and a hooker.

Greg sums it up. "Nobody wanted to go. I didn't want to go either. But I'm glad I went, even though it doesn't help you practically one little bit." Steve notes that a lot of people felt they just had too much to do, but Larry points out, "there's never a good time" for soft training such as this. Sure, responds Steve, "but some times are better than others." Greg counts up the cost. "Fifteen people for two full days — that's a full man-month and a half." Ed says he didn't learn anything new.

In Deric's absence, John picks up the gauntlet. How does KL Group go the next step, he asks, without trying to help its people grow as managers and leaders? "It was an application day," he says. "We can speak the speak, but can we do the do?" Greg offers the last word by saying that he thinks, "the management sophistication of the company went up a few notches" as a result of the course. One gets the feeling, however, that the debate between the short-term, product-oriented thinkers and the longer-term company strategists is not over yet.

This meeting is almost finished. But this group meets again as early as Wednesday, from 8:00 to 12:00, when they are scheduled to discuss annual evaluations and reviews of all members of staff. It's a freewheeling, no-holds-barred, closed-door meeting and a long-standing tradition they are obviously loath to give up — even though, at sixty people, KL Group would seem too large now for all its top managers to expect to be able to participate in in-depth discussions about every member of the staff. They already acknowledge that they may need more than four hours for this, which means they will probably have to schedule another meeting after that one. The growing burden is felt by everyone. As Larry says, "we're going to be pretty sick of each other by the end of the week."

Next Monday morning, with vacations and trade shows kicking in, only three of the seven managers will be here. Should they meet? The answer is no. It will be the first Monday morning without a management meeting since Larry instituted them three months ago. Not a bad record, actually. The next meeting, Larry announces, will be Monday, March 17. "Everybody has to wear green."

THE ORGANIZATION MEN

By now I knew enough about KL to recognize this company as a model for growth firms across the country. Successful companies everywhere are finding that their good fortune is causing unanticipated problems of all kinds such as managing larger and more diverse groups of people, dealing with unfamiliar industries or customer groups, regular requirements for more cash, expansion into exotic foreign markets and so on. Most of these problems, of course, are those for which the founders have little training, and possibly even less interest. The test of a company's ability to survive and keep growing is the way management responds to these challenges. And in Ed and Greg's logical, planned and strategic solutions to these problems, I detected a model for companies of all sizes, in all industries.

After the meeting, I spend some time with Larry Goldberg, probably the man who, more than any other, represents the future of KL. If it is to succeed in the new markets it is tackling, it will be due to new, professional staff such as Larry who bring valuable management expertise and an outside perspective. No one discounts the accomplishments or potential of the two founders of the company. They built a world-class software developer out of a narrow family of products. But it is the savvy and experience of people like Larry, Steve and Deric who determine whether the hottest start-up companies will actually survive and thrive.

Larry always wanted to get into the technology business. Even at university studying to become an accountant, he took all the computer courses he could cram in. After a short stint at Price Waterhouse in 1980, he joined a technology consulting firm, and later crossed over into management of a sister company that sold real estate software and had ballooned from five employees to over 200. That experience seemed perfect for KL, which was looking for a senior financial person to manage its own growth trajectory. Having seen a lot of single-product software companies fail to grow successfully into sustainable larger organizations, Larry today has only praise for the way Kiessling managed the company without him. "Greg has so far very effectively been able to make the leap from family company to real company," he says. "He's added good people to his senior management team, and he's given them real authority and responsibility. And he's very careful. He doesn't just hire people; he talks to everyone in the company, to make sure they're onside."

Besides taking over the books and processes, Larry has another job: planning the future of KLG Direct, the company's direct-selling venture. As KL moves from the low-volume, $2,000-and-up world of UNIX products to Windows and Java, it needs to build new delivery media and information systems, he says. Currently, the only way customers can buy the Java products is by downloading them from KL's Web site, although a physically packaged version will follow soon. For the future, however, says Larry, "we want our customers to do everything with us electronically."

Why is KLG Direct Larry's baby? Selling on-line is primarily an information systems challenge, he explains, and he had a lot of experience developing systems at his previous company. But it could be that there's another agenda at work. He says KL needs new management information systems, to collect and share information across the company. This is his chance to put together a new company-wide MIS, including more sophisticated housekeeping systems for such things as payroll and purchase orders, that will help KL take the next step to corporate maturity. "We'll be the glue that holds all the systems together," he says. "This will help us become a marketing- and sales-driven organization." As with everything at KL Group, Larry's timetable is daunting. His job is to have a plan in place by March 31 and to begin implementation by June 30.

Another discipline now being beefed up at KL is customer service. Tom Wilkinson, who used to run the Toronto customer service group for Sun Microsystems, was hired three months ago to build a more sophisticated service culture at KL. Although KL's price points are declining, Greg Kiessling wants the company to be known for still providing the same top-quality service it offered the buyers of its $2,000 XRT products. "That means more than answering phones," he says. It includes solving people's problems promptly and efficiently and building a better database by surveying customers more frequently. For instance, every tenth caller will be asked to take part in a survey about their satisfaction with their entire KL experience. "It's part of the culture building," says Greg.

"Customer service has to be measurable. Until now, we had no way to say that our customers are happier than they were a year ago. Other companies, know this. We don't."

In sales, Deric Moilliet, thirty-eight, sees his primary task as not just selling product, but building the company too. "I'm here to motivate, train and coach the sales staff. That's how you keep good people," he says. "People will stay as long as they're learning." Deric was handpicked by Kiessling for the job. In the 1980s, Greg and Deric worked for Sun Microsystems of Canada. Deric knew Greg as the technical engineer who would go along on Deric's sales calls to answer the tough technical questions. In 1989 they both left Sun, Deric to join Sybase Canada Ltd., a developer of client-server software. In January 1995, Greg invited Deric to lunch and pulled an old headhunter's trick. He asked Deric if he could name a few people who might make a good sales manager for KL. Deric dropped a few names before Greg said, "I'd like you." Deric was taken aback. He thought KL a little small for his talents. "Greg is so understated, I didn't realize how well he was doing. He doesn't call you up and say, 'we have forty people here now.' I thought it was maybe still five." At any rate, he signed a non-disclosure agreement and got a look at KL's books, which convinced him then and there. Still, he wanted to go out on a high, so he waited until he landed a $5-million-deal in mid-1995 before leaving Sybase to go to work for KL.

For the first sixty days, Deric didn't do anything. "When you have people who are successful, they're going to ask, 'Who is this guy? Why's he trying to change things?'" Then he started slowly, putting in a sales forecasting system (there wasn't one before) before helping push the company into the Java market place. Because it is so new and ill-defined, he says, "Java is the riskiest market for us, but the one with the most potential. Now we have to figure out a way to dominate; you have to be number one or number two in this market or you're not going to go anywhere."

LOOKING AT THE LONG TERM

With such fast-changing markets and opportunities, where does KL Group see itself in five years' time? Don't ask. Don't ask anyone in high-tech that. Larry Goldberg gives the standard industry answer: things are just changing too fast for anyone to even guess. "Where will the industry be in five years? That's like trying to predict what the weather will be like three weeks from next Tuesday. We look nine months ahead, not five years." Roughly, though, he says KL's aim is to offer a diverse set of products and product lines. Most will be developed in-house, but some may be picked up through acquisitions of like-minded software companies. It's primarily a defensive strategy, he explains. "We don't want to be in a position where Microsoft can crush us if they ever decide to do what we do."

Greg Kiessling adds his own long view. "We've gone from having to choose one new product a year to having to make decisions on five or six new products in the next few months," he says. "We don't want to be a $100-million company with one product, like Hummingbird," he says (referring to another **PROFIT 100** company, Toronto-based Hummingbird Communications Ltd., which holds the lion's share of the market for the PC-UNIX connectivity software upon which KL's UNIX line depends). "We want twenty to forty products. We view that to be the only sustainable model."

Which brings us back to the going-public option. He sees increasing numbers of mergers and acquisitions taking place as part of the inevitable shake-out of smaller players in his industry, and he wants KL to be prepared to move fast as a buyer. The best way to buy other companies is with shares, he notes, rather than cash. Even though they're convertible into cash, issuing new shares doesn't actually cost a company anything up front. So, while he doesn't seem particularly eager to go public for fear of the changes it will bring to KL's freewheeling style, he's hoping to pull it off for strategic reasons. At any rate, thanks to last fall's "beauty contest" (his term for the line-up of brokers and investors who came by to size up KL), he says the company has the contacts now to either go public, or raise private capital if a deal comes up in the meantime. "If we need a million dollars in a few days, we now know who to go to."

TRANSITIONS AT THE TOP

KL's long-term product plans are entrusted to the soft-spoken Ed Lycklama, the junior-partner co-founder who is now almost entirely freed up from day-to-day operations. As the mastermind behind KL's first product line and the man who led the charge into Windows and Java, "he's the catalyst in the product-planning process," says Greg. Ed now hangs his hat with the R&D staff on the fourth floor, in a high-ceiling brick office that offers a sunny view into the *Toronto Sun* building across King Street. The room is cluttered with computer magazines of all shapes and sizes.

Ever since Steve Rosenberg joined the company in June 1995, Ed has acted as the technology eyes and ears of the company, with a mandate to seek out new technologies. Perhaps Ed has the ideal job: being paid to surf the Net, read magazines, and come up with the product strategies that will keep KL on the cutting edge two or three years from now.

Still, Ed admits kind of wistfully that this a big change from the old days when he was up to his neck in code. "In some cases I miss being involved in product development," he says. He remained technical product manager for Olectra Chart until last summer when he handed the responsibilities off to two other people. Then he took six weeks' holidays. "I recognized the transition was coming," he says. "I wanted a clean break before moving to a higher level." As a husband and father of two, he says his new job offers more freedom and more fun, "and in some ways it's less stressful."

While Ed is now much further removed from KL's marketing and administrative nerve centre on the third floor, the transition he has made is nothing compared to the one that has confronted, and still confronts, his co-founder. Greg Kiessling, too, is learning that running a growing company actually means a continuing, and sometimes wrenching, process of disengagement. That's not all bad. He still remembers licking stamps and buying photocopiers in KL's early days. But more and more, he has had to give up the sales and marketing duties he loves to concentrate on being a leader. Although he gave up responsibility for sales to Deric a year and a half ago, he has remained in charge of KL's XRT products, the traditional mainstay of the company. But now he knows that's got to go, too. "I'm looking for someone to take that on," he says. "I will move out of product management. It will be hard to adjust to, but it's the right thing to do." He also expects to hire a vice-president of marketing in another year or so, distancing him even further from his roots. He now realizes that the president's job is strategy, mentoring and leadership, "helping articulate who we are and what we're doing and helping ensure the right structure is in place to help people do their job."

He, too, is spending more time reading and thinking, although his business reading still tends towards technology-based magazines such as *Red Herring* and *Upside,* rather than the *Harvard Business Review*, which he sheepishly admits he probably should start to read. He is also spending more time going to management and industry seminars and networking events. In late March he was scheduled to attend a conference geared specifically to high-tech companies trying to advance to the next level. For a hands-on techie, he says, "I'm now realizing these soft events are important."

But Greg has one other big project in the works: putting together a board of experts who would take an interest in the company and use their industry knowledge, experience and contacts to help KL with its new challenges. The question he's still wrestling with, however, is whether it should be an advisory board or a full-fledged legal board of directors. "It's part of our 'ready-to-go-public' mandate," he says. He wants people who can advise the company on tactics, critique its performance, help set strategy and introduce them to all the right people in customer, technical, financial or distribution organizations. Tongue-in-cheek, he says, "we want people who can question our strategy, but not unduly." But he's serious about wanting this to be a real commitment. He intends to reward his advisors with KL stock, whether the company goes public or not.

Ask Greg Kiessling about the management team he's put in place at KL and he'll smile the shy grin of someone who knows he's done good work. "We may be a little top-heavy for this size of company now, but we've got the people in place for the next few years. Our management team is really rocking."

SELLING THE FOX

Monday at 3:30, it's time for the conference call from the Global Technology Giant. Things are kind of confusing. It seems GTG wants to create some Java applications to give to their corporate clients to help them better access GTG's services. But details are sketchy. So far, GTG is playing its cards close to its chest. When Janis from GTG calls, Greg makes his colourful announcement: "The fox is in the lair. Code Red." He is quickly joined in his office by Steve Rosenberg and three JClass product developers. We all crowd around the speakerphone as Janis, who is obviously in charge, announces, "I'm very interested in Live Table, especially in terms of the volume-functionality behind it. Tell us everything about it." Then she asks for more information on JClass Chart and JClass BWT, a collection of components that includes an outliner.

In Denver, Deric Moilliet, the sales VP suddenly thrust into the role of a product manager, does his level best, using demo programs downloaded from KL's Web site onto his laptop. But already he's getting the third-degree from Janis and ten other GTG developers. One of their first questions concerns the outliner. "We want to have trees with 300,000 nodes. Is that a problem?" Well, says Deric, "It's theoretically possible." Janis wants to know, "Can I click on a column and move it around?" Deric says, "Yes and no. You can drag, but there are no nice visuals."

That seems to be a problem. Janis asks a few more questions, most of them picking up very quickly on the deficiencies of KL's evolving Java software. Greg is starting to suspect someone has briefed her on what to say, possibly to embarrass KL. But he doesn't let his suspicions show. At one point, after another canny question reveals yet another shortcoming, he talks to the speakerphone himself, "It sounds like you'd be a good customer for us. You'd definitely have our ear, and features that you're looking for would definitely be on our priority list [for future upgrades]."

But if this is the wave of business of the future, as John Selles suggested this morning, the outlook isn't good. Confusion reigns. Although both sides have downloaded the same demo, neither can really follow what the other is doing. Plus, when Greg gets on the phone to talk to Janis directly, it cuts off the speakerphone so no one else can hear the Denver side of the conversation. Someone dials in to the conversation from the speakerphone in the next office, so everyone runs Keystone Kops-like into the next office to follow the dialogue. But in that office you can't see the computer screen on Greg's desk, so people are continually darting back and forth trying to follow what's going on.

Janis asks more questions, most of which are clearly beyond Deric. Can the software generate maps? Is balloon help available? "We plan to have it," responds a developer. Can chart labels include percentages? In Denver, Deric tries to regain control by asking textbook salesman questions such as, "Can you tell us the three things most important to you in choosing us or the other guys?" Janis doesn't want to get specific. She turns the question around and asks what makes KL products superior to the competition. Greg steps up confidently to the speakerphone. "We're 100% focused on GUI components," he says in a calm, reasoned tone. "We were the first company committed to that, we were the first company with a Java product. We're working with all the key Java tool vendors: Borland, Microsoft et cetera. You're trying to make a very fast technology decision. If you do have the time, we urge you to really study the products. There's a lot of depth to our products." He declines the opportunity to say anything negative about the competition.

After a few more comments, Janis asks for an evaluation copy of KL's software. Everyone starts to look a little more relaxed. But then the people at GTG in Denver actually start arguing among themselves. Some of them want to take up Greg's offer to study the products a little more closely, while Janis is insisting, "We have no choice. We have to make a decision tomorrow morning." Someone else argues that another day spent evaluating software wouldn't be the end of the world. Greg grins and mimics a boxer's moves as the debate continues. GTG may be a multibillion dollar corporation, but I am more impressed by the cool competence of this young Toronto company than by the way GTG has mismanaged this technology decision. From the last-minute call on Friday to the current argument, they don't look very organized or sound very professional.

Again, Deric tries to wrap things up. "Clearly, neither vendor has 100% of your solution," he says. "I will be first to admit that we don't have everything ("We do!" whispers Steve in Toronto), but our company is committed to this work." Janis brings things to a close by saying that her group "has a business decision and a technical decision" to make. When Deric suggests that GTG give them some specs so that KL can look at what they want and decide whether it's a core feature worth integrating into the product, the Toronto team beams. But when Deric goes on to say, "It's a tough decision. I wish I could make it for you, but I can't," Greg hisses at him to shut up. Fortunately the speakerphone is off, so he can't be heard.

With a hearty "thank you all," Janis hangs up. "Well," says Greg, "that was confusing." As the software developers file out of the office, one of them mutters, "I think Deric missed some closing opportunities."

So, does the teleconference/Internet demo represent the future of business? No way, says Greg. "That's a really ugly way to sell." Still, he won't lose sleep worrying about it. Earlier today, a salesperson on the XRT side landed a US$100,000 site-licence deal with 3Com Corp., a fast-growing computer networking company in Santa Clara, California. It's more than twice the size of the potential GTG contract, and it's further proof that the UNIX product line can still bring home the bacon.

JAVA FOR BREAKFAST

At 8:00 a.m. Tuesday, it's meeting time again. This is the Java marketing breakfast, featuring Greg, Ed, Steve and the members of the Java development team, held at the local Golden Griddle Pancake House a few blocks west on Jarvis Street. This time there's no written agenda. The point is to talk about product developments, customers and marketing ideas. At first, though, all anyone wants to do is hear from Deric who is back from Denver. He had flown there first thing Monday morning and was back in Toronto by 11:00 p.m. He is still shaking his head over the road trip. "They want this application up and running in October," he says, to concerned looks all round.

Deric feels the need to explain what was going on, as if the chaos at GTG wasn't evident even across the phone lines. "I was trying to bring structure to the meeting, but Janis kept hopping around the Web. I couldn't control things." The good news is that price is not an issue. Overall, he estimates he got through to maybe three of GTG's ten team members. But he's not impressed with their inability to get their act together. "I don't think they're as smart as we think they are."

"They were asking us very tough questions," notes Greg Kiessling, raising his theory. "Nobody would have known they were weak points — unless they knew. Maybe Rogue Wave clued them in." Deric suggests that maybe it was Sun, which turns out to have done a lot of homework before recommending KL to GTG. "They went on the Web, analysed various companies, talked to customers," he says. "We never knew it."

Deric maintains that the first thing he told the GTG team was that he had come to Denver as a show of good faith, not because he could answer all their technical questions. KL isn't set up to do a lot of personal demos, but now Deric is wondering whether that might not be the company's next big thing. "Could we learn something from that?" he asks. "As we switch from four products to three product lines, we're going to be more and more attractive to the corporate market. We may have to get more involved in face-to-face selling." Clearly, even for highly successful companies in the vanguard of management and technology, there are always more questions than answers.

Munching on bacon and eggs and drinking orange juice and real java, the team is about to move on to real business. But first, Greg asks whether it would be worthwhile for someone to take half an hour to write a demo program for GTG that would demonstrate KL's ability to handle 300,000 nodes. Deric volunteers to e-mail Janis as soon as he gets back to the office and ask her if there's anything they can do to help GTG reach a decision. In particular, he suggests, maybe it would be useful to discuss further GTG's idea of a topographical maps tool. "OK," says Ed, but he wants to expand it beyond maps to include building floor plans and other graphical layouts. At KL the opportunities and the ideas just keep coming.

SNARING THE FOX

Two weeks later, I call Deric for an update on the GTG project. "I've just been notified that we got the contract," he says. "As unorthodox as they were, things worked out in the end." He confirms that the contract will be worth at least US$40,000, and possibly twice that amount.

The deal went through even though KL was unable to meet GTG's request that it prepare a demo answering some of the potential client's concerns. "We just had no time to do it," says Deric. Since GTG didn't need the product until May 15, two months away, KL proposed an alternative. It simply pledged to upgrade the product by that date to add those desired features. "We can't demo it by Monday," Deric said. Based on the quality of the rest of KL's products, he said, "you're just going to have to take it on faith."

Even in this brave new world of teleconferencing and Internet demos, that was good enough for GTG. In fact, that was exactly what they were looking for. Apparently, KL's products made it a favourite from the beginning, but GTG didn't know enough about this tiny Canadian company. What kind of a partner would it be? Would they understand GTG's needs and go out of their way to serve them? By promising to change the entire product to meet GTG's requirements, KL proved it had the right stuff to begin a relationship. "It was kind of a test, in a way," concludes Deric. "We thought the test was to demo the functionality, but it was the relationship they were interested in."

In the end, perhaps Code Red did point towards changes in the future of business. As usual, though, it had nothing to do with the technology. It was about the people.

A FINAL SECRET

Clearly, much of this is not new. The basics of business — providing an innovative product, understanding customers, and communicating effectively up, down and beyond the organization — have not changed in a hundred years. What has changed, however, is the importance of these basic disciplines. The pace of business today is accelerating. Competition is intensifying, and customers are demanding ever-increasing quality and value. To succeed, companies must master these fundamentals of business, faster and more effectively than ever. The alternative is to fall behind your competition, a woeful fate which more and more spells certain stagnation or even failure.

The good news, of course, is that these disciplines can be learned. And as the PROFIT 100 demonstrates, they can be extraordinarily effective. Most of Canada's top growth entrepreneurs had no conception of setting the world on fire when they started their business or released their first product. They were just doing what comes naturally: serving customers and meeting their changing needs. As they institutionalize their customer focus, their respect for their employees, and their thirst for innovation, these growth leaders are proving that the rewards of savvy entrepreneurship are greater than ever.

No one can predict with certainty that the future of the PROFIT 100 companies will be as bright as their past. Advancing technology, new competitors and ever-shifting markets have a way of humbling even the best and the brightest. The one golden guarantee, however, is this. As our very first look at the PROFIT 100 demonstrated, there is no end to potential market niches. From health food to hot tubs, from GUI components to kids' clothing, Canada's Fastest-Growing Companies prove there is a breathless diversity of paths leading to business success — and accessible global markets for those who choose their routes wisely.

The lesson of the PROFIT 100 is that business success can strike everywhere, in almost any sector of any industry, for those who respect the fundamentals, display a flair for innovation, and share their passion with their people. Unfortunately, there are too few people in Canada currently who understand this concept and can pass on this upbeat message to nervous would-be entrepreneurs, or to the unemployed or underemployed young people still casting about for a way to make a living.

The success of the PROFIT 100 stands not just as a role model for other entrepreneurs, but as a symbol of the success that's possible in Canada today. But now the secret's out. Pass it on.

APPENDIX

THE PROFIT 100

Canada's Fastest-Growing Companies

Who are Canada's hottest growth companies? This 1997 PROFIT 100 list provides a recent glimpse of the newest players in the new economy.

RANK	COMPANY	LOCATION	DESCRIPTION	1996 SALES	5 YEAR GROWTH (%)
1	Oasis Technology Ltd.	North York, ON	Funds transfer software	$13,395,289	10113.79
2	Shikatronics Inc.	LaPrairie, PQ	Computer memory products	$41,971,950	7701.48
3	Hummingbird Communications Ltd.	North York, ON	X-server software	$102,060,000	5978.62
4	The G.A.P Adventures Inc.	Toronto, ON	Adventure tour operator	$4,058,000	3626.73
5	Iris Power Engineering Inc.	Etobicoke, ON	Industrial testing equipment	$5,282,338	3534.37
6	Media Express Telemarketing Corp.	Montreal, PQ	Call centre services	$8,014,165	3444.85
7	Brigdon Resources Inc.	Calgary, AB	Oil and gas	$3,258,000	3150.46

RANK	COMPANY	LOCATION	DESCRIPTION	1996 SALES	5 YEAR GROWTH (%)
8	Image Processing Systems Inc.	Scarborough, ON	Machine-vision systems	$10,100,000	3086.12
9	Datalog Technology Inc.	Calgary, AB	Oil-field monitoring	$15,114,000	2800.96
10	Virtek Vision Corp.	Waterloo, ON	Machine-vision systems	$5,616,212	2514.70
11	Tropical Treets (Caribbean Ice Cream Co. Ltd.)	North York, ON	Food products distributor	$3,431,516	2488.87
12	Theme Holdings Ltd.	Richmond, BC	Casual wear retailer	$4,530,000	2375.41
13	Prime Way Ltd.	Welland, ON	Housewares developer and distributor	$3,777,241	2323.45
14	Pebble Hill Industries Inc.	Burnaby, BC	Beer and winemaking supplies	$3,140,112	2240.62
15	Kee Transport Group Inc.	Mississauga, ON	Supplies drivers to trucking fleets	$4,795,661	2183.65
16	S&P Data Corp.	North York, ON	Call centre services	$28,684,000	2089.95
17	Total Care Technologies Inc.	Kelowna, BC	Healthcare scheduling software	$4,410,679	2085.51
18	Northern Micro Inc.	Nepean, ON	Computer systems integrator	$35,266,000	2066.22
19	Yogen Früz World-Wide Inc.	Markham, ON	Fast-food franchisor	$30,038,623	2026.73
20	Les Systèmes Zenon Inc.	Longueuil, PQ	Computer systems integrator	$9,130,241	1981.07
21	PointOne Graphics Inc.	Toronto, ON	Printing and graphics services	$3,256,118	1971.15
22	IntelaTech Inc.	Mississauga, ON	Electronics sales and distribution	$15,143,349	1949.97
23	ABC Communications Ltd.	Quesnel, BC	Telecom sales and service	$2,220,848	1949.96
24	Online Business Systems	Winnipeg, MB	Computer consulting	$5,272,207	1937.65
25	Andyne Computing Ltd.	Kingston, ON	Info-retrieval software	$16,517,000	1894.81
26	Unibroue Inc.	Chambly, PQ	Microbrewery	$16,700,000	1864.71

RANK	COMPANY	LOCATION	DESCRIPTION	1996 SALES	5 YEAR GROWTH (%)
27	Barrington Petroleum Ltd.	Calgary, AB	Oil and gas	$90,483,000	1858.08
28	Aurora Microsystems Distribution Inc.	Copper Cliff, ON	Computer reseller	$4,549,000	1819.41
29	Lemire & Habrich Consultants Inc.	St-Laurent, PQ	CAD/CAM sales and consulting	$20,057,720	1799.98
30	KL Group Inc.	Toronto, ON	Software tools developer	$9,332,248	1730.47
31	McGill Multimedia Inc.	Windsor, ON	Multimedia producer	$5,491,854	1722.98
32	Urbco Inc.	Calgary, AB	Real-estate developer	$8,558,824	1647.29
33	KIK Corp.	Concord, ON	Cleaning products manufacturer	$56,491,076	1646.87
34	A1 Computers Ltd.	Edmonton, AB	Computer retailer	$4,352,241	1606.30
35	Canderm Pharma Inc.	St-Laurent, PQ	Skin-care products manufacturer	$11,226,273	1507.81
36	Gage Applied Sciences Inc.	St-Laurent, PQ	Data-acquisition systems manufacturer	$4,407,160	1404.69
37	Gajdecki Visual Effects	Toronto, ON	Special effects producer	$2,768,302	1359.21
38	Pacific Asia Technologies Inc.	Toronto, ON	Food preservation technology	$4,707,185	1328.31
39	Logical Design Inc.	Richmond Hill, ON	IBM AS/400 systems consultants	$3,479,887	1314.30
40	Canadian Medical Legacy Corp.	Vancouver, BC	Medical products sales and distribution	$2,985,000	1285.81
41	Unique Systems Corp.	Calgary, AB	Computer systems integrator	$19,174,000	1284.40
42	Rand A Technology Corp.	Mississauga, ON	CAD/CAM sales and consulting	$175,374,000	1283.62
43	South of the Border (Imports Inc.)	Antigonish, NS	Imported giftware retailer	$1,399,752	1262.69
44	Trump Systems Inc.	Bolton, ON	Computer network sales and consulting	$3,631,246	1249.54
45	Teknor Industrial Computers Inc.	Boisbriand, PQ	Industrial computer manufacturer	$33,250,000	1246.70

RANK	COMPANY	LOCATION	DESCRIPTION	1996 SALES	5 YEAR GROWTH (%)
46	Camoguid Inc.	St-Théodore d'Acton, PQ	Industrial parts manufacturer	$7,276,247	1225.91
47	Silent Witness Enterprises Ltd.	Surrey, BC	Video surveillance equipment	$8,321,174	1223.63
48	Henry Hicks & Associates Ltd.	Kentville, NS	Financial planning services	$3,924,572	1223.21
49	Queue Systems Inc.	Markham, ON	Technology consulting	$3,528,169	1220.40
50	Northumberland Package Handling Ltd.	Port Hope, ON	Material handling systems	$3,830,164	1219.64
51	SLP Automotive Canada	Lachine, PQ	Automotive sub-assembly	$5,405,860	1171.62
52	L.E. Cherry & Associates	Markham, ON	Mail order computer sales	$2,539,997	1133.98
53	Vantage Securities Inc.	Vancouver, BC	Financial planners	$11,963,000	1120.71
54	Phonettix Intelecom Ltd.	Richmond Hill, ON	Call centre services	$27,154,189	1039.52
55	Les Aliments Fontaine Santé Inc.	St-Laurent, PQ	Innovative food products manufacturer	$6,157,508	1008.32
56	FirstService Corp.	Toronto, ON	Business and consumer services	$171,370,000	1007.87
57	MDC Corp.	Toronto, ON	Integrated communications services	$233,133,000	1000.31
58	Les Entreprises Métallex	Aylmer, PQ	Steel fabricator and installer	$1,558,635	993.33
59	Macrodyne Technologies Inc.	Woodbridge, ON	Industrial press manufacturer	$2,048,726	984.34
60	Paradon Computer Systems Ltd.	Victoria, BC	Computer systems integrator	$7,638,580	980.42
61	Endpoint Research Ltd.	Toronto, ON	Clinical trial management services	$3,588,756	974.86
62	Cooke Aquaculture Inc.	St. George, NB	Salmon products	$18,816,491	965.32
63	Call-Net Enterprises Inc.	North York, ON	Long-distance reseller	$712,600,000	936.58
64	La Scala Audio/Video Interiors Ltd.	Vancouver, BC	Home-theatre installation	$2,603,992	933.49

RANK	COMPANY	LOCATION	DESCRIPTION	1996 SALES	5 YEAR GROWTH (%)
65	Ascent Power Technology Inc.	Concord, ON	Electrical equipment manufacturer	$68,536,000	922.93
66	Chai-Na-Ta Corp.	Langley, BC	Ginseng products	$34,430,000	888.23
67	Spider Manufacturing Inc.	Kelowna, BC	Wiring accessories manufacturer	$1,017,766	883.06
68	Cangene	Corp.Winnipeg,	MBPharmaceutical manufacturer	$19,185,739	846.88
69	Auto Control Medical Inc.	Mississauga, ON	Medical products distributor	$25,055,000	844.05
70	Magnotta Winery Corp.	Vaughan, ON	Winemaker and retailer	$11,308,027	843.33
71	MPact Immedia Corp.	Montreal, PQ	Electronic commerce software	$11,025,479	843.08
72	Canway Ltd.	Ottawa, ON	Carpet and upholstery cleaning	$39,514,960	840.83
73	Nor-Built Construction	Amherstburg, ON	Home builder	$3,350,125	823.28
74	Softub Canada	Val Caron, ON	Hot tub manufacturer and marketer	$2,446,575	818.69
75	CRS Robotics Corp.	Burlington, ON	Robot systems manufacturer	$21,070,000	790.81
76	Locator Group Inc.	Orangeville, ON	Local business directory publisher	$8,237,000	778.66
77	MSM Transportation Inc.	Bolton, ON	Trucking and freight services	$17,020,758	767.08
78	Priva Inc.	Anjou, PQ	Adult incontinence products	$2,359,122	752.74
79	ITI Information Technology Institute	Halifax, NS	Technology training	$5,168,491	743.71
80	Tescor Energy Services Inc.	North York, ON	Energy performance contracting	$30,727,700	741.70
81	Corel Corp.	Ottawa, ON	Graphics and office suite software	$450,177,000	737.34
82	OpenAire Inc.	Mississauga, ON	Pool enclosures and solaria	$2,858,485	730.74
83	Fulcrum Technologies Inc.	Ottawa, ON	Text-retrieval software	$60,181,000	729.40

RANK	COMPANY	LOCATION	DESCRIPTION	1996 SALES	5 YEAR GROWTH (%)
84	Just Kid'n Children's Wear Ltd.	Langley, BC	Clothing manufacturer and retailer	$1,883,592	718.57
85	Puresource Inc.	Guelph, ON	Natural food products	$10,209,521	718.07
86	New Systems Solutions Ltd.	Ottawa, ON	Information systems consulting	$4,392,877	706.50
87	C.M. Oliver Inc.	Vancouver, BC	Financial services	$75,000,000	706.45
88	Vidir Machine Ltd.	Arborg, MB	Motorized shelving manufacturer	$5,813,097	703.89
89	Philip Services Inc.	Hamilton, ON	Industrial services recycling	$802,490,000	698.95
90	Unity Business Machines Ltd.	Victoria, BC	Office equipment sales and service	$1,970,000	693.97
91	Avant-Garde Engineering (1994) Inc.	L'Assomption, PQ	Hydraulic scaffolding manufacturer	$3,279,010	688.56
92	Kingsway Financial Services Inc.	Mississauga, ON	Specialty insurer	$140,610,000	673.26
93	CBCI Telecom Inc.	Montreal, PQ	Videoconferencing systems manufacturer	$41,796,000	668.03
94	ITEC Screenprinting Inc.	Dorval, PQ	Touch-sensitive keypads and switches	$2,298,000	666.00
95	InsulPro Industries Inc.	Surrey, BC	Insulation contracting	$30,891,500	662.03
96	Fantom Technologies Inc.	Welland, ON	Vacuum cleaner manufacturer and marketer	$98,428,527	658.08
97	The Packaging Group	Concord, ON	Flexible packaging for food industry	$12,660,097	656.73
98	Statpower Technologies Corp.	Burnaby, BC	Electrical inverters and battery chargers	$20,246,000	641.61
99	Transpro Freight Systems Ltd.	Mississauga, ON	Trucking and freight services	$11,374,633	627.73
100	A.R.C. Accounts Recovery Corp.	Victoria, BC	Account collection and consulting	$3,209,230	609.75

INDEX OF COMPANY NAMES

HAVE YOU EVER HAD A GREAT BUSINESS IDEA...

...but didn't know what to do with it?

Or perhaps you already run a successful business, but you could always benefit from great ideas shared by other successful entrepreneurs.

Then try **PROFIT**, the Magazine for Canadian Entrepreneurs. It's written for *you*.

Published six times a year, each issue is packed with specialized information and advice designed to take you and your company to new heights of success. This award-winning magazine gives you the entrepreneurial *success stories* that **inspire** you, the *business post mortems* that **guide** you, and the *trends, briefs and strategies* that can help you **achieve** everything you want to with your million dollar idea.

Discover for yourself great advice on ... Marketing ... Management ... Technology ... Finance ... Niches ... Exporting ... Raising capital ... Insightful one-on-one profiles of successful entrepreneurs ... The annual **PROFIT 100**, our assessment of Canada's fastest-growing companies ... plus much more of value to anyone with a great business idea!